Applied Innovation and Technology Management

Technology is not just limited to technology companies. Managing innovation and technology is no longer a luxury and needs to be understood by all sectors around the world and by both technical and non-technical managers. This book series explores existing and emerging technologies that address current challenges within innovation and technology managements. Each title is developed to provide a set of frameworks, tools and methods that can be adopted by researchers, managers and student in engineering, innovation and technology fields. Research, policy and practice-based books in the series cover topics such as roadmapping, portfolio management, technology forecasting, R&D management, health technologies, bio technologies, transportation management, smart cities, and open innovation, among many others

Nebojša Stojčić

Elusive Innovation

Promises, Failures and Policies for Emerging Innovation Systems

Springer

Nebojša Stojčić
Faculty of Economics and Business
University of Dubrovnik
Dubrovnik, Croatia

ISSN 2662-9402 ISSN 2662-9410 (electronic)
Applied Innovation and Technology Management
ISBN 978-3-032-14899-5 ISBN 978-3-032-14900-8 (eBook)
https://doi.org/10.1007/978-3-032-14900-8

This Springer imprint is published by the registered company Springer Nature Switzerland AG
The registered company address is: Gewerbestrasse 11, 6330 Cham, Switzerland

Preface

Innovation has become one of the defining ideas of our time. It is celebrated in strategies, championed in political speeches and treated as an essential recipe for growth and resilience. The rhetoric is powerful and the promise enticing: Innovate and prosperity will follow. But the reality often tells a different story. In many emerging innovation systems, despite decades of reform, increasing investment and integration into global markets, the results remain underwhelming. Ambitious policies lead to modest results, innovation strategies rarely extend beyond paper, and national ecosystems struggle to move beyond peripheral positions in global value chains. The paradox is that knowledge has never been as easily accessible as it is today, yet the gap between aspiration and achievement in innovation has never been so wide. It is this paradox, the gap between discourse and outcome, that motivated the writing of this book.

My engagement with these questions has been both professional and personal. Over the years of academic research, policy advising and collaboration with practitioners, I have repeatedly encountered the same recurring puzzle: Why is innovation so hard to achieve, even when the ingredients seem to be there? I have observed firms that were formally integrated into global markets but failed to build lasting innovation capabilities. I have seen public research organisations that have scientific achievements but struggle to engage with industry or society. I have seen well-funded programmes and strategies that looked convincing but collapsed under the weight of fragmented institutions, political cycles or lack of trust. These experiences suggested that failure was not accidental, but structural. Innovation was not absent in these contexts, but elusive. Always promised, always anticipated, but rarely transformative.

This book argues that innovation failure in emerging innovation systems is not only due to individual mistakes or poor decisions. Rather, it reflects systemic weaknesses in the way knowledge is accessed, absorbed and applied. When institutions discourage risk-taking, when policies reward compliance instead of learning and when global integration produces dependency rather than capability, the outcome is predictable. Failure becomes embedded in the system itself. But failure need not be destructive. In more resilient contexts, failure is a feedback mechanism that encourages reflection, adaptation and reform. In fragile systems, on the other hand, it leads to retreat, risk aversion and stagnation. This book is, therefore, not only about diagnosing failure, but also about how emerging economies can turn this failure into a source of renewal. The central argument is simple: Systems that can learn from failure can also learn to innovate.

Innovation is not just about competitiveness or growth. It is also about inclusivity, about who benefits from technological change and who is left behind. Emerging economies cannot afford innovation systems that reinforce inequality, concentrate opportunities in a handful of enclaves or neglect societal needs in the pursuit of narrow economic goals. In this sense, inclusivity is not an optional extra, but a key requirement for resilience and legitimacy. A system that excludes large segments of its population, be it women, small businesses or marginalised regions, cannot truly innovate in a sustainable way. By placing equity, participation and societal missions into the centre of innovation policy, countries can build systems that are not only more effective, but also more equitable. This book, therefore, insists that inclusion is not treated as a side issue, but as a central element of innovation.

At the same time, this book is not a story of despair. Across emerging economies, we find remarkable cases of ingenuity and persistence: entrepreneurs creating global businesses from small towns, policymakers experimenting with mission-oriented strategies and institutions defying expectations and delivering real impact. These are not yet system-wide transformations, but they are vital reminders that innovation is possible even under difficult conditions. They show that the problem is not the lack of talent or ideas, but the lack of structures that allow them to spread, connect and endure. The task ahead of us is to transform these islands of excellence into learning ecosystems. This requires policies that guide rather than dictate institutions that connect rather than isolate, and strategies that are anchored in long-term development missions rather than adhering to short-term external templates.

This book is aimed at a diverse readership. For policymakers, it offers a call to move beyond slogans and fragmented reforms and develop strategies that combine vision with institutional design and long-term learning. For academics, it integrates insights from evolutionary economics, innovation systems theory and institutional development into a framework for understanding systemic failure. For practitioners and entrepreneurs, it serves as both a reality check and a roadmap that reminds us that innovation is not just about success stories, but about the messy, iterative processes that precede them. Above all, the book is an invitation to see innovation not as a race to replicate others, but as a collective, inclusive process of experimentation, learning and adaptation. If there is one lesson, it is this: Innovation in emerging economies is not absent but elusive. The challenge is to make it real, durable, inclusive and transformative.

Dubrovnik, Croatia
2025

Nebojša Stojčić

Declaration of Competing Interests The author declares that there are no competing interests, financial or non-financial, that could be perceived as influencing the content of this book. The analyses, arguments and conclusions presented are solely those of the author and are not influenced by any personal or institutional relationships.

Contents

1 Introduction: The Elusive Promise of Innovation 1

2 Understanding Innovation Failure 7
- 2.1 Introduction 7
- 2.2 Innovation and Failure in Evolutionary Economics 8
- 2.3 National and Sectoral Innovation Systems 10
- 2.4 Absorptive Capacity and Capability Theory 12
- 2.5 Institutional Economics and Path Dependence 14
- 2.6 Contemporary Views on Innovation Failure in Globalized Innovation Networks 16
- 2.7 Typologies of Innovation Failure 18
- 2.8 Failure vs Experimentation in Innovation 22
- 2.9 Implications for Emerging Innovation Systems 25
- 2.10 Conclusion 27
- References 28

3 Bottlenecks in Knowledge Transfers 31
- 3.1 Introduction 31
- 3.2 Mechanisms of Knowledge Transfer 33
- 3.3 Structural Barriers to Knowledge Diffusion 37
- 3.4 Intellectual Property and the Limits of Spillovers 40
- 3.5 Case Studies in Knowledge Transfer 43
- 3.6 Conclusion 47
- References 48

4 Weaknesses of Domestic Innovation Systems 51
- 4.1 Introduction 51
- 4.2 Fragmentation and Disconnected Subsystems 54
- 4.3 Institutional Inertia and the Absence of Adaptive Governance 56
- 4.4 Skills Mismatch and Weak Human Capital Linkages 59
- 4.5 Weak Demand for Innovation 62

4.6 Absence of Feedback, Evaluation and Iterative Learning 65
4.7 Conclusion 67
References 68

5 The Role of Multinational Enterprises 71
5.1 Introduction 71
5.2 MNEs as Drivers of Innovation 73
5.3 MNEs as Knowledge Gatekeepers 76
5.4 Dependence on Foreign Firms for Innovation 80
5.5 When Multinationals Contribute to Domestic Technological Capacity 83
5.6 Conclusion 86
References 87

6 Towards Innovation Sovereignty 89
6.1 Introduction 89
6.2 Rethinking Dependency in a Globalised Innovation System 92
6.3 Policy Space and Institutional Capabilities for Innovation Sovereignty 95
6.4 Building Domestic Technological Capabilities 99
6.5 Selective Integration: Balancing Openness and Control 102
6.6 Conclusion 105
References 106

7 Rethinking Industrial and Innovation Policy for the Twenty-First Century 109
7.1 Introduction 109
7.2 Beyond Horizontal vs Vertical: Reframing the Policy Toolkit 112
7.3 Building Innovation Systems that Learn 114
7.4 Missions, Platforms and Ecosystems 117
7.5 Instruments that Align Finance, Risk and Purpose 121
7.6 Policy Capacity and Governance for Innovation 125
7.7 Conclusion 129
References 130

8 Inclusive Innovation and a Participatory Future 133
8.1 Introduction 133
8.2 Dimensions of Exclusion in Innovation Systems 136
8.3 Concepts and Principles for Inclusive Innovation 140
8.4 Participation as a Method: Co-design, Co-production and Democratic Innovation 143
8.5 Policies for Inclusion: What Governments Can Do 146
8.6 Avoiding the Pitfalls: When Inclusion Becomes a Buzzword 150
8.7 Conclusion 152
References 153

9 Governing Innovation in the Age of Uncertainty 157
9.1 Introduction 157
9.2 The Nature of Contemporary Uncertainty 160
9.3 Anticipatory Governance and Strategic Foresight 162
9.4 From Agility to Institutional Resilience 165
9.5 Trust, Legitimacy and Public Engagement 169
9.6 Governing Transformative Innovation: Towards a New Policy Ethos 172
9.7 Conclusion 175

About the Author

Nebojša Stojčić is a Professor of Economics at the University of Dubrovnik whose work bridges research, policy and practice in the fields of innovation, industrial development and economic transformation. His research is shaped by the challenges faced by economies in transition from production-driven to innovation-driven growth, particularly in Central and Eastern Europe and other emerging regions. By examining why some countries, regions and industries succeed in building innovation capacity while others remain constrained, he seeks to uncover the systemic factors that determine whether innovation flourishes or remains elusive. Throughout his career, he has combined academic research with active participation in international projects and policy initiatives, working with governments, businesses and development agencies, as well as international organisations such as the World Bank and UNIDO. His studies have been published in leading international journals and frequently cited in debates on innovation and industrial policy at national and supranational levels. Recognised among the top 2% of academics worldwide in Stanford University's citation rankings, he also plays an active role in higher education leadership. In addition to these tasks, he remains deeply committed to teaching and mentoring the next generation of researchers.

Chapter 1
Introduction: The Elusive Promise of Innovation

> The difficulty lies not so much in developing new ideas as in escaping from old ones. (John Maynard Keynes)

From Silicon Valley garages to national catch-up strategies, stories of innovation often revolve around success, breakthroughs achieved against the odds, visionary leadership and moments of transformation. These accounts inspire, but they also distort. They gloss over the false starts, the structural constraints and the mundane institutional work that quietly underpins technological change. Failure, in contrast, is rarely given serious analytical attention. It is treated as an embarrassment to be explained away, rather than a central feature of innovation itself. In policy and academic discourse alike, the focus remains on inputs and outcomes, not on the uncertain, iterative processes in between. But it is precisely in those processes, where ideas falter, adjustments are made, and systems are tested, that real capability is forged. Understanding innovation requires moving beyond heroic narratives and paying attention to the slow, uneven and often frustrating work of building systems that can adapt, learn and endure over time.

In the second half of the twentieth century, a small group of East Asian economies embarked on an industrial transformation that defied conventional expectations. With limited natural resources, modest domestic markets and underdeveloped scientific infrastructures, they sought entry into some of the world's most complex technological sectors such as semiconductors, automotive and advanced machinery. The early stages were anything but smooth. Capability gaps were wide, quality inconsistent and the learning curve steep. Entire production systems had to be understood, adapted and stabilised under unfamiliar conditions. Imported technologies rarely fit neatly into local contexts, requiring continual adjustment and operational improvisation. Yet failure did not signal retreat. Instead, it became part of the process. Engineers and technicians learned on the job, often through reverse engineering, collaboration with foreign partners and painstaking trial and error. What emerged from this uncertainty was not just incremental progress, but the foundation for a deeper shift towards an industrial base that could learn, adjust and evolve.

This transformation was neither accidental nor simply a by-product of market liberalisation. It was actively designed through national strategies that combined state

N. Stojčić, *Elusive Innovation*, Applied Innovation and Technology Management,
https://doi.org/10.1007/978-3-032-14900-8_1

direction with market incentives into what some have called "governed experimentation." Governments used a mix of industrial policy, targeted finance and performance monitoring to create an ecosystem that demanded results. However, the support came with conditions. Firms were protected from foreign competition but also pushed to meet export targets, absorb new technologies and demonstrate continuous upgrading. Bureaucracies were empowered to coordinate across sectors and align resources towards strategic objectives. Policies went beyond correcting market failures and sought to cultivate market-shaping institutions, embed learning incentives and steer innovation towards nationally defined goals. The result was not just rapid industrialisation, but the construction of adaptive innovation systems. Today, this legacy is both a touchstone and a challenge for emerging innovation systems around the world offering inspiration but also exposing how difficult it is to replicate success without strong institutions, strategic coherence and long-term commitment.

Despite decades of reform, increased openness and participation in global value chains, innovation systems in many emerging economies remain structurally weak and institutionally fragmented. Domestic firms often operate with outdated technologies, low productivity and limited engagement in R&D. Universities and public research institutes produce scientific output, but frequently lack the channels, incentives or partners needed to connect with industry or societal needs. In regions such as Central and Eastern Europe, decades after EU accession and substantial investment in research infrastructure, many innovation ecosystems still struggle to build meaningful linkages between academia and business. Initiatives remain overly reliant on EU funding cycles, and reforms tend to emphasise compliance over creativity. In Latin America, sub-Saharan Africa and other parts of the world struggling to transition from production-driven to innovation-driven growth, similar patterns are visible where national innovation policies exist on paper, but the institutions meant to implement them are under-resourced, politically constrained or disconnected from real-world technological demands.

Despite these systemic constraints, flashes of frontier innovation have still emerged often from unexpected corners of emerging world. In Central and Eastern Europe, some of the region's most remarkable breakthroughs have been driven less by coordinated policy or institutional capability and more by the vision and persistence of individual inventors and entrepreneurs. Croatia's Rimac, starting from a garage-built electric car, grew into a global leader in high-performance EV technology. Estonia's Skype redefined global communication before being acquired by major international players. Bulgaria's Telerik, born as a small developer tool company, caught the attention of Progress Software, while Poland's CD Projekt transformed from a local game distributor into a world-renowned studio. Other examples include Croatia's Infobip, now a global cloud communications platform; Hungary's Prezi, which reinvented presentation software; and Croatia's Agrivi, bringing advanced farm management solutions to international markets. These ventures navigated funding gaps, scarce research infrastructure and uncertain market acceptance. Yet they remain enclaves of excellence, impressive in their own right, but largely disconnected from broader innovation ecosystems. Their stories highlight the ingenuity and resilience of individuals, while highlighting that without systemic support, such successes are difficult to replicate and rarely transform the innovation landscape as a whole.

Rather than resolving these challenges, global integration has often exacerbated them. Foreign technology continues to arrive through trade, investment and imported equipment, but its impact is frequently contained within multinational subsidiaries or embedded in turnkey solutions that offer little space for local adaptation. Firms in manufacturing zones or supplier networks follow global specifications but lack incentives or capabilities to innovate beyond them. Even where public investment in innovation is present, it is too often short-term, fragmented across agencies or overly focused on formal metrics like patent counts or start-up numbers. In the Western Balkans, for instance, innovation programmes often reflect donor priorities rather than domestic developmental needs. The result is a deepening paradox, the one where in a world awash with digital tools, global knowledge flows and institutional templates, many countries remain stuck in low-innovation equilibria, integrated into global systems, but without the agency to shape them or learn meaningfully from them.

This book begins with a central question: Why do some countries succeed in building innovation systems that generate learning, experimentation and long-term technological upgrading while others remain persistently constrained? Conventional explanations such as limited financial resources, institutional weakness or poor policy implementation offer partial insights. However, they often fail to capture the deeper, systemic dynamics at play. The book argues that innovation failure in emerging economies is rarely the result of isolated missteps. It is structural phenomena that emerge from how global knowledge is accessed, filtered and absorbed or excluded. It reflects the presence or absence of critical institutional capabilities such as the ability to learn from failure, to coordinate actors around shared developmental missions and to bridge the persistent divide between knowledge production and application.

In many emerging innovation systems, the gap between ambition and outcome cannot be explained solely by underinvestment or weak implementation. It lies in how innovation systems are imagined and operationalised. Policies often focus on measurable inputs such as research funding, start-up support or infrastructure development, but fail to build the relationships and feedback loops that turn those inputs into long-term capability. Coordination across ministries and agencies is frequently limited, and evaluation systems tend to prioritise administrative compliance over learning and adaptation. Institutions that should act as bridges between research, industry and public policy are often weak, missing or misaligned with national priorities. As a result, innovation becomes an isolated activity, fragmented across sectors and disconnected from development strategy. Even when ambitious agendas are announced whether in digital transformation, green growth or advanced manufacturing they often remain aspirational, lacking the institutional mechanisms to turn vision into action. This book seeks to understand, and ultimately help overcome, that disconnect.

We begin by revisiting the puzzle of technological catching-up. Why have some countries, like those in East Asia, managed to enter high-technology sectors and climb the value chain, while others remain stuck in low-productivity, resource-intensive or peripheral niches? What differentiates success from stagnation? This section explores the economic, institutional and political conditions that enable latecomer economies to break into complex industries. We also examine the mythologies that surround catching-up narratives, how headline successes sometimes obscure the long, nonlinear process of building technological depth. From there, we shift to the dynamics of knowledge transfer. What happens when technology crosses borders? Why does it often fail to embed itself meaningfully in domestic ecosystems? Here we engage critically with foreign direct investment, a mechanism often celebrated for its developmental potential, but one whose learning effects are highly conditional. We also revisit the concept of absorptive capacity, not just as a technical function, but as a system-wide capability to internalise, adapt and reapply knowledge in contextually relevant ways.

Next, we turn to the internal dynamics of national innovation systems. What makes them cohere, and what causes them to fracture? This part of the book examines how domestic actors, universities, firms, research institutes, public agencies and civil society interact, coordinate and sometimes collide. We analyse the institutional architectures that underpin innovation systems, focusing on the importance of intermediaries, policy alignment and long-term coordination mechanisms. We challenge the narrow view that innovation is confined to elite tech start-ups or isolated centres of excellence and instead argue that system-wide innovation emerges from dense, interactive networks of actors operating under shared expectations and mutual accountability. We ask what kinds of institutional configurations are most conducive to inclusive, adaptive innovation, particularly in resource-constrained or politically fragmented settings. And we raise a final, normative question: How can innovation systems be built not only to serve economic goals, but also to contribute to broader agendas of resilience in the face of shocks, equity across social groups and sustainability over time?

By tackling these questions, the book addresses a diverse readership. For policymakers, it offers an invitation to move beyond slogans and isolated reforms, and towards a systemic approach that connects vision to institutional design and learning processes. For researchers, it integrates insights from innovation studies, development economics, political economy and comparative institutional analysis, offering a cross-disciplinary framework for studying and strengthening innovation systems. For development practitioners and business leaders, it offers both a reality check and a roadmap, an argument for looking beyond patent counts or start-up tallies to assess whether innovation policies are building long-term capacity. Above all, the book offers a provocation: What if innovation failure is not an unfortunate deviation from a natural trajectory but a predictable result of how global and national innovation systems are currently structured? And what if rethinking these systems is not only possible, but essential?

The solution, we argue, lies not in replicating familiar success stories, though they offer important lessons, but in fundamentally reimagining what success means in the context of innovation. It means moving beyond the pursuit of metrics and models borrowed from elsewhere, and instead embracing a vision rooted in learning, adaptation and purpose. Innovation systems capable of learning from failure, tailoring interventions to local realities and cultivating broad-based participation do not emerge fully formed. They are forged through deliberate political commitment, institutional experimentation and iterative, at times uncomfortable, coordination among diverse actors. This journey is rarely linear. It involves setbacks, recalibrations and tensions between competing goals. But it is precisely within this complexity that the seeds of sovereignty, resilience and long-term developmental agency can take root.

The capacity to shape innovation pathways on one's own terms, rather than passively absorb global trends, is not the privilege of a few, but a possibility for many, provided the right foundations are laid. Even in systems constrained by limited resources, fragmented institutions or peripheral positions in the global economy, there remains room to manoeuvre, to experiment and to build. With the right scaffolding, institutions that connect rather than isolate, policies that guide rather than prescribe, and a strategic horizon anchored in inclusive missions, emerging economies can chart innovation trajectories that serve societal goals as much as market imperatives. This book is about how to initiate that shift and, more importantly, how to sustain it over time. It is a call to reframe innovation not as an imported template, but as a locally embedded, collectively constructed and continually evolving process of development.

Chapter 2
Understanding Innovation Failure

Ever tried. Ever failed. No matter. Try again. Fail again. Fail better. (Samuel Beckett)

Abstract Innovation is often celebrated as the engine of progress, yet just as often it stumbles, leaving behind abandoned projects, wasted resources and frustrated ambitions. This chapter begins by challenging the comforting notion that failure is merely accidental. From an evolutionary lens, failure is shown to be part of the natural turbulence of technological change, where uncertainty and selection shape winners and losers. The narrative then moves into the realm of innovation systems where the absence of coordination or weak absorptive capacities can transform individual setbacks into systemic paralysis. Institutions, with their legacies and rigidities, add another layer of constraint, while globalisation and the rise of value chains and platforms reveal how opportunities can be offered but kept just out of reach. By weaving these perspectives together, the chapter tells a larger story that innovation failure is not an exception, but a recurring shadow that accompanies every promise of progress.

2.1 Introduction

In innovation policy, failure is often treated as a technical problem to be solved, a weak business model, a faulty prototype or an ineffective subsidy. But in emerging innovation systems, failure goes deeper. It is not just the result of a bad bet or a missed market opportunity. It reflects structural weaknesses, institutions that lack capabilities or discourage risk-taking, firms that lack problem-solving routines, and ecosystems fragmented by mistrust and misalignment. In such an environment, a single failed initiative can have ripple effects that dry up funding, erode political support and harden the culture of caution. Chapter 2 starts from this uncomfortable truth. It argues that innovation failure is not an exception, but a systemic outcome embedded in the way innovation is organised, promoted and supported. Rather than treating failure as something to be avoided or hidden, this chapter looks at what failure tells us about what is missing, what is misaligned and what needs to change for innovation to take root.

N. Stojčić, *Elusive Innovation*, Applied Innovation and Technology Management,
https://doi.org/10.1007/978-3-032-14900-8_2

Drawing on theories ranging from evolution to innovation systems to institutional economics, the chapter explores why innovations fail and how such failure differs across contexts. A typology of technical, market, institutional and systemic failure is introduced, not to classify problems, but to help the reader diagnose them more accurately. A broken product can be a sign of a technical misstep but when promising technologies falter due to poor regulation or lack of demand, it is a systemic failure. The chapter argues that emerging innovation systems face distinctive challenges of thinner institutional buffers, less room for error and fewer opportunities to learn from setbacks. In such contexts, failure is more frequent and more costly. However, if dealt with openly and constructively, failure can become a feedback mechanism that exposes bottlenecks, reveals blind spots and triggers reform. The chapter provides both a conceptual framework and practical insights to understand failure not as an endpoint but as a starting point for rebuilding innovation systems that are more resilient, adaptive and inclusive.

2.2 Innovation and Failure in Evolutionary Economics

In evolutionary economics, innovation is regarded as uncertain, cumulative and path-dependent (Edquist, 1997). In contrast to neoclassical models, which see innovation as a rational response to incentives, evolutionary theory views it as a process of trial, error and learning (Metcalfe, 1998). Failure is not an anomaly, but a central component of the development of technological change. Schumpeter's (1934) concept of creative destruction summarizes this dynamic by arguing that economic progress is created by waves of innovation that destroy existing firms and industries. In this view, the failure of firms, technologies or entire industries is not a flaw, but a necessary result of renewal and transformation. The system develops through selection and adaptation (Knudsen, 2002). However insightful and foundational, Schumpeter's romanticized portrayal of entrepreneurial failure neglected the importance of organizational learning, institutional frameworks and cumulative capability building, all of which are essential to how innovation occurs. In contemporary literature failure is increasingly recognized not only as inevitable, but also as an important contributor to innovation and long-term economic resilience.

In their seminal work The Evolutionary Theory of Economic Change, Nelson and Winter (1982) expand this framework and argue that firms are not rational optimisers, but boundedly rational actors that innovate through routines and search under uncertainty. In this framework, innovation is a process of experimentation in which some attempts succeed and many fail. Whether an innovation survives depends on both internal capabilities and external selection pressure from markets and institutions. Failure is therefore not an aberration, but a natural part of innovation. Firms work with incomplete information and test new technologies or methods in an environment that they do not fully understand. Nelson and Winter also emphasised the cumulative nature of innovation where firms with deep routines and experience are more likely to succeed. This leads to a systemic asymmetry. Firms or economies that lack prior capabilities are more prone to failure, not because they are irrational, but because they are structurally disadvantaged in their ability to learn, adapt and compete.

Another important contribution of evolutionary theory is the concept of technological trajectories and path dependence (Dosi, 1982). Technologies develop along certain paths that are characterised by early decisions, institutional arrangements and market structures. Once a particular trajectory becomes dominant, alternative paths may become economically or politically unviable, even if they are technologically superior. This has a significant impact on the failure of innovations. Firms and economies can become locked into sub-optimal technologies due to sunk costs, vested interests or external network effects. Efforts to break out of such trajectories, for example by introducing radically new technologies, often fail not because of technical shortcomings but because the system as a whole resists change. This is a particular challenge for emerging economies. If their innovation systems are centred on low value-added activities, path dependency can make the transition to more knowledge-intensive sectors more difficult. Failure in such contexts is not just firm level, but a phenomenon at system level.

In evolutionary thinking, failure is only valuable if it leads to learning. A failed product, a failed strategy or a failed policy can contribute to long-term fitness if the organisation or system can internalise the lessons learned and adapt accordingly. This is why institutions are important. In well-functioning innovation systems, failures are analysed, discussed and incorporated into the knowledge base. Feedback loops between firms, regulatory authorities, research organisations and funders help to avoid repeated mistakes. In dysfunctional systems, on the other hand, failures are ignored, blamed on individuals or repeated without change. The difference lies not in the presence or absence of failure but in the ability to learn from them. Nelson (1993) later emphasised this point in his work on the co-evolution of technology and institutions. He noted that advanced economies benefit from an institutional infrastructure ranging from patent systems to vocational training to publicly funded research and development that enhances the ability of firms to experiment safely and productively. Emerging economies often lack such infrastructures, making failure more costly and learning more difficult.

Evolutionary economics asks us to view failure as a critical feature of the development of innovation. From this perspective, innovation is a process of search under uncertainty, where success depends not only on effort, but also on the depth of accumulated capabilities and the strength of supporting institutions (Nelson, 2008; Schot & Steinmueller, 2018). Failure is inevitable, but it only becomes detrimental when systems are unable to learn, adapt and respond. This perspective is particularly relevant for emerging economies, where the failure of innovation is all too often explained by poor decisions or lack of ambition. In reality, chronic failure is more a reflection of structural weaknesses such as thin knowledge base, limited organisational routines, fragmented institutions and weak feedback mechanisms. If we understand innovation as an evolutionary process, we can move beyond blaming actors and focus instead on building systems that learn. The next section builds on this foundation and turns to innovation systems theory to explore how these systemic weaknesses manifest themselves.

2.3 National and Sectoral Innovation Systems

While evolutionary economics emphasises learning, routines and path dependence at the firm level, it also laid the foundation for a broader shift in the way economists and policymakers understand innovation, not as the result of isolated firm behaviour, but as the result of interactions within a system (Metcalfe, 2005). This insight gave rise to the National Innovation Systems (NIS) approach, which is arguably one of the most influential frameworks for understanding why innovation succeeds in some countries and fails in others. In this section, we review the origins and core concepts of the NIS framework, examine its relevance for emerging economies and introduce the related concept of sectoral innovation systems, which provides a more detailed insight into the differences in failure across industries. Together, these approaches shift our attention from isolated causes of failure (e.g. firm incompetence or market distortions) to systemic weaknesses in coordination, incentives and institutional architecture (Woolthuis et al., 2005).

Until the 1980s, policymakers largely advocated a linear model of innovation: Scientific research would lead to inventions, which in turn would lead to economic success (Trott, 2017). This view suggested that investment in R&D would naturally lead to economic growth. But reality has challenged this logic. Some countries with strong science systems struggled to innovate, while others with modest R&D investments flourished due to stronger networks and institutional coordination. This discrepancy gave rise to the concept of National Innovation Systems (NIS), developed by scholars such as Christopher Freeman (1987), Bengt-Åke Lundvall (1988) and Richard Nelson (1993). The NIS framework emphasised that innovation does not emerge from isolated efforts, but from the interaction between different actors, firms, universities, public institutions, financial institutions, within a supportive institutional context (Lundvall, 2016). Freeman's study of post-war Japan showed how coordinated policy, education and trust-based firm networks enabled the technological catch-up process. Lundvall also emphasised that innovation is a socially embedded, interactive process driven by learning-by-doing and learning-by-interacting, not just by scientific breakthroughs.

One of the most valuable insights from the National Innovation Systems approach is the focus on systemic failure, not on the failure of individual firms or technologies, but on the networks and institutions that shape innovation. This failure is often not due to bad intentions or weak ideas, but to structural failures. In some cases, the problem lies in inadequate infrastructure. For example, without reliable broadband connections, efficient transport or a stable energy supply, innovation may find it difficult to flourish. In other cases, the institutions themselves constrain progress through weak protection of intellectual property, unpredictable political signalling or cumbersome bureaucracy that discourages experimentation. These are not only policy failures but also signals of systems that lack the coherence and continuity needed to foster innovation. Even when resources are available, they often flow through fragmented channels or support activities that are poorly aligned with national priorities.

Equally disruptive are failures in interaction and capability. When universities, businesses and government agencies do not work together effectively, knowledge remains trapped in silos. In many countries, for example, researchers are incentivised to publish rather than commercialise, while industry players often view universities with suspicion. Funding programmes to bridge these gaps are often short-lived or poorly structured, which exacerbates the mistrust. Meanwhile, many firms and institutions lack the internal capacity to absorb and apply external knowledge, rendering even the best technology transfer ineffective. These forms of failure do not mean that innovation is technically impossible, but they do mean that the system lacks the scaffolding to help promising ideas cross the "valley of death" between research and practical application. Without stronger coordination mechanisms, deeper trust and better aligned incentives, innovation remains fragmented, fragile and prone to repeated failure.

Applying the NIS framework to emerging economies demonstrates both its benefits and its limitations. It shows the importance of building institutions that support innovation, such as funding agencies, scientific institutions and intellectual property offices. But it also requires a level of coordination and institutional development that many low- and middle-income countries have not yet achieved. Early NIS studies focused mainly on countries such as Japan, Sweden or the United States, where innovation actors already operate within relatively networked systems. In contrast, many emerging economies are more fragmented, with modern export sectors coexisting with informal markets and government policies often not aligned with the realities of the economy. Copying institutional models from wealthier countries often does not lead to results. What we need are approaches that take local conditions and histories seriously (Cimoli et al., 2009). One answer is to analyse functional innovation systems, which examine whether core tasks such as knowledge creation or market formation are actually carried out, regardless of formal structures.

While national innovation systems are a valuable tool for understanding how countries organise innovation, they are not uniform structures. Different sectors operate under different technological, regulatory and market conditions. This has led to the development of the Sectoral Innovation Systems (SIS) framework introduced by Malerba (2002), which focuses on the diversity of innovation dynamics in different industries. In the pharmaceutical industry, innovation is characterised by long development times, strict regulations and dependence on formal R&D. In contrast, the ICT sector moves fast, driven by digital platforms, open standards and rapid iterations. Agriculture, on the other hand, depends on natural conditions and access to land and water. As a result, the failure of innovation in one sector often has very different causes than in another. A policy that supports digital innovation may be ineffective in agriculture or manufacturing if it does not take sector-specific barriers into account. A targeted innovation policy requires an understanding of how these differences influence the conditions for business success.

To sum up, innovation systems, whether at national or sectoral level, often fail not because of weak actors, but because of poor coordination, lack of connections or inappropriate priorities. A firm may have the right idea and the right technology, but without the institutions and networks to support funding, research collaboration and market access, it may still fail. The lesson here is not that one sector is easier than another, but that different sectors require different support structures. Both the NIS and SIS frameworks point to a deeper truth. Innovation policy is not about isolated interventions, but about aligning systems to support learning, collaboration and problem solving. In the next section, we turn from systems to organisations and explore why some are better equipped to innovate than others, even in similar circumstances.

2.4 Absorptive Capacity and Capability Theory

In many emerging innovation systems, the challenge is not access to knowledge or technology, but the ability to adopt and build on it. Technologies often enter the country through foreign direct investment, trade or licencing, but local firms often lack the ability to adapt and apply them effectively. This is where the concept of absorptive capacity, introduced by Cohen and Levinthal (1990), becomes important. Defined as the ability of a company to recognise, assimilate and apply external knowledge, absorptive capacity depends heavily on prior learning and experience. Firms with weak R&D, limited capabilities and superficial problem-solving routines are less able to benefit from knowledge flows (Pietrobelli & Rabelotti, 2011). For example, many Eastern European countries attracted a lot of foreign capital after joining the EU, but achieved uneven innovation results due to low internal capabilities. Absorptive capacity is not just a firm level issue as its consequences bear systemic implications. Without investment in education, training and learning at the firm level, national innovation systems remain ill-equipped to benefit from globalisation and technological diffusion (Strelkov et al., 2025).

Following the seminal work of Cohen and Levinthal, later scholars have shown that absorptive capacity is not fixed but evolves as firms learn and interact. Zahra and George (2002) have made a useful distinction between potential and realised absorptive capacity. The former refers to the acquisition and absorption of knowledge, while the latter involves the transformation and utilisation of knowledge for commercial purposes. This distinction is important because many firms, especially in emerging innovation systems, are able to access external knowledge through training, networks or foreign direct investment, but struggle to translate it into performance. Without complementary internal structures such as capable management, adaptable routines and effective knowledge-sharing mechanisms, the potential absorptive capacity remains unutilised. For example, public procurement contracts in emerging economies often include requirements for knowledge transfer, but these rarely lead to meaningful change if the recipient firms lack the systems to internalise what they have learned. This explains why policies that focus solely on external incentives such as R&D tax credits or encouraging foreign direct investment often fall short without building internal capacity.

While absorptive capacity emphasises the importance of learning from external sources, technological capabilities theory broadens the focus to the accumulation of skills and know-how at the firm level over time. Scholars such as Lall (1992), Bell and Pavitt (1993) and Kim (1997) emphasise that innovation in developing countries depends on building a multi-layered set of capabilities that includes not only the use of existing technologies, but also the improvement and eventual creation of new technologies. Lall distinguishes between production capabilities (the ability to operate technologies), investment capabilities (the ability to design and manage production systems) and innovation capabilities (the ability to improve or invent technologies). In many emerging economies, firms have acquired basic production capacities but remain stuck at this level and are unable to move up the value chain. This leads to what researchers call "shallow integration" into global value chains where firms participate in assembly or manufacturing but gain little in terms of knowledge (Langbein, 2020; Steinfeld, 2004). South Korea took a different path, investing heavily in domestic learning, R&D and internal firm development to climb the technological ladder (Hobday, 1995; Hobday et al., 2004). In contrast, many countries liberalised and welcomed foreign investment without building domestic capacity in parallel, resulting in limited technological upgrading (Cimoli et al., 2009; Stojcic, 2024).

The development of absorptive capacities and technological capabilities is often presented as firm responsibility, but in practice these learning processes are strongly characterised by systemic conditions. Firms rely on national education and training systems to access skilled labour, while their willingness to make long-term investments depends on macroeconomic stability and consistent policy support (Bell & Pavitt, 1993). Collaboration and learning are influenced by the presence or absence of innovation networks, clusters and public–private partnerships (Malerba, 2002; Mazzucato, 2013). When this system-level support is weak or poorly aligned, even motivated firms have difficulty investing in innovation. Knowledge may circulate within the system, but if there are no mechanisms for connection and absorption, it cannot be translated into firm-level capabilities. As a result, many emerging innovation systems are persistently underperforming despite formal reforms and increasing global integration.

Systemic weaknesses often lead to what scholars refer to as "capability traps", i.e. situations in which firms and institutions remain stuck in low-performing cycles due to poor governance, limited resources and weak learning incentives (Andrews et al., 2017). In such contexts, even a well-designed innovation policy can make little difference. Firms may have access to R&D funds, but are not in a position to utilise them. Public–private partnerships may exist in form, but not in function. Imported technologies may arrive, but they fail to learn locally in a meaningful way. Without targeted investment in capabilities such as skilled labour, management expertise and internal learning routines, the failure of innovation becomes self-reinforcing (Stojcic, 2024). Absorptive capacity and technological capabilities are not a luxury, but prerequisites for turning access to knowledge into results. When policies ignore this, the result is often low participation in global value chains and persistent underperformance. The next section explores how these challenges are rooted in history and institutions, compounding the difficulty of breaking free.

2.5 Institutional Economics and Path Dependence

Like most aspects of human behaviour and living, technological progress is not independent of its environment, but is shaped by institutions, the rules, norms and governance structures that determine how innovation unfolds. Institutions influence how firms behave, how markets function, how knowledge is exchanged and how risks are dealt with. As we already argued, the failure of innovation in emerging economies often has less to do with poor decisions and more to do with structural constraints due to institutional weaknesses and historical legacies. These constraints, such as weak enforcement of rules, misaligned incentives or institutional voids create path dependence, making change difficult. As North (1990) famously described, institutions are the "rules of the game", encompassing both formal laws and informal norms. When institutions work well, they reduce uncertainty and support innovation through mechanisms such as strong intellectual property rights, transparent funding and regulation that keeps pace with technological change. But in many emerging innovation systems, these support mechanisms are absent or flawed, making innovation riskier, less rewarding and more prone to failure or stagnation.

The absence or dysfunction of key market-supporting institutions in emerging economies is often described with the concept of institutional voids (Liedong, 2020; Matus-Ruiz et al., 2025; Stojcic et al., 2025). In innovation contexts, these voids manifest themselves in different ways as lack of early-stage funding, weak or non-existent certification bodies, fragmented university–industry collaboration and poor contract enforcement. Such voids create a risky environment, particularly for start-ups that depend on reliable infrastructure to test and scale new technologies. These are not just technical shortcomings, but also wider governance gaps and institutional weaknesses. In many African and Southeast Asian countries, promising ventures fail not because of flawed ideas, but because the systems needed to grow them are lacking. These challenges are particularly acute for small and medium-sized enterprises (SMEs), which often lack the networks, capital or political influence to navigate unstable institutional landscapes, making innovation in these environments costly, uncertain and often short-lived (Stojcic et al., 2024).

While policy debates tend to focus on formal institutions such as laws, regulations and funding structures, informal institutions also play a crucial role in shaping the dynamics of innovation (Petraite et al., 2022). These include cultural norms, trust in public systems and societal attitudes towards risk and failure. In some countries, failure is accepted as part of the innovation process. In others, there is a social stigma attached to it that discourages experimentation and entrepreneurial ambition. Informal trust is equally important since innovation systems thrive when firms, universities and public organisations share information and collaborate freely. However, in low-trust environments, collaboration breaks down and innovation is fragmented or duplicated. A vivid example of this can be seen in many post-socialist countries in Eastern Europe, where persistent mistrust between academia and industry has weakened innovation ecosystems. Even where there are formal incentives for collaboration, these often fail to materialise because the informal norms underpinning sustainable collaboration have eroded or have never been fully established.

Path dependence illustrates how historical institutional decisions shape today's innovation systems and often steer them in sub-optimal directions. The concept was originally used to explain emergence of dominant technologies such as QWERTY keyboards or VHS tapes, but it is now also applied to political and institutional developments. In the field of innovation, path dependence can manifest itself as policy lock-in (continued funding of outdated sectors), skills lock-in (education systems that are not aligned with current needs) or organisational lock-in (firms clinging to outdated routines). Many emerging countries inherit institutional structures that are shaped by colonial, socialist or protectionist history and continue to influence innovation behaviour. The example of post-socialist countries of Eastern Europe speaks profoundly in favour of such reasoning as the collapse of centralised research systems in the 1990s left a vacuum that has never been fully replaced (Švarc & Dabić, 2021). Copying policies from more advanced economies often fails when these institutional foundations are absent and promising reforms become disjointed and ineffective measures.

Although institutional structures can be rigid, they are not immutable. Institutional change occurs in different ways, e.g. through top-down reforms led by governments, through grassroots adjustments driven by entrepreneurs or civil society, or through transnational pressure from international organisations. Innovation systems are not about flawless institutional design, but about the ability to adapt to changing technological and societal needs by adjusting rules, incentives and relationships. Systems that can evolve in this way are better able to learn from failure and avoid repeating them. A good example that we will often revisit in this book is Finland, which faced severe disruption in the 1990s after the collapse of trade with the Soviet Union. Instead of stagnating, the country focused its innovation system on ICT, expanded cooperation between universities and industry and invested in governance bodies such as TEKES. The result was a resilient, adaptable innovation model. Emerging economies may not be able to copy the Finnish way, but the general lesson that institutional adaptability is essential for innovation success holds nevertheless.

Institutional economics and the concept of path dependence show that the failure of innovation is often not due to poor strategies or underperforming firms, but to deeper structural constraints. Historical legacies, entrenched routines and misaligned institutions can limit collaboration, discourage risk-taking and stifle learning. For emerging economies, these challenges are significant, but not insurmountable. Institutional weaknesses may shape the playing field, but they do not dictate the outcome. Through targeted reforms, inclusive governance and targeted investment in formal rules and informal norms, countries can build innovation systems that are more adaptable and resilient. The ability to learn from failure depends not only on having good ideas, but also on the surrounding institutions that either support or suppress experimentation. In the following section, we shift the focus from institutions to broader systemic pressures and examine how globalisation, platform-based economies and shifting geopolitical dynamics are changing the conditions for innovation success or failure in emerging innovation systems.

2.6 Contemporary Views on Innovation Failure in Globalized Innovation Networks

While classical theories of innovation systems, absorptive capacity and institutions continue to play a central role in explaining success and failure, contemporary global economy adds new layer of complexities that challenge these frameworks. Innovation today takes place in a fragmented, highly interconnected environment characterised by global value chains, cross-border knowledge flows, platform-based ecosystems and increasing geopolitical tensions (Petraite et al., 2022). These dynamics influence not only how innovations are created and disseminated, but also who benefits and who is left behind. In many emerging economies, access to technology has never been better, yet failure to innovate remains widespread. This paradox points to a deeper structural problem: Emerging economies are integrated into global networks, but not necessarily on terms that enable meaningful learning or capability development (Stojcic, 2021). In this section, we explore how four interrelated forces, the rise of global value chains, the platformisation of innovation, growing innovation asymmetries and resurgent techno-nationalism, shape today's innovation landscape and help explain persistent failure in catch-up contexts.

Global value chains (GVCs) have become the dominant structure of the global economy, enabling firms from emerging economies to integrate into international production networks by specialising in tasks such as assembly, packaging or logistics. While this model provides access to capital, technology and management practices, it often does not lead to real learning relevant for building of domestic innovation capabilities (Stojcic & Matic, 2024). This phenomenon can be seen as thin integration, a participation with limits to upgrading. As several scholars have shown over the past two decades (Hobday, 1995; Humphrey & Schmitz, 2002; Lee, 2019; Stojcic, 2021; Stojcic et al., 2025), leading firms, typically located in advanced economies, often retain control over high-value functions such as R&D, branding and product design, while outsourcing standardised, low-margin activities. Knowledge is only shared to ensure operational efficiency, not to foster the development of local capabilities. As a result, suppliers are often seen as interchangeable, which reduces the incentives for meaningful investment in their growth. South East Asia or Central Eastern Europe abound with examples of countries that have attracted large multinational investment, while domestic firms remain on the periphery in the innovation process (Stojcic et al., 2025). Without a proactive policy, there is a risk that participation in GVCs will increase dependency instead of enabling a technological catch-up process.

The rise of digital platforms has fundamentally reshaped the innovation landscape. These platforms now mediate access not only to markets and consumers, but also to data, infrastructure and innovation environments through APIs, app stores and cloud services (Kenney & Zysman, 2016). While they lower barriers to entry for some players, particularly start-ups and digital entrepreneurs, they also concentrate control over critical resources, standards and decision-making (Srnicek, 2017). For emerging economies, this creates a paradox. On the one hand, platforms enable new opportunities in emerging sectors, while on the other, domestic firms often become peripheral players, data providers, resellers or developers operating under opaque algorithms and governance systems controlled elsewhere. Innovation decisions are centralised, while local ecosystems remain dependent and constrained. Failure is, thus, not a lack of activity, but a lack of autonomy in such setting. Without platform sovereignty or regulatory influence, countries struggle to influence innovation outcomes or secure their digital future.

While access to knowledge has expanded worldwide, the ability to turn this knowledge into innovation is still very unevenly distributed. Technologies such as artificial intelligence, biotechnology and green energy are not freely shared goods, but are subject to intellectual property rights, complex licences, export restrictions and tacit know-how that is difficult to transfer. This leads to strong innovation asymmetries. Advanced economies dominate upstream research and retain control of key platforms, while many emerging economies remain downstream users, unable to change or build on fundamental technologies. Patent thickets, restrictive licences and non-compete agreements limit the scope for local innovation. Lee (2019) and Lee and Lim (2001) describe several dependency traps in which countries, sectors and firms in East Asia trying to build innovation capacities were faced with the choice of either remaining tied to external providers or decoupling from them. In short, access to technology does not guarantee innovation autonomy and makes emerging systems vulnerable to disruption and failure.

Innovation is no longer just an economic issue, but one that is increasingly intertwined with geopolitics. Over the past decade, technological rivalry, particularly between the United States and China, has led to a wave of export controls on strategic technologies, bans on foreign firms in critical infrastructure,and efforts to reshape supply chains through onshoring or "friendshoring" These changes pose significant risks for emerging economies. Technological alliances are becoming increasingly exclusive, forcing third countries to align themselves politically, which can limit their access to innovation. Countries that are highly dependent on foreign research partnerships or imported technologies now face increased uncertainty as geopolitical tensions disrupt academic collaboration and technology flows. In such an environment, the failure of innovation may not be due to internal inadequacies, but to external exclusion, where strategic competition, rather than capability, determines who gets to innovate and who gets left behind.

While we will revisit these issues in more detail through several of following chapters, it can be concluded already that emerging innovation systems today face the paradox of a global economy that appears open but is characterised by deep asymmetries in knowledge, control and access. Participation in global value chains, digital platforms and international research networks can foster growth, but only if countries retain the ability to absorb, adapt and control the knowledge that flows through them. This has led to an increasing focus on "innovation sovereignty", the ability to define national innovation pathways, reduce technological dependency and ensure strategic autonomy. Achieving this does not require isolation, but rather targeted investment in domestic capabilities, a regulatory framework that protects local ecosystems and diplomatic engagement to secure access to key technologies. Without these efforts, countries run the risk of falling into a dependent role that is vulnerable to both internal fragmentation and external shocks. The failure of innovation in this context is not just a domestic problem but reflects structural imbalances in the global innovation landscape. The next section looks at a framework for a more systematic diagnosis of such failure.

2.7 Typologies of Innovation Failure

The failure of innovations is not a single phenomenon, but a spectrum of problems with different causes, consequences and effects. Some failures are due to technical errors, such as products that do not work or processes that underperform (Baxter et al., 2023; Hyll & Pippel, 2016). Others result from misunderstood markets, where innovations fail to meet demand or come too early or too late (Block et al., 2017; Guzzini & Iacobucci, 2017; Miller, 2003). Still others are due to institutional weaknesses such as poor regulation, lack of incentives or misaligned funding structures (Radosevic et al., 2023; Stojcic, 2024). Systemic failure reflects deeper problems, fragmented ecosystems, broken connections or lack of coordination between key players (Metcalfe, 2005; Woolthuis et al., 2005). Especially in emerging economies, where resources are limited and the margin for error is small, it is important to understand the nature of failure. This section presents a typology of four interrelated types of failure: technical, market, institutional and systemic. Although they differ analytically, these often overlap in practice. A technical failure can lead to market failure just as institutional failures can lead to systemic failures. Recognising these dynamics helps policymakers and practitioners to develop more targeted and effective innovation strategies.

Technical failure occurs when an innovation is flawed in terms of design, engineering or implementation despite its ambitions (Baxter et al., 2023). This is common in high-risk R&D environments, but in emerging systems the consequences are often even more acute. Failures may be due to immature technology, inadequate testing or unrealistic expectations given local capabilities. India's Aakash tablet is a classic example. Its goal of providing affordable access to education was undermined by poor performance and reliability, largely due to inadequate design validation. Similarly, the Boeing 737 Max history shows that even advanced firms are prone to technical failures when commercial pressures override engineering standards. In many low-capacity innovation systems, the likelihood of technical failure is increased due to weak testing infrastructure, limited prototyping environments and a lack of design and system integration capabilities. Projects that look promising on paper fail in practice not because of bad ideas, but because the underlying technological systems needed to support them are underdeveloped or missing.

Even if a product works, it can fail if it cannot attract or retain users. Market failure in innovation occurs when a technically sound solution fails to gain commercial traction due to poor timing, lack of infrastructure, misjudged user needs or ineffective pricing (Bleda & del Rio, 2013). Google Glass, for example, had advanced features but suffered from high costs, social stigmatisation and privacy concerns, which ultimately led to its rejection by the broad mass of consumers. In many developing countries, market failures are particularly common, not because innovations are ineffective, but because delivery systems are weak or demand is underdeveloped. Electric vehicles (EVs) face this barrier in many regions, where the lack of charging infrastructure and consumer finance makes adoption difficult. It is often not possible to transfer innovations from high-income countries to lower-income countries where purchasing power, the cultural environment or service networks are very different. In these cases, the problem is not the product itself, but a lack of an ecosystem of support, so the failure is systemic rather than isolated.

Technical failure and market failure are analytically distinct, but in practice they often intertwine. A product may fail in the market because it was poorly designed or because users were not ready for it. Sometimes market feedback can lead to technical improvements, creating an important feedback loop for innovation. In many emerging innovation systems, however, this loop is broken. Entrepreneurs receive little information about why an idea failed, procurement systems discourage iteration and investors penalise risk without giving a second chance. As a result, innovation failure becomes a terminus rather than a source of learning. This is in contrast to high-performing innovation ecosystems where failure is treated as part of the learning cycle. In emerging markets, building this adaptability through better data systems, iterative funding models and more open procurement processes is critical. Only then can systems move from failure as loss to failure as learning and from isolated missteps to cumulative progress.

Institutional failure occurs when the rules governing innovation, laws, policies, norms and governance structures, either fail or actively stand in the way of progress towards innovation goals (Woolthuis et al., 2005). In contrast to technical failure or market failure, which can be limited to specific technologies or sectors, institutional failure distorts the entire innovation environment. In many emerging innovation systems in Central and Eastern Europe, such failure is due to weak coordination between government agencies, short-term political cycles and limited strategic foresight (Stojcic, 2024; Stojcic et al., 2025). Institutions tasked with supporting innovation, such as funding bodies, research councils and regulators, often operate in silos, follow conflicting mandates or are politically captured. Even when the R&D infrastructure is in place, the policy environment can lack the stability and coherence required for long-term capability building. As a result, innovators face conflicting incentives, fluctuating priorities and fragmented governance. All of this creates uncertainty, increases transaction costs and reduces the willingness of firms and researchers to invest in high-risk, high-reward innovations.

Institutional failure manifests itself in many forms. One common problem is policy incoherence, where the strategies of education, industry and academia contradict rather than support each other. Another is the dysfunctionality of regulation, particularly in fast-developing sectors such as fintech or artificial intelligence, where outdated, unclear or inconsistently enforced rules lead to uncertainty and discourage investment. In such an environment, firms often operate in legal grey areas and risk sudden policy U-turns, despite offering valuable and often indispensable services.

An even worse form of institutional failure is corruption and rent-seeking, when public funds earmarked for innovation are distributed based on political connections or personal networks rather than merit. Innovation funds and grant programmes in many emerging systems have come under criticism for lacking transparency and accountability and have undermined trust in public funding mechanisms. However, not all institutional barriers are formal. Informal norms such as excessive risk aversion, top-down decision-making or discriminatory social expectations can be equally obstructive. Taken together, these institutional weaknesses undermine trust, fragment coordination and slow down innovation dynamics.

Even well-intentioned innovation policies often fall short if the institutional foundations are weak or uncoordinated. An effective innovation policy requires not only ambitious goals, but also cross-ministerial coordination, transparent funding mechanisms and robust systems for evaluation and learning. In the absence of these elements, there is a risk that innovation policy becomes a performative policy, well-articulated in strategy documents but disconnected from practical outcomes. Programmes can be announced with great fanfare but fail to have a lasting impact due to budget uncertainties, administrative fragmentation or politicised implementation. Promising projects often stall before they can realise their full impact, leading to a cycle of inflated expectations and subsequent disappointment. This erosion of credibility discourages both public and private sector engagement. Entrepreneurs lose confidence in public support systems, firms reduce their investment in long-term research and development, and innovation becomes increasingly focused on a small group of players or reliant on foreign inputs. Over time, the system stagnates, not so much because there is a lack of ideas, but because the institutions that are supposed to support them are not working.

One of the most critical forms of institutional failure is inflexibility, the inability of institutions to evolve in response to new technological or market conditions. Innovation is dynamic by nature, yet many regulatory systems remain static and apply outdated rules to new technologies such as AI, biotechnology, fintech or digital platforms. Countries such as Singapore and Estonia have addressed this problem by introducing regulatory sandboxes where firms can test innovations under supervised conditions, enabling both regulators and companies to learn in real time. In contrast, many emerging markets either over-regulate prematurely or leave entire sectors in limbo, creating uncertainties that discourage investment. Institutional readiness, the ability to respond quickly, transparently and intelligently to innovation challenges, is crucial but often overlooked. It is not enough to increase R&D budgets or improve STEM education. If institutions are unable to support, regulate and adapt to innovation processes, these investments will yield little. Inflexible institutions not only block innovation but also waste scarce resources and undermine public confidence in reform.

Ultimately, institutional failure is one of the most persistent and damaging barriers to innovation in emerging systems. It affects everything from who gets funded to the risks that are taken and whether ideas survive the pilot phase. It's not just about weak laws or poor implementation, but also about deeper structural issues such as power imbalances, historical legacies and a lack of inclusive governance. Dealing with institutional failure requires systemic reforms: improving transparency, building capacity and creating feedback loops that allow systems to learn and evolve. It is important that institutions are not seen as neutral intermediaries, but as products of political and social structures. Building institutional readiness means ensuring that innovation policies are not only well designed, but also credible, fair and aligned with national development goals. Next, we turn to systemic failure, the most comprehensive category. We examine what happens when the entire innovation ecosystem is fragmented or misaligned, and why even strong ideas and capable actors can fail in such an environment.

Systemic failure occurs when the components of an innovation system, firms, research organisations, governments, financial actors and intermediaries, exist but do not work together. In contrast to technical failure or market failure, systemic failure reflects a breakdown in the relationships, feedback loops and coordination mechanisms that allow innovation to flourish. While many emerging economies have formal institutions, R&D policies and increasing public spending, the entire ecosystem is fragmented and uncoordinated. This leads to duplication of effort, inefficiency and missed opportunities. In this sense, the innovation system becomes less than the sum of its parts. Woolthuis et al. (2005) identify various subtypes of systemic failure, including structural gaps (e.g. lack of regulations or procurement mechanisms), coordination gaps and cultural or trust deficits. In many contexts, SMEs are excluded from national programmes, universities operate in isolation and financial institutions avoid innovation risks. Systemic failure is, thus, not caused by a single actor, but by the lack of connections between them.

Examples of systemic failure can be found in regions such as the Western Balkans and parts of Central and Eastern Europe, where countries have invested in innovation strategies, infrastructure and institutional reforms, but struggle to create coherent systems. Universities are often incentivised to prioritise international publications over collaboration with local firms. Small and medium-sized enterprises lack the absorptive capacity, resources or confidence to engage in collaborative research and development, while government agencies operate in silos with overlapping mandates and fragmented funding mechanisms. Innovation intermediaries such as cluster organisations or science parks exist on paper, but are often underfunded, poorly connected to industry or lack credibility with key stakeholders. The result is a policy landscape that contains many of the expected ingredients, but lacks the coordination or trust needed to translate them into meaningful outcomes. These cases show that the failure of innovation is not always due to missing elements, but to weak coordination between system components.

One of the most damaging effects of system failure is its tendency to be self-reinforcing. When actors work in isolation, the benefits of collective learning and coordination are lost. Over time, public agencies avoid risky projects in favour of safe, incremental initiatives, firms withdraw from public programmes that appear inefficient or irrelevant and universities focus on global metrics rather than local impact. These behaviours create a capability trap in which the ambition to innovate across the system continues to decline. The result is stagnation not only in outcomes but also in aspirations. The problem is exacerbated by the absence or weakness of intermediary organisations that bridge the gap between business, academia, funders and policymakers. These include innovation centres, technology transfer offices, cluster coordinators and industry associations. In well-functioning systems, they facilitate matchmaking, reduce transaction costs and strengthen trust. In many emerging systems, however, they are underfunded, under-resourced or simply absent, leaving key innovation players stuck in isolation.

Because systemic failure is widespread and often invisible, it is frequently misdiagnosed. Politicians may blame market rejection for a failed product when the real problem was a lack of institutional support or regulatory clarity. Universities can be criticised for their lack of engagement with industry, even though public incentives discourage them from doing so. Dealing with systemic failure requires tools that focus on relationships, not just actors. These include system mapping to identify who interacts with whom, stakeholder platforms to encourage co-creation of innovation, and empowered co-ordination bodies to align fragmented policy efforts. The OECD's (2024) Agenda for Transformative Science, Technology and Innovation (STI) policies calls for reflexivity, i.e. the ability of systems to assess whether their structures support inclusive and sustainable innovation. Systemic failure is a kind of meta-failure that exacerbates technical, market and institutional weaknesses. A brilliant product can fail because of flawed regulation. A capable start-up may fail because public procurement favours incumbents. In these cases, fixing innovation problems means rethinking the whole system, not just improving individual parts.

Innovation failure is rarely a single event, but a complex process that can occur in different phases and at different levels of the system. By distinguishing between technical, market, institutional and systemic failure, we get a more precise framework to understand why innovations fail and what kind of interventions are needed. Technical failure often requires improved design and engineering, market failure requires demand-side measures and supportive infrastructure, institutional failure requires governance reform and coherent policy and systemic failure emphasises the need for coordination, trust and shared direction. In practice, most failures are hybrids that stem from overlapping causes, particularly in emerging economies where firm capabilities, institutions and system-wide linkages are often weak at the same time. The goal is not to eliminate failure, which is inevitable and necessary in innovation but to enable systems to learn from it. The next chapter looks at a critical source of failure in this context, the bottlenecks in knowledge transfer in an increasingly interconnected but unequal global economy.

2.8 Failure vs Experimentation in Innovation

Innovation and failure have always had an uneasy relationship. In public and policy discourse, failure is often seen as a negative outcome, evidence of poor judgement, inefficiency or wasted resources. This view reinforces a culture of risk aversion and penalises experimentation, particularly in emerging economies where resources are scarce. In the innovation literature, however, failure has a different status as it is not only expected, but essential. Trial and error, setbacks and iterative learning are central to how new ideas develop and improve (Ferreira et al., 2020; Khanna et al., 2016). The crucial difference lies in the way failure is presented and utilised. If it is treated as dysfunction, it leads to blame and withdrawal. When it is seen as discovery, it becomes a catalyst for adaptation and learning. This section explores this tension and examines how organisations and innovation systems can understand failure not as a signal to quit, but as a resource for building resilience, refining strategy and strengthening long-term capacity for meaningful innovation.

Innovation is fundamentally a process of trial and error, characterised by uncertainty, experimentation and adaptation. It is about venturing into the unknown, developing new technologies, products or business models without guaranteed outcomes. In this context, failure is not an anomaly, but an integral part of the development of innovation. Scholars such as Nelson and Winter (1982) and March (1991) have emphasised that firms innovate under conditions of bounded rationality and incomplete knowledge. Instead of optimising perfectly, they search, test and learn, often by failing first. The key is not to eliminate failures, but to build the capacity to learn from them through feedback mechanisms, iterative design and institutional support (Greco et al., 2020). Industries that lead in innovation are not those that avoid failures, but those that systematise them, reflect on them and adapt accordingly. Innovation systems that allow for trial and error rather than penalising it tend to be more resilient, flexible and able to make sustainable progress over time.

Not all failures are created equal. Some serve as important learning moments, while others lead to wasted resources and repeated mistakes. The concept of "intelligent failure" introduced by Sitkin (1992) refers to failures that occur in novel contexts, on a manageable scale, with clear learning objectives and subsequent reflection. These failures help organisations to refine their strategies, discard ineffective approaches and improve future performance. Amy Edmondson (2011) has expanded on this idea by identifying the cultural conditions that favour intelligent failure. Organisations with high levels of psychological safety, where employees feel safe to report mistakes, tend to develop stronger feedback loops and systems for codifying lessons learned. Transparency, open dialogue and systematic follow-up make failure an asset rather than a liability. Such environments foster a "learning orientation" where experimentation is encouraged and missteps are not seen as incompetence, but as part of the innovation journey. The presence of these characteristics often distinguishes adaptive organisations from stagnant ones.

In contrast, unproductive failures are more common in systems where learning is weak or not encouraged. These failures occur when experiments are poorly designed, lessons are ignored, or the same mistakes are repeated due to institutional amnesia (Narduzzo & Forrer, 2024). Often the root problem is not incompetence, but systemic failures such as misaligned incentives that prioritise results over learning, cultures that penalise failure and information silos that prevent knowledge sharing. A recurring example is the "pilot project syndrome" that can be observed in many public innovation programmes. Initiatives are launched without learning from previous endeavours, leading to a cycle of redundancy and frustration. What separates productive failure from unproductive failure is often the presence or absence of robust evaluation mechanisms. Real-time monitoring, independent audits and open stakeholder feedback are essential to turn failures into learnings. Yet in many emerging innovation systems, these mechanisms are weak or non-existent. Without institutionalised learning processes, failure becomes opaque and isolated, depriving innovation systems of much-needed adaptive feedback.

The cultural and institutional attitude towards failure plays a decisive role in the development of innovations. In addition to technical design and organisational routines, the way in which societies perceive and react to failure influences whether people are willing to take risks, experiment and learn from setbacks. Cultural norms operate on multiple levels, from personal beliefs to organisational habits and national policy frameworks and together define a region's innovation climate. In the United States, failure is often viewed as a learning opportunity and rite of passage for entrepreneurs. Mantras such as "fail fast, fail forward" reflect a culture that tolerates and even celebrates failure if it leads to growth. This mindset lowers the psychological cost of risk-taking and encourages second chances, especially in ecosystems like Silicon Valley. In contrast, Japan's emphasis on precision, hierarchy and social harmony creates an environment where failure is tainted with stigma and shame, leading to risk aversion and a reluctance to acknowledge or publicly address setbacks.

In Europe, the picture is more heterogeneous. Countries such as the UK and the Netherlands have adopted a more open attitude to failure, while others, such as Germany and France, remain more cautious and risk averse. Recent policy changes in the EU, particularly around mission-oriented innovation (Mazzucato, 2018), recognise failure as an expected outcome of ambitious experimentation. However, deeply entrenched bureaucratic structures often hinder the institutionalisation of learning from failure. In most emerging innovation systems, the consequences of failure are more severe. Entrepreneurs often face not only the loss of their reputation, but also financial ruin or legal consequences, especially in countries with weak safety nets. This risky environment discourages experimentation and encourages conservatism. In the public sector, fear of political backlash for failed programmes leads to defensive behaviour where failures are hidden or suppressed rather than addressed. As a result, innovation systems suffer from a lack of transparency and accountability, making it difficult to learn lessons from failure or build a culture that allows for learning and adaptation.

Cultural attitudes to failure are rarely a stand-alone phenomenon but are reinforced and perpetuated by institutional structures. In many countries, strict bankruptcy laws, punitive credit systems and media reports that stigmatise failure contribute to an environment in which even intelligent, well-intentioned failure becomes a serious liability. Entrepreneurs are discouraged from taking bold risks and instead turn to safer, less transformative ventures. This institutional reinforcement of risk aversion means that innovation systems often underperform not because of a lack of ideas, but because of a lack of psychological and legal freedom to experiment. Changing this dynamic requires more than good policy. It requires institutional reforms in areas such as bankruptcy law, regulatory oversight and public communication. Creating a climate in which failure is recognised as part of learning rather than treated as a moral or legal failure is an essential prerequisite for adaptive innovation. However, this cultural change becomes possible only when institutions model openness, tolerance and a commitment to long-term learning over short-term blame.

While culture shapes attitudes to failure, organisations and governments can actively design systems that treat failure as a source of learning rather than a reason for punishment. High-performing firms often institutionalise learning by conducting innovation audits, root cause analyses and post-mortem reviews, processes that uncover what went wrong and why, without assigning personal blame. These mechanisms are particularly important in industries where the stakes are high, such as aerospace, software development and healthcare. However, they are rarely used in SMEs in emerging economies, where time, training and trust are limited. Governments can also enable learning through sandbox policies that allow innovators to test new technologies in a controlled, low-risk environment. Examples such as Singapore's AI governance sandbox and Kenya's flexible approach to mobile money regulation show how experimentation can be encouraged without sacrificing oversight. These models emphasise safe conditions, feedback loops and early stakeholder engagement all of which are design elements that help innovation systems become more adaptable, inclusive and resilient in the face of uncertainty.

Adaptive innovation systems are those that can learn from failure, adapt to new conditions and improve over time. Building such systems requires institutional memory, a repository of past experiences that prevents the repetition of mistakes, reflexive governance, policy frameworks that evolve based on learnings and outcomes, and inclusive processes that involve different stakeholders, especially those affected by failed initiatives. In a resource-constrained environment, these goals may seem ambitious, but even modest measures such as documenting failed grants, publishing evaluation reports or organising open learning sessions can foster a culture of continuous improvement. For emerging economies, this change is critical. Innovation and failure are not opposites but rather two sides of the same coin. Societies must learn to view failure not as a final judgement but as a source of insight. This requires a rethinking of the definition of success, the evaluation of programmes and the support of entrepreneurs. The next section looks at why failure carries greater weight in emerging innovation systems and why recovery needs to be intentional and well supported when possible.

2.9 Implications for Emerging Innovation Systems

The failure of innovation is never trivial, but in emerging economies the consequences are often more serious and far-reaching. These systems usually operate under conditions of institutional weakness, limited financial resources and an underdeveloped innovation infrastructure (Stojcic, 2024). When failures occur in such an environment, they can drain scarce public resources, discourage future experimentation and reinforce the perception that innovation is too risky to pursue. Unlike in mature systems, where failures can be absorbed, analysed and redirected, emerging systems often lack mechanisms such as robust evaluation frameworks, institutional memory or adaptive policy instruments to turn failures into learnings. As a result, failures can become system-wide setbacks instead of serving as a springboard for improvement. This section summarises the lessons learned so far to explore why innovation failure is not only more likely in emerging economies, but also more damaging. It highlights the structural vulnerabilities that amplify their impact and discusses what is needed to strengthen the resilience of systems that are still in the process of technological catch-up.

In mature innovation systems, failure is often cushioned by institutional redundancy including multiple sources of funding, flexible labour markets and legal protection mitigate setbacks. In contrast, emerging economies operate with thin ecosystems and few second chances. A failed start-up can mean the end of an entrepreneur's career while a collapsed public R&D programme can dry up funding for years. Because the system lacks buffers, each failure carries disproportionate weight. The loss of a single initiative can derail momentum, discredit entire policy approaches or discourage future experimentation. This fragility amplifies the costs of failure, turning what could be a manageable setback in a developed system into a sector-wide crisis. Without institutional depth, emerging economies have more at stake, less room to manoeuvre and limited options for recovery. Failure becomes a systemic threat, not just to individual players, but to the entire technological catch-up process and long-term development planning.

An important reason why failure is so consequential in emerging innovation systems is the lack of a learning infrastructure. In high-performing systems, failure leads to feedback after which evaluations form the basis for future programmes, post-mortems impart lessons and institutions adapt. In many emerging contexts, these mechanisms are absent or weak. Political cycles interrupt continuity, documentation is neglected and turnover erases organisational memory. Programmes fail quietly, only to be relaunched under a new name and with the same flaws. Innovation policies repeat the mistakes of the past not out of ignorance, but because the systems lack the ability to remember. This learning gap undermines credibility, discourages stakeholder participation and wastes scarce resources. It also perpetuates inefficiency as reforms are implemented without reference to past outcomes. Building institutional memory through evaluations, knowledge repositories and stakeholder learning platforms is critical for resilience. Without this memory, failures remain a one-off event rather than a source of strategic adaptation. Innovation systems that cannot learn from mistakes are doomed to repeat them.

Political and reputational dynamics exacerbate the problem. In many emerging economies, innovation failure is highly visible and easily politicised. A failed public initiative can trigger media backlash or parliamentary investigations and discourage officials from supporting risky or novel ventures. As a result, the bureaucracy tends to be incrementalist, favouring low-risk projects over transformative ones. Similarly, entrepreneurs who suffer a failure and whose reputation is damaged make it difficult to re-enter the market or secure future investment. In close-knit business circles, a single failure can result in a long-term stigma. This environment encourages caution, suppresses ambition and reduces the system's tolerance for experimentation.

The feedback loop is damaging as fewer bold initiatives are funded, fewer lessons are learnt and fewer breakthroughs are achieved. In this environment, innovation systems become conservative by default, not because of a lack of talent or ideas, but because the institutional and cultural climate penalises failure rather than seeing it as a necessary part of progress.

The failure of innovations is not only more frequent in emerging innovation systems but also has more serious consequences. Without the buffers and redundancies of mature ecosystems, failure can bring entire sectors to a standstill, undermining trust and entrenching risk-averse behaviour. It undermines institutional learning, discourages experimentation and can block strategic pathways for technological upgrading. For these reasons, understanding and dealing with failure must be prioritised not only by policymakers and researchers, but by all actors within the innovation system. Emerging economies cannot afford to hide or dismiss failures, rather, they must view them as valuable feedback and triggers for course correction. Dealing with failures in a transparent and constructive way provides an opportunity to reshape incentives, rebuild trust and improve long-term resilience. The next and final section of this chapter summarises the key findings from our analysis and paves the way for Chapter 3, which turns to one of the most persistent barriers to innovation success, the one of knowledge transfer bottlenecks.

2.10 Conclusion

The failure of innovation is often misunderstood as a singular, visible event, as a poorly functioning product, an unsuccessful policy or a failed start-up. But as this chapter has argued, failure is rarely that simple. In many cases it is a systemic signal embedded in the underlying architecture of innovation systems. We have explored how failure arises not only from flawed technologies or inappropriate markets, but also from institutional failure, fragmented ecosystems and cultural resistance to risk. The typology of technical, market, institutional and systemic failure provided us with tools to diagnose these failures more accurately. We also explored how failure can be productive, by promoting adaptation and learning, or unproductive, by reinforcing stagnation. Crucially, we found that failure reveals the health of a system. In coordinated, well-resourced environments, it leads to feedback and evolution. In fragile systems, it triggers a retreat. This is especially true in emerging innovation systems, where the costs of failure are high and the opportunities to recover are far more limited.

Understanding failure is only the first step. If we want to build stronger innovation systems, we also need to ask ourselves why innovation often fails to materialise in the first place. One of the most persistent and damaging culprits is the knowledge transfer bottleneck. Despite decades of globalisation, access to knowledge is still very unevenly distributed. Technologies, ideas and expertise often do not reach the firms, institutions and regions that need them most. In emerging systems that are highly dependent on imported knowledge, whether through foreign direct investment, licencing or technical co-operation, these breakdowns are especially damaging. They delay learning, deepen technological dependence and undermine local innovation capacity. Chapter 3 addresses this challenge. It examines why knowledge transfer fails, where it gets stuck and what can be done to improve its flow. From absorptive capacity and institutional readiness to global power asymmetries, we examine the structural barriers that impede knowledge diffusion and consider how emerging innovation systems can redesign these systems to support inclusive learning and long-term technological sovereignty.

References

Andrews, M., Pritchett, L., & Woolcock, M. (2017). *Building state capability: Evidence, analysis, action.* Oxford University Press.

Baxter, D., Trott, P., & Ellwood, P. (2023). Reconceptualising innovation failure. *Research Policy, 52*(7), 104811.

Bell, M., & Pavitt, K. (1993). Technological accumulation and industrial growth: Contrasts between developed and developing countries. *Industrial and Corporate Change, 2*(2), 157–210.

Bleda, M., & del Rio, P. (2013). The market failure and the systemic failure rationales in technological innovation systems. *Research Policy, 42*(5), 1039–1052.

Block, J. H., Fisch, C. O., & van Praag, M. (2017). The Schumpeterian entrepreneur: A review of empirical evidence on the antecedents, behaviour and consequences of innovative entrepreneurship. *Industry and Innovation, 24*(1), 61–95.

Cimoli, M., Dosi, G., & Stiglitz, J. E. (Eds.). (2009). *Industrial policy and development: The political economy of capabilities accumulation.* Oxford University Press.

Cohen, W., & Levinthal, M. (1990). Absorptive capacity: A new perspective on learning and innovation. *Administrative Science Quarterly, 35*, 128–152.

Dosi, G. (1982). Technological paradigms and technological trajectories. *Research Policy, 11*(3), 147–162.

Edmondson, A. C. (2011, April). Strategies for learning from failure. *Harvard Business Review.*

Edquist, C. (1997). *Systems of innovation.* Routledge.

Ferreira, J. J. M., Fernandes, C. I., & Ferreira, F. A. F. (2020). Wearing failure as a path to innovation. *Journal of Business Research, 120*, 195–202.

Freeman, C. (1987). *Technology, policy and economic performance: Lessons from Japan.* Pinter.

Greco, M., Grimaldi, M., & Gricelli, L. (2020). Interorganizational collaboration strategies and innovation abandonment: The more the merrier? *Industrial Marketing Management, 90*, 679–692.

Guzzini, E., & Iacobucci, D. (2017). Project failures and innovation performance in university-firm collaborations. *The Journal of Technology Transfer, 42*, 865–883.

Hyll, W., & Pippel, G. (2016). Types of cooperation partners as determinants of innovation failures. *Technology Analysis & Strategic Management, 28*(4), 462–476.

Hobday, M. (1995). *Innovation in East Asia: The challenge to Japan.* Edward Elgar.

Hobday, M., Rush, H., & Bessant, J. (2004). Approaching the innovation frontier in Korea: The transition phase to leadership. *Research Policy, 33*(10), 1433–1457.

Humphrey, J., & Schmitz, H. (2002). How does insertion in global value chains affect upgrading in industrial clusters. *Regional Studies, 36*(9), 1017–1027.

Kenney, M., & Zysman, J. (2016). The rise of the platform economy. *Issues in Science and Technology, 32*(3), 61–69.

Khanna, R., Guler, I., & Nerkar, A. (2016). Fail often, fail big, and fail fast? Learning from small failures and R&D performance in the pharmaceutical industry. *Academy of Management Journal, 59*(2), 436–459.

Kim, L. (1997). *Imitation to innovation. The dynamics of Korea's Technological Learning*. Harvard University Press, Boston.

Knudsen, T. (2002). Economic selection theory. *Journal of Evolutionary Economics, 12*(4), 443–470.

Lall, S. (1992). Technological capabilities and industrialization. *World Development, 20*(2), 165–186.

Langbein, J. (2020). Shallow market integration and weak developmental capacities: Ukraine's pathway from periphery to periphery. *Review of International Political Economy, 27*(5), 1126–1146.

Lee, K. (2019). *The art of economic catch-up: Barriers, detours and leapfrogging in innovation systems*. Cambridge University Press.

Lee, K., & Lim, C. (2001). Technological regimes, catching-up and leapfrogging: Findings from the Korean industries. *Research Policy, 30*(3), 459-483.Hyll.

Liedong, T. A., Peprah, A. A., & Eyong, J. E. (2020). Institutional voids and innovation governance: A conceptual exposition of the open versus closed architecture choice. *Strategic Change, 29*(1), 57–66.

Lundvall, B. A. (1988). Innovation as an interactive process: from user-producer interaction to the national system of innovation. In G. Dosi et al. (Eds.), *Technical change and economic theory* (pp. 349–370). Pinter.

Lundvall, B. A. (2016). *The learning economy and the economics of hope*. Anthem Press.

Malerba, F. (2002). Sectoral systems of innovation and production. *Research Policy, 31*(2), 247–264.

March, J. G. (1991). Exploration and exploitation in organizational learning. *Organization Science, 2*(1), 71–87.

Matus-Ruiz, M., Saka-Helmhout, A., & Carillo, J. (2025). How institutional voids are experienced and enacted through social innovation initiatives by multinationals in emerging markets. *International Business Review, 34*(2), 102382.

Mazzucato, M. (2013). *The entrepreneurial state: Debunking public vs. private sector myths*. Anthem Press.

Mazzucato, M. (2018). Mission-oriented innovation policies: Challenges and opportunities. *Industrial and Corporate Change, 27*(5), 803–815.

Metcalfe, J. S. (1998). *Evolutionary economics and creative destruction*. Routledge.

Metcalfe, J. S. (2005). Systems failure and the case for innovation policy. In P. Llerena & M. Matt (Eds.), *Innovation policy in a knowledge-based economy*. Springer.

Miller, D. (2003). An asymmetry-based view of advantage: Towards an attainable sustainability. *Strategic Management Journal, 24*(10), 961–976.

Narduzzo, A., & Forrer, V. (2024). Nurturing innovation through intelligent failure: The art of failing on purpose. *Technovation, 131*, 102951.

Nelson, R., & Winter, S. (1982). *An evolutionary theory of economic change*. Harvard University Press.

Nelson, R. (1993). *National innovation systems*. Oxford University Press.

Nelson, R. R. (2008). Economic development from the perspective of evolutionary economic theory. *Oxford Development Studies, 36*(1), 9–21.

North, D. C. (1990). *Institutions, institutional change and economic performance*. Cambridge University Press.

OECD (2024). *OECD agenda for transformative science, technology and innovation policies* (OECD Science, Technology and Industry Policy Papers, No. 164). OECD Publishing.

Petraite, M., Mubarak, M. F., Rimantas, R., & von Zedtwitz, M. (2022). The role of international networks in upgrading national innovation systems. *Technological Forecasting and Social Change, 184*, 121873.

Pietrobelli, C., & Rabellotti, R. (2011). Global value chains meet innovation systems: Are there learning opportunities for developing countries? *World Development, 3*(7), 1261–1269.
Radosevic, S., Kanellou, D., & Tsekouras, G. (2023). The experimentation-accountability trade-off in innovation and industrial policy: Are learning networks the solution? *Science and Public Policy, 50*(4), 655–669.
Schot, J., & Steinmueller, W. E. (2018). Three frames for innovation policy: R&D, systems of innovation and transformative change. *Research Policy, 47*(9), 1554–1567.
Schumpeter, J. A. (1934). *Theory of economic development.* Harvard University Press.
Sitkin, S. B. (1992). Learning through failure—The strategy of small losses. *Research in Organizational Behavior, 14*, 231–266.
Srnicek, N. (2017). *Platform capitalism.* Polity Press.
Steinfeld, E. S. (2004). China's shallow integration: Networked production and the new challenges for late industrialization. *World Development, 32*(11), 1971–1987.
Stojcic, N. (2021). Collaborative innovation in emerging innovation systems: Evidence from Central and Eastern Europe. *The Journal of Technology Transfer, 46*, 531–562.
Stojcic, N. (2024). Innovation failure, training for innovative activities and public support for innovation: Multi-annual evidence from emerging European innovation systems. *Research Policy, 53*(8), 105059.
Stojcic, N., & Matic, M. (2024). A journey toward global value chain upgrading: Exploring the transition from backward to forward integration. *Technology in Society, 76*, 102435.
Stojcic, N., Dabic, M., & Musteen, M. (2024). With a little help from my friends: Institutional obstacles, networking and SME exporting in emerging European and Asian economies. *International Business Review, 33*(3), 102258.
Stojcic, N., Vujanovic, N. & Radosevic, S. (2025). Resource sharing in enterprise groups and innovation failure: Emerging innovation systems perspective. *The Journal of Technology Transfer*. Online first.
Strelkov, A., Hirzalla, F., & Samokhvalov, V. (2025). Paths (not) taken: Promoting R&D in Central and Eastern Europe. *Journal of Contemporary Central and Eastern Europe, 33*(1), 69–85.
Švarc, J., & Dabić, M. (2021). Transformative innovation policy or how to escape peripheral policy paradox in European research peripheral countries. *Technology in Society, 67*, 101705.
Trott, P. (2017). *Innovation management and new product development* (6th ed.). Pearson.
Woolthuis, R. K., Lankhuisen, M., & Gilsing, V. (2005). A system failure framework for innovation policy design. *Technovation, 25*, 609–619.
Zahra, S. A., & George, G. (2002). Absorptive capacity: A review, reconceptualization and extension. *The Academy of Management Review, 27*(2), 185–203.

Chapter 3
Bottlenecks in Knowledge Transfers

The single biggest problem in communication is the illusion that it has taken place. (George Bernard Shaw)

Abstract Behind every successful innovation lies the ability to absorb, adapt, and apply knowledge. Yet for many firms and economies, this flow of knowledge is anything but smooth. This chapter tells the story of how promising ideas often falter when they meet the barriers of weak absorptive capacities, fragmented systems, and shallow learning routines. It explores how firms may gain access to new technologies through trade, foreign investment, or collaborations, but without the skills and structures to internalise them, opportunities remain unrealised. At the systemic level, poor coordination between universities, firms, and policy frameworks compounds these weaknesses, creating bottlenecks that stifle diffusion. Global value chains add another twist: Integration may bring access, but often on terms that limit local upgrading. By unpacking these dynamics, the chapter reveals why knowledge, the most celebrated currency of the innovation age, so often slips through the fingers of those who need it most.

3.1 Introduction

In the idea of globalisation, knowledge moves effortlessly across borders. Engineers collaborate in real time from different parts of the world, technical standards spread instantly, and research articles are accessible to anyone with an internet connection. This optimistic view suggests that in a globalised world, knowledge is frictionless, weightless and universally accessible. It is a vision that underpins much of the innovation and development policy agenda: As countries open up, liberalise trade, attract foreign direct investment and reform intellectual property regimes, knowledge will naturally flow inwards. It will then spread throughout the domestic economy and drive technological upgrading and inclusive growth. But the reality rarely matches this script. In many emerging innovation systems, the mere presence of global knowledge does not lead to local learning. Integration into global networks often leads to

N. Stojčić, *Elusive Innovation*, Applied Innovation and Technology Management,
https://doi.org/10.1007/978-3-032-14900-8_3

exposure to knowledge, but not absorption. What is assumed to be a pipeline of opportunities often turns out to be a dead end with unrealised potential.

Despite decades of integration, many emerging economies continue to struggle with weak technological diffusion and limited innovation capacity. Foreign firms operate within national borders but rarely collaborate effectively with local suppliers or research organisations. Intellectual property accumulates but remains unutilised due to a lack of technical capabilities. Universities and industry may be formally linked, but these partnerships often remain symbolic rather than substantive. Knowledge enters the system but does not circulate, adapt or become embedded in local practice. These missing links between knowledge inflows and indigenous innovation ecosystems are among the most persistent causes of failure in catch-up processes. The difference lies not only in the quantity of knowledge, but also in the quality of the connection. Without the mechanisms, incentives and capabilities to process, adapt and apply external knowledge, many countries remain bystanders to global innovation rather than participants. The result is a dependence on external actors and an underutilised domestic innovation base.

Knowledge transfer is not a marginal issue for emerging economies but is central to their development strategies. In contrast to advanced economies competing at the technological frontier, most latecomers focus on acquiring, adapting and upgrading existing technologies. Their innovation challenge is less about discovery and more about implementation; they need to learn to produce better, more efficiently and with higher value. Mechanisms such as foreign direct investment, licencing, public–private partnerships and joint research initiatives promise access to global expertise, production methods and innovation networks. They offer the prospect of leapfrogging stages of industrial development. In practice, however, these channels often fall short. Technologies are imported, but skills are not. Learning-by-doing is hindered by weak feedback loops and superficial interdependencies. Local firms assemble products that they do not fully understand. This gap between access and absorption turns what should be a stepping stone into a stumbling block and raises the question of why knowledge, though available, so often fails to lead to development outcomes.

One of the main reasons for this underperformance lies in a long-standing myth that knowledge spillover is automatic. Early economic models assumed that if a multinational firm enters a market, local firms would inevitably benefit through imitation, labour mobility or competitive pressure. However, empirical studies have shown that spillovers are neither automatic nor guaranteed (Görg & Greenaway, 2004; Smeets, 2008; Stojcic & Orlic, 2020). Whether knowledge actually spreads depends on many conditions including but not limited to the strategies of foreign firms, the absorption capacity of domestic firms, the density of collaboration networks and the broader institutional environment. Without a targeted policy and proactive engagement, spillovers can be limited or even negative, crowding out local firms without a learning process taking place. As a result, knowledge remains locked in proprietary processes, protected by intellectual property rights or locked in management routines that are inaccessible to outsiders. This asymmetry challenges the notion that globalisation builds capabilities on its own. It shows that knowledge is not just a public good, but a controlled, negotiated and contested resource.

This chapter analyses these frictions, asymmetries and bottlenecks in the knowledge transfer process. It shows how mechanisms such as foreign direct investment, licencing and strategic partnerships work in practice and what hinders their effectiveness in emerging systems. We examine how capability gaps, institutional weaknesses and strategic behaviours of global firms constrain local learning. Particular attention is paid to intellectual property regimes that are designed to protect innovation but often limit the ability of latecomers to adapt or improve imported technologies. The chapter also draws on real-world examples, from South Korea's success in orchestrating technological learning to Brazil's struggle with superficial integration and India's mixed experience with pharmaceuticals and software. At the centre of this discussion is a simple but crucial question: What does it take to move from having knowledge to having skills? The answer lies not in access alone, but in the systems that support change. Chapter 3 explores how these systems can be built.

3.2 Mechanisms of Knowledge Transfer

The idea that emerging economies can catch up technologically by acquiring knowledge has long characterised development thinking. Unlike fixed assets such as land or minerals, knowledge is seen as inherently mobile and replicable. In theory, it can be passed on through blueprints, training programmes or collaboration with more advanced firms. This assumption has driven industrial policy and reform for decades: open markets, welcome foreign investment, improve intellectual property regimes and innovation will follow. Governments have often placed great faith in these pathways, expecting that the presence of foreign firms, access to technology licences or involvement in international research networks will automatically lead to local learning and long-term upgrading. But the historical record is sobering. Many countries have established the formal architecture of knowledge transfer, investment laws, innovation centres and university alliances without a corresponding growth in innovation capacity. The problem lies not in access alone, but in the systems that transform access into learning.

To better understand this discrepancy, this section examines three important channels of international knowledge transfer: foreign direct investment (FDI), licences and joint ventures, and strategic partnerships. These mechanisms have been promoted worldwide because they can bring in capital, familiarise domestic firms with global standards and embed new knowledge in local ecosystems. In practice, however, they have had very different effects in different countries and sectors. Success depends not only on the mechanism itself, but also on the conditions under which it works. Capacity gaps in domestic firms, weak institutional support for learning and the protective strategies of multinational corporations often limit the scope of knowledge spillovers. What looks like a knowledge transfer opportunity on paper may be of little value in practice if local actors are not equipped, or permitted, to absorb and adapt the technology. As we will see, effective knowledge transfer calls for more than just participation. It requires focused effort, complementary investment and a broader strategy of capability building.

Attracting FDI has long been one of the favourite strategies for accessing foreign knowledge in emerging innovation systems (Stojcic & Orlic, 2020). Policymakers have invested heavily to create attractive conditions for multinational companies through investment promotion agencies, tax exemptions, streamlined regulations and the development of special economic zones (Stojcic et al., 2022). Their hopes were that foreign firms will not only bring in capital, but also act as conduits for technology transfer, managerial upskilling and integration into global value chains. Such logic was compelling as multinational companies operate with advanced equipment, exacting quality standards and state-of-the-art organisational methods (Fujita & Thisse, 2002; Vujanovic et al., 2022). Local workers gain experience in a high-performance environment, suppliers must upgrade to meet new requirements, and domestic firms can improve their own operations by observing best practices (Aitken & Harrison, 1999; Markusen & Trofimenko, 2009). This dynamic forms the basis of the FDI-led model of technological upgrading that underpins many national development strategies in Asia, Latin America, Eastern Europe and parts of Africa.

However, the optimistic narrative of automatic spillovers has rarely materialised as smoothly as expected. While multinational companies often have superior knowledge and skills, they do not necessarily share them (Javorcik, 2004; Stojcic et al., 2025). In many countries, foreign firms operate as enclaves with minimal involvement beyond their own supply chains and internal systems. They may import most of their inputs, employ foreign staff in key technical positions and limit their supplier relationships to low-complexity transactions. The technologies and processes they use are often embedded in proprietary systems that are protected by strict internal protocols or contractual safeguards. Even if local labour is employed, its use may be limited to low-skilled tasks with little opportunity to access core competencies. As a result, the foreign firm remains a "black box" that is technologically advanced but largely impenetrable. In such cases, the presence of foreign direct investment can boost production and exports without contributing meaningfully to domestic learning or skills development, leaving the local innovation system underserved.

Recognising these risks, host governments have experimented with a range of measures to make knowledge spillovers more likely. Some countries enact local content rules to force multinationals to source inputs domestically. Others are investing in supplier development programmes and encourage foreign firms to work with local partners on quality standards, logistics and process improvements. In some cases, foreign investors are required to conduct research and development locally or enter into technology sharing agreements. However, the effectiveness of these measures varies greatly. In all contexts, it is clear that the success of foreign direct investment as a knowledge transfer tool depends besides the technological capabilities of the investor also on the absorptive capacity of the host country. Local firms must be able to recognise, adapt and apply what they observe or receive (Antonelli et al., 2022; Vujanovic et al., 2022). Without a strong domestic base of skills, technical infrastructure and institutional support, even the most advanced multinational becomes an isolated "island of excellence", productive in its own right but disconnected from the broader development process.

While foreign direct investment brings in knowledge through organisational presence, licencing and joint ventures offer more contractual routes for technology access. Licencing, in particular, appears to be a shortcut for countries or firms seeking rapid modernisation. It offers legal rights to utilise established products, processes or designs without having to take the long, uncertain route of in-house development. But the promise of licencing often fades when it comes to implementation. What is transferred are blueprints, user manuals and standardised procedures, while the crucial know-how, the tacit knowledge embedded in experience, routines and context, remains with the licensor (Martinez & Zuniga, 2017). For firms with robust engineering teams and prior experience, codified knowledge may suffice. But for firms in weak innovation systems, the result can be hollow modernisation made of imported machines that cannot be adapted and processes that are followed but not improved. Without hands-on learning and problem solving, licenced technology remains technically available but operationally ineffective and strategically underutilised.

Joint ventures, on the other hand, promise a more relational and potentially deeper form of knowledge interaction (Jiang et al., 2024). When foreign and domestic partners share ownership, operations and strategic objectives, there is scope for collaboration that goes beyond transactional exchange. Joint development, joint staffing and mutual learning become possible in day-to-day operations. In theory, joint ventures can serve as learning platforms where local firms gradually acquire competences from their more experienced partners. However, this ideal is often compromised by asymmetries of power and purpose. Foreign firms may enter into joint ventures not to share knowledge, but to fulfil regulatory requirements or gain access to local markets. In such cases, they may deliberately limit access to their core technologies or retain key functions abroad as we will discuss in Chapter 5. Meanwhile, domestic firms, especially those lacking technical depth or bargaining power, may not be able to gain meaningful insights. Without aligned incentives and sufficient absorptive capacity, joint ventures risk becoming a legal agreement for market entry rather than a genuine mechanism for knowledge diffusion.

China provides a notable example of how joint ventures can be strategically utilised for capability building when accompanied by targeted government intervention (Jiang et al., 2024; Lu et al., 2017). For decades, China required foreign car manufacturers to establish joint ventures with local firms as a condition for market entry. Initially, many of these agreements resulted in limited spillover effects as foreign firms retained control over key technologies. But over time, the Chinese government refined its approach, introducing stricter rules on local content, directing investment towards state-owned enterprises with clear innovation mandates and ensuring that joint ventures contribute to long-term learning objectives. The result was the emergence of competitive domestic automotive and electric vehicle companies, many of which have their roots in joint venture experiences. Former joint venture employees have become entrepreneurs or engineers in Chinese firms, bringing with them the skills, routines and knowledge gained through collaboration. The example of China shows that the transfer of knowledge through joint ventures is not automatic. It requires a coordinated policy, institutional learning objectives and the sustainable development of domestic capabilities.

In addition to market-oriented mechanisms such as foreign direct investment or licencing, collaborative models offer alternative ways of transferring knowledge that are often in the public interest rather than for direct commercial benefit (Stojcic, 2021). These include university–industry partnerships, international research consortia, donor-funded development programmes and hybrid public–private initiatives. In principle, such collaborations enable domestic institutions to learn alongside global experts, jointly develop solutions and gradually strengthen their own innovation capacities. They promise a more equitable flow of knowledge, where learning is reciprocal, iterative and embedded in real problem solving. The focus shifts from simple technology acquisition to deeper capability building. However, the success of these partnerships is far from guaranteed. Misalignments are not uncommon as universities may prioritise academic outcomes while firms push for rapid commercialisation, donors often favour short-term results over long-term institutional development and public–private partnerships often exclude SMEs or marginalised actors. Moreover, technologically advanced partners in asymmetric partnerships may intentionally withhold critical know-how, retain control over key design decisions or limit access to tacit knowledge to maintain competitive advantage (Lee, 2019; Stojcic, 2021; Stojcic et al., 2025). Such knowledge asymmetries, whether intentional or structural, undermine collaborative potential and reduce the scope for true learning and upgrading. Without long-term commitment, inclusive governance and mechanisms to build trust and reciprocity, collaboration risks becoming a symbolic act that produces reports, conferences or pilot projects, but little systemic change.

Another of the important but underestimated barriers to effective knowledge transfer is the distinction between codified and tacit knowledge. Codified knowledge, which is contained in patents, manuals, blueprints or software, is relatively easy to document, transfer and scale. Tacit knowledge, on the other hand, which is based on experience, intuition and real-time problem solving, is much more difficult to access or reproduce. It lives in people, routines and corporate cultures. It is acquired through practice, mentorship and immersion, not through documents or downloads. Emerging markets often gain access to the codified "what" but lack the tacit "how." Licence agreements transfer designs but not the craftsmanship to modify them. Joint ventures may provide proximity to advanced firms, but not the deep engagement required to internalise their routines. Foreign direct investment may bring sophisticated machinery, but not the operational knowledge to adapt it locally. This tacit gap leads to many innovation systems operating on the surface and adopting technologies without fully understanding or owning them.

This asymmetry has serious consequences. Without tacit knowledge, the innovation process becomes superficial as firms can acquire advanced tools, but have difficulty improving, adapting or repairing them when problems arise. Products remain static, services do not evolve and processes cannot respond flexibly to new challenges. Over time, this not only hurts competitiveness of companies, but also the national ability to build a resilient innovation system. The conclusion is that for knowledge transfer to lead to real technological upgrading, it must be deliberate, embedded and tailored to the absorptive capacities of local actors. This requires more than transaction contracts or episodic partnerships; it calls for long-term commitment, capacity building and institutions that facilitate learning by doing. The history of the catching-up process shows that the most successful cases, whether in East Asia, Eastern Europe or parts of Latin America, are those where tacit learning was built into the design of transfer mechanisms. The next section looks at why this often fails, the structural barriers that hinder or distort knowledge absorption.

3.3 Structural Barriers to Knowledge Diffusion

If the mechanisms of knowledge transfer are the vessels through which technology and expertise should flow, then structural obstacles are the invisible reefs that silently interrupt the journey. These barriers rarely lead to visible breakdown, but they steadily undermine the effectiveness of even the best-designed policies by blocking absorption, disrupting feedback loops and preventing foreign knowledge from being embedded in domestic systems. In emerging innovation ecosystems, these barriers are particularly persistent and deeply entrenched. They explain why, despite decades of openness to foreign direct investment, international partnerships and licencing agreements, many countries struggle to translate access to knowledge into results. Knowledge arrives, but it does not spread, does not develop and does not become embedded in local firms or institutions. This section shifts the focus from the mechanisms of knowledge transfer to the systemic weaknesses that mitigate their impact, underdeveloped absorptive capacity, institutional fragmentation and the absence of key intermediaries. Understanding these barriers is crucial for developing more effective strategies for technological catch-up.

The most fundamental barrier to knowledge diffusion in emerging economies is the lack of absorptive capacity (Stojcic, 2021; Stojcic & Orlic, 2020). While the term often conjures up images of R&D labs or the technical skills of engineers, it goes much deeper. As already argued in chapter, absorptive capacity encompasses organisational routines, the ability to assess and internalise external knowledge, the habit of learning through feedback and institutional memory that allows past experiences to shape current decisions. In many emerging economies, firms do not lack access to external knowledge, but an incentive to absorb it. A company may obtain a licence, install advanced machinery or even enter into a joint venture, but fail to adapt its processes, retrain its staff or change its culture to allow it to learn. Without routines that support experimentation or reflection, new knowledge is seen as noise rather than an opportunity. In such an environment, innovation endeavours rarely last. They remain on the periphery of the firm's core activities or fade away after the first setback.

Capacity shortfalls in emerging economies often originate in mismatches between knowledge sources and the structures meant to channel them into productive use

(Bykova et al., 2023). Education systems may deliver strong theoretical training but fall short in applied problem-solving, project-based learning, or the technical adaptability demanded by fast-changing industries. Vocational programmes, where present, frequently rely on outdated curricula and limited engagement with employers. Research institutions may produce high-quality publications, yet their findings remain disconnected from commercialisation pathways due to weak technology transfer offices or limited understanding of market needs. These gaps in the "last mile" of capability development are compounded by missing or underdeveloped learning infrastructures such as mentoring schemes, professional accreditation systems, and technical standard-setting bodies that could otherwise anchor knowledge in the local context. As a result, foreign technologies and know-how acquired through investment, licensing or partnerships often undergo only superficial assimilation: The tools arrive, but the practices and adaptations that make them effective remain absent.

Innovation systems can also be hampered by weak connective tissue between their actors. The relationships linking universities, firms, regulators and funding agencies are frequently sporadic or purely transactional (Stojcic, 2024). A multinational may wish to build a local supplier base but finds no centralised register of capable firms. A university may excel in niche research fields but have no dedicated channels for engaging industry partners. Public funding for collaborative R&D may exist, yet complex procedures or limited outreach prevent take-up by businesses. Moreover, coordination failures are not confined to the horizontal level, i.e. between sectors or regions, but extend vertically across tiers of government, where overlapping strategies and jurisdictional ambiguities dilute the impact of otherwise sound policies. In this fragmented landscape, knowledge flows tend to dissipate rather than accumulate, and opportunities for joint problem solving remain underexploited.

An important reason for this fragmentation is the weakness or absence of innovation intermediaries. These are the intermediaries, translators and facilitators that support the flow of knowledge across institutional boundaries (Noviaristanti et al., 2024; Zhang & Liu, 2024). In high-performing innovation systems, there are many forms of intermediaries: cluster organisations that coordinate firms, technology parks that provide start-ups with infrastructure and mentors, public procurement agencies that create demand for innovation and think tanks that translate research into policy (Caloffi et al., 2023). In many emerging economies, such institutions are rare, under-resourced or misaligned (Hyvarinen et al., 2024). Technology transfer offices may exist nominally but lack staff who understand both science and business. Industry associations can be dominated by old firms and resist disruptive innovation. If there are no intermediaries, collaboration becomes ad hoc and superficial. Even when potential partners want to work together, they often lack a trusted intermediary to structure the relationship. This leads to a paradoxical situation where the ecosystem is full of players and ideas, but the knowledge does not go beyond its origin.

Apart from institutional weaknesses, the incentives that drive behaviour within innovation systems are often fundamentally misaligned. Reward schemes in academia frequently give advantage to priorities other than collaboration with industry and commercialisation of research results. Government officials are penalised for failed projects but hardly rewarded for taking calculated risks. Firms focus on quarterly profits, not long-term capability building. Multinationals operating in emerging markets may be judged on cost savings rather than the development of the local ecosystem. This misalignment means that knowledge transfer, even when technically feasible, is often strategically avoided. Innovation becomes a compliance exercise rather than a transformative process. Everyone knows that collaboration could be beneficial, but no one is incentivised to take the first step. The result is inertia. Knowledge spreads not because stakeholders are unwilling to learn, but because the costs of engagement outweigh the benefits.

When all these structural barriers come together, the result is a system in which knowledge arrives but fails to land. Multinational firms establish operations, but their practices remain locked behind factory walls. Licences are acquired but used ineffectively. Collaborative projects are launched but quickly fizzle out. The mechanisms are in place on paper but the substance of learning fails to materialise. Worse still, the system often lacks the feedback loops necessary to recognise and correct these errors. Innovation programmes are recycled without meaningful evaluation and those involved repeat the same partnerships with the same results without realising the past shortcomings. Without learning, failure becomes routine and normality. In such an environment, innovation systems stagnate. The promise of catching up technologically remains unfulfilled, not because of a lack of effort or ambition, but because of persistent structural decoupling. Breaking this cycle requires more than just reforms at the margins, but a comprehensive rethink of how innovation ecosystems are designed, managed and supported.

The diffusion of knowledge does not happen automatically or simply because it is written into policy but must be intentionally encouraged through the design of institutions, incentives and networks. In many emerging economies, the persistent failure to disseminate and embed knowledge is not due to a lack of interest or effort, but to systemic constraints that hinder learning. These include limited absorptive capacity in firms and public institutions, fragmented innovation ecosystems that isolate key actors, an issue that we revisit in next chapter, the weakness or absence of intermediaries that translate and communicate knowledge, and incentive structures that discourage experimentation and collaboration. In addition, large parts of the economy, especially in the informal sectors, are completely excluded from formal innovation systems. These problems are not just technical failures, they are the legacy of historical, political and institutional choices. To understand them, we need to move beyond idealised models of knowledge flow and grapple with the reality of how power, structure and access determine who gets to innovate. The next section examines how intellectual property regimes add another layer of complexity to this already difficult landscape.

3.4 Intellectual Property and the Limits of Spillovers

Intellectual property rights have become one of the most contested frontiers in the global innovation economy. Once seen primarily as instruments for rewarding creativity, they are now powerful tools for governing access to knowledge. Patents, copyrights, trade secrets and similar protection mechanisms define not only who owns an idea, but also who is authorised to use it, under what conditions and at what cost. These regimes increasingly shape the contours of technological inclusion and exclusion. For firms and institutions in developing countries, the challenge is not only to acquire knowledge, but also to overcome a dense architecture of legal and contractual barriers. Important information is often locked behind paywalls, embedded in proprietary standards or completely withheld by non-disclosure agreements. Even where technologies are visible, the know-how required to adapt or replicate them remains inaccessible. In this environment, intellectual property no longer acts as a bridge to innovation, but as a gatekeeper that reinforces the asymmetry between the owners of knowledge and those trying to catch up.

Intellectual property rights are not inherently beneficial or harmful. They are policy instruments whose impact depends entirely on how they are structured and applied in particular economic and institutional contexts. In theory, intellectual property rights incentivise innovation by granting temporary exclusivity and allowing inventors to recoup their investment. But in practice, especially in many emerging innovation systems, the global intellectual property regime often acts as an obstacle rather than a bridge. It prevents domestic firms from reverse-engineering or adapting foreign technologies, increases the cost of access to critical knowledge and limits policy space for industrial development and public health. These consequences are not accidental, but the result of a system that is centred on the interests and capacities of innovation leaders rather than laggards. For countries that are still building their innovation ecosystem, strict adherence to this framework can limit learning and entrench dependency. The result is a kind of legal lock-in that undermines the very technological catch-up process that the global intellectual property system is supposed to support.

A core feature of intellectual property rights is that they grant exclusivity from the outset. Patents, copyrights and trade secrets give firms the legal authority to exclude others from using, adapting or commercialising their innovations. In principle, this protects innovation and ensures the profitability of investments. In practice, however, especially in industries such as pharmaceuticals, semiconductors or biotechnology, this can block the learning and adoption of technologies. Patents may disclose the basic invention, but the tacit knowledge, the "know-how" that is essential for imitation, is often withheld or hidden in trade secrets. In addition, multinational firms often pursue defensive strategies by building up a "patent thicket" that makes innovation related to existing technologies costly, or they refuse licences altogether. Others attach conditions that prohibit local adaptation or restrict export markets. These tactics are rational for intellectual property owners, but they fragment global learning and stifle cumulative innovation. For emerging economies, they limit the scope for local firms to experiment, adapt and grow by creating a legal ceiling on technological development.

In addition to the above, the global IP system is not evenly enforced. Industrialised countries tend to dominate global forums such as the World Intellectual Property Organisation (WIPO) and the WTO's TRIPS Council. They also have more legal means to challenge infringements, be it through investor-state dispute settlement mechanisms or bilateral trade agreements. Meanwhile, emerging economies often lack the ability to challenge unfair intellectual property claims, defend local innovators or negotiate fair licencing terms. This imbalance distorts innovation policy. Strong countries can shape the rules in their favour, while weaker countries must comply or risk sanctions. Even within a country, intellectual property enforcement often favours large firms over smaller, informal innovators who have no access to legal advice or formal protection. These asymmetries make intellectual property an instrument of exclusion that acts less as a bridge to innovation and more as a wall separating knowledge holders from knowledge seekers.

Over the last four decades, the global intellectual property (IP) landscape has changed fundamentally. What was once a patchwork of national laws has been harmonised under the Agreement on Trade-Related Aspects of Intellectual Property Rights (TRIPS), which was signed in 1994 as part of the WTO. For many emerging economies, compliance with the TRIPS Agreement was part of a broader liberalisation and integration into the global trading system. Countries were obliged to introduce minimum standards for the protection of intellectual property in various sectors such as pharmaceuticals, software and industrial design. Some countries even went beyond the TRIPS agreement by introducing stricter rules such as data exclusivity and patent term extensions. These changes were intended to promote domestic innovation and attract foreign investment but often had mixed results. Countries with a strong innovation ecosystem benefited, but those that had yet to develop their capabilities found their options limited. With stronger protection and limited local absorption capacity, opportunities for imitation, reverse engineering and incremental learning diminished, slowing rather than accelerating technological catch-up.

For all of the above reasons, in today's knowledge-based economy, intellectual property is more a geopolitical tool than just legal protection. Firms protect intellectual property to maintain their market dominance. Countries use intellectual property as leverage in trade negotiations. Patent portfolios determine who sets technological standards and who merely adopts them. This reality poses a dilemma for emerging innovation systems. Either adhere strictly to global IP standards and risk dependency or resist and risk isolation. Many find themselves in a bind as they are forced to demonstrate compliance with IP norms to attract foreign investment, even if this compliance limits local learning. Navigating this terrain requires strategic thinking. Some countries are experimenting with open innovation platforms, investing in public research or building sovereign patent pools that negotiate access to key technologies. The goal is not to abolish the IP system, but to recalibrate it to protect real innovation while ensuring that IP regimes do not entrench global inequality or block the path for laggard economies.

However, history shows that strict enforcement of intellectual property has rarely been accompanied by a successful technological catch-up process. Countries such as the United States in the nineteenth century, Germany in the early twentieth century and South Korea in the 1970s and 1980s all took a flexible approach to intellectual property. They tolerated imitation, invested in reverse engineering and delayed full compliance with intellectual property regulations until domestic firms had grown strong. South Korea's success was not based on early compliance with global IP standards, but on state-led strategies that enabled learning that often took place outside formal licencing agreements (Lee, 2016; Lee & Kim, 2010). It was only when local firms became competitive that Korea strengthened its IP regime. Today, this development window has narrowed. Under the TRIPS agreement, even the least developed countries are expected to grant full patent protection in most sectors. This "one-size-fits-all" approach ignores the radically different innovation capacities of countries and forces many into legal compliance without the tools or institutions to benefit from them (ICTSD, 2009). The result is stagnation instead of structural change.

This tension is particularly problematic in contexts where capability building depends on the ability to learn from existing technologies rather than inventing entirely new ones. Strong intellectual property rights can incentivise research in advanced economies and the transfer of knowledge and technology to emerging innovation systems (Gentile, 2020; Kanwar, 2012; Yang & Maskus, 2009), but they can also prevent local firms from reverse engineering, adapting or improving imported technologies. In addition, strict patent enforcement can hinder generic competition, drive up costs in critical sectors such as healthcare and limit the use of publicly funded research. Even in partnerships or licence agreements, intellectual property rights can be used to limit the scope of knowledge sharing or impose restrictive conditions on local use. The problem is not the existence of intellectual property rights per se, but the way they are designed and enforced and how they are harmonised with the development needs of less technologically advanced countries. Without flexible, context-dependent frameworks, there is a risk that intellectual property rights will deepen the divide between knowledge holders and knowledge seekers and entrench global hierarchies instead of enabling technological convergence.

The pharmaceutical sector illustrates this conflict between innovation protection and access. Prior to the TRIPS agreement, many developing countries only recognised process patents, which allowed firms to produce affordable generics through alternative manufacturing routes. This enabled countries such as India and Brazil to build a strong domestic pharmaceutical industry. However, TRIPS required the protection of both product and process patents, making the manufacture of generic versions of patented medicines illegal. India's compliance with the TRIPS agreement was coupled with clever legal provisions such as Section 3(d), which prevents the patenting of minor modifications to existing drugs. In this way, India has been able to maintain access to essential medicines and become a major supplier of low-cost generic drugs globally. However, this balancing act has attracted criticism from multinational firms and foreign governments. Trade disputes have arisen, exposing geopolitical tensions over intellectual property. The pharmaceutical sector shows how intellectual property regimes can undermine public health and industrial development if they are not tailored to the realities of local capabilities and social needs.

What above tells us is that if intellectual property is to support global development, it must be reimagined. This does not mean that protection must be abolished altogether, but that incentives and access must be rebalanced. Several reforms are possible. First, strengthen TRIPS flexibilities, such as compulsory licences, for public health and other strategic sectors. Second, invest in local patent offices and legal assistance for innovators in the Global South. Third, support open source models, patent pools and licencing consortia that expand access to enabling technologies. Fourth, recalibrate innovation metrics so that policy incentives reward socially useful innovation and not just the number of patents. Crucially, innovation policy needs to shift from a narrow focus on protection to a broader focus on capability building. The goal is not just to acquire more intellectual property, but to ensure that knowledge systems serve inclusive growth, technological learning and long-term resilience. Rewriting the rules of intellectual property for development means challenging the notion that protection and progress are always in harmony and designing a system that recognises innovation as a shared endeavour.

If knowledge is to truly serve development, it must be made accessible not only in legal theory but also in institutional practice. This requires rethinking the relationship between intellectual property and the broader goals of inclusive innovation, capacity building and long-term resilience. Protection should not come at the expense of dissemination, and exclusivity must be balanced by mechanisms that support adaptation, experimentation and cumulative learning. For emerging economies, this means that they need to design intellectual property strategies that are contextualised, development-oriented and strategically flexible, emphasising not only legal compliance but also local capacity building. Innovation should be seen as a collective endeavour and not a zero-sum game of controlling ownership. In the next section, we explore how this dynamic unfolds in practice by looking at the contrasting experiences of South Korea, Brazil, India and Central and Eastern Europe. These countries provide rich case studies of how knowledge transfer strategies combined with coherent policies and institutional learning can help or hinder efforts to build domestic innovation capacity.

3.5 Case Studies in Knowledge Transfer

The previous sections have shown that the transfer of knowledge is anything but automatic. It depends on the mechanisms through which it is mediated, on the institutions that mediate it, and on the power dynamics that determine its flow. These abstract principles take on deeper meaning when viewed through the lens of real national experiences. In this section, we explore four contrasting cases: South Korea, Brazil, India and the countries of Central and Eastern Europe. Each of these territories represents a different way in which emerging economies have sought to acquire, absorb and adapt foreign knowledge. Their strategies have ranged from state-led learning and joint ventures to market liberalisation and policy experimentation. Their constraints have ranged from geopolitical pressure to institutional fragmentation and limited absorptive capacity. However, one lesson can be learnt from all these different developments: Knowledge transfer is successful when it is embedded in long-term capability development, guided by strategic intent and reinforced by systems that transform access into learning. Where these elements are missing, knowledge often fails to take root.

South Korea is a paradigmatic example of a strategic technological catch-up process (Soh et al., 2023). In the 1960s, the country was a low-income agricultural economy with virtually no technological infrastructure. By the early 2000s, it had become a global innovation leader in sectors such as semiconductors, shipbuilding and consumer electronics. This transformation was not the result of passive exposure to foreign investment or open markets. Rather, it was the result of a targeted government strategy, selective exposure to global knowledge and intensive firm level to build absorption capacity. Korean firms such as Samsung and Hyundai did not rely primarily on foreign direct investment. Instead, they relied on technology import through licencing, reverse engineering and targeted collaborations. The state restricted foreign ownership in key sectors to ensure that domestic firms retained control over learning. Companies invested heavily in organisational learning, built up internal R&D and sent engineers abroad. Knowledge transfer was not incidental, but the central development goal, pursued with strategic coherence and long-term commitment.

The Korean state played a decisive coordinating role. It identified strategic sectors, provided targeted support and incentivised firms to adopt and build on foreign technologies. Learning was structured and mission-driven: Technologies were not imported to be used as they were, but as platforms for experimentation, modification and subsequent innovation. Firms internalised these imperatives. Chaebols rotated engineers across business units and embedded R&D into the core operations. Over time, Korean firms transitioned from technology adopters to global innovators. This transformation was underpinned by a carefully orchestrated approach to global integration: Trade and intellectual property liberalisation came only after a strong domestic innovation base had been established. The Korean case cannot be easily replicated, but it highlights important lessons, particularly that knowledge transfer requires not only openness, but also strategic intent and significant investment in learning infrastructure. In Korea, knowledge did not just arrive, it was captured, transformed and converted into long-term national capabilities.

Brazil offers a more ambivalent portrayal (de Quieiroz et al., 2025). As one of the largest economies in the Global South, the country has long attracted foreign investment in sectors such as the automotive industry, agribusiness and natural resources. However, this continued exposure to global capital and technology has not led to a corresponding increase in domestic innovation capacity. Much of Brazil's industrial base has been shaped by multinational companies that tend to import key components, centralise R&D activities abroad and operate with management models that limit integration with local suppliers and institutions. As a result, cutting-edge technologies often coexist with shallow local linkages, resulting in enclaves of excellence with limited spillover effects. Domestic firms, especially small and medium-sized enterprises, consistently struggle to meet the technical, quality and coordination standards required to participate in global value chains. This discrepancy is exacerbated by weak institutional mechanisms for supplier development, insufficient investment in absorptive capacity and limited coordination between universities and industry.

Although Brazil has well-respected public institutions such as EMBRAPA in agricultural research and FINEP in innovation financing, the broader innovation ecosystem in Brazil remains fragmented and inconsistent. The political landscape fluctuates between periods of active industrial policy and phases of liberalisation, leading to a lack of long-term coherence and consistency. While there has been public support for innovation, including grant programmes, credit instruments and tax incentives, these have often been implemented in isolation, without a unified strategy for technological upgrading across all sectors. The gap between federal initiatives and sub-national capabilities has also hindered implementation, particularly outside the major industrial centres. Crucially, the role of foreign direct investment has remained largely extractive or efficiency orientated, with no incentives for technology transfer or local capacity building. Compared to countries such as South Korea, where industrial policy provides for strategic coordination between the state and domestic firms to drive technological learning, the Brazilian model has been relatively passive and dependent on external actors. Policies have rarely required multinationals to invest in local innovation networks and have not consistently supported domestic firms in moving up the value chain. As a result, the Brazilian innovation system is polarised with foreign firms acting as isolated poles of technological sophistication and much of the domestic corporate sector remaining technologically stagnant. In this context, the inflow of knowledge has not been matched by the institutions and incentives necessary for its embedding, adaptation and diffusion. Learning, where it occurs, remains the exception rather than the rule.

India presents a more complex and mixed case. Its success in pharmaceuticals and IT is not the result of comprehensive liberalisation or state control, but of sector-specific strategies and adaptable legal and institutional measures (WHO, 2017). In the pharmaceutical sector, India benefited from a pre-TRIPS patent regime that protected manufacturing processes but not end products. This legal structure enabled Indian firms to reverse-engineer patented drugs using alternative methods and thus develop extensive expertise in process innovation. Over time, these firms grew to become global suppliers of affordable generic drugs. Even after joining the TRIPS agreement, India utilised legal flexibilities such as Section 3(d), which restricts patent evergreening, to maintain access to essential medicines and safeguard domestic production. Public–private partnerships and investment in regulatory infrastructure have further strengthened the sector's competitiveness. India's pharmaceutical strategy shows that learning by imitation and adaptation can be very effective when supported by legal ingenuity and institutional investment, even within the constraints of the global intellectual property system.

In IT services, India leveraged its English-speaking workforce, strong higher education system and global diaspora to become a hub for outsourced software development. Firms like Infosys and TCS initially built their capabilities through contract work for Western clients, gaining experience in project management, coding standards and client interaction. Over time, some firms have moved into higher value-added services, including consulting and systems integration. However, this model remains limited in terms of product innovation and much of the sector's growth has been driven by labour arbitrage rather than profound technological change. India's manufacturing sector has not seen comparable growth and challenges remain in areas such as coordination between research institutions and industry, skills mismatch and infrastructure deficits. Nevertheless, the Indian experience shows that strategic sectoral specialisation, flexible IP policies and targeted capability building can lead to globally competitive outcomes. It shows that a catch-up process is possible without completely following the path of earlier industrialised nations.

The experience of Central and Eastern European (CEE) countries is a cautionary tale of the limits of knowledge transfer through foreign ownership. After the fall of socialism, countries such as Poland, Hungary and the Czech Republic have adopted market liberalisation, privatisation and foreign direct investment as central pillars of their development strategy (Bykova et al., 2023; Stojcic, 2024). Western European firms, particularly from the automotive and electronics sectors, relocated their production to the region in order to benefit from the lower costs. While this integration brought job creation and export growth, the benefits for development were uneven. In many cases, the local subsidiaries of foreign firms functioned as low-cost production centres with little autonomy or innovation mandate. R&D remained concentrated in the Western headquarters. Local firms, excluded from the core activities of the value chain, were relegated to a peripheral role. Universities were strong in basic research but had few links to industry, and public innovation policies struggled to establish meaningful collaboration. The result was advanced manufacturing without knowledge spillover and economic upgrading without innovation capacity.

Some CEE countries have endeavoured to reverse this pattern. Slovenia focused on domestic ownership and innovation-driven growth, while Estonia invested in digital governance and public sector modernisation. But overall, the region illustrates the dangers of "dependent modernisation" The assumption that foreign ownership would lead to knowledge transfer proved optimistic, especially when there were no measures to promote local learning. EU accession brought important benefits such as access to finance, harmonisation of regulations and infrastructure investment, but also limited the scope for industrial policy through competition rules and restrictions on state aid. What was missing in many cases was domestic capacity building, namely support for local suppliers, investment in labour training and coordination between universities, firms and public agencies. Without this, the region developed a strong export base but weak innovation ecosystems. The CEE case reminds us that knowledge transfer is not a mechanical consequence of openness, but requires institutions, policies and incentives that turn access into absorption and presence into performance.

These four cases illustrate the range and fragility of the results that knowledge transfer can produce. South Korea demonstrates the power of a deliberate strategy and long-term investment in domestic learning. Brazil illustrates the dangers of assuming that a foreign presence will automatically lead to spillover effects. India shows how legal flexibility, sectoral focus and public–private coordination can help achieve global competitiveness even under structural constraints. Central and Eastern Europe, on the other hand, shows the limits of integration without capability development, where foreign ownership can increase production but not local innovation. In all these experiences, the central realisation is clear and argues that access to global knowledge is not enough. Success depends on the architecture of the system that receives the knowledge, its institutions, incentives and learning infrastructure. Knowledge transfer must be actively designed, supported and embedded in a broader capacity building strategy. In the concluding section of this chapter, we highlight the main reasons why knowledge transfer often fails and explore what policymakers in emerging economies can do to move from passive access to productive transformation.

3.6 Conclusion

The belief that knowledge flows easily across borders, especially in a globalised economy, has shaped the development strategies of many emerging economies. Policies are based on the assumption that attracting foreign investors, signing technology licencing agreements and fostering international partnerships will almost automatically lead to domestic learning, capacity building and innovation. But as this chapter has shown, the reality is much more complicated. Knowledge does not simply travel and it must be translated, absorbed and integrated into local systems. And in many emerging innovation systems, this process fails. The mechanisms are in place, foreign direct investment, licencing, partnerships, but the learning they promise often does not materialise. Instead of driving change, they lead to low engagement, weak spillover effects and long-lasting dependency.

We have seen that these failures are not just accidental, but systemic. At the firm level, many domestic companies lack the routine and experience to internalise external knowledge. At the institutional level, innovation ecosystems are often fragmented, poorly coordinated and lack effective intermediaries. At a strategic level, global firms and intellectual property regimes work to protect proprietary advantages rather than share them. Crucially, these failures are not evenly distributed. They are more pronounced in systems that have not invested in absorptive capacity, that view integration as an end in itself, or that accept global norms such as TRIPS without developing counterweights to protect domestic learning. The case studies in this chapter make this clear. South Korea succeeded, not because it was more open, but because it was more strategic. Brazil and parts of Central and Eastern Europe opened up quickly but failed to build the institutions needed to turn access into innovation. India was successful where it was selective and less adaptable where it was not.

The conclusion is both sobering and hopeful. Sobering because many emerging economies are now stuck in a passive mode of knowledge absorption, dependent on external technologies without the ability to adapt or build on them. Hopeful because these outcomes are not predetermined. With the right institutional reforms, learning-centred policies and system-wide coordination, knowledge transfer can be transformed from a one-way transfer to a dynamic process of co-creation and upgrading. To achieve this transformation, however, one must go beyond the mechanisms of transfer and look at the deeper architecture of innovation systems. As we will explore in the next chapter, many failures in knowledge absorption are not only due to barriers at the border but have their roots in domestic weaknesses such as underdeveloped innovation infrastructure, fragmented research systems, weak links between academia and industry, and misaligned incentives. Chapter 4 looks inwards. It asks what makes a domestic innovation system strong or weak and how internal characteristics, rather than external linkages, determine countries' long-term ability to learn, adapt and innovate.

References

Aitken, B. J., & Harrsion, A. E. (1999). Do domestic firms benefit from direct foreign investment? Evidence from Venezuela. *American Economic Review, 89*(3), 605–618.

Antonelli, C., Crespi, F., & Quatraro, F. (2022). Knowledge complexity and the mechanisms of knowledge generation and exploitation: The European evidence. *Research Policy, 51*(8), 104081.

Bykova, A., Dobrinsky, R., Grieveson, R., Grodzicki, M. J., Hanzl-Weiss, D., Hunya, G., Korpar, N., Leitner, S., Moshammer, B., Sankot, O., Strohm, B. C., Tverdostup, M., & Zavarska, Z. (2023). *Industrial policy for a new growth model: A toolbox for EU-CEE countries* (WIIW Research Report 469). The Vienna Institute for International Economic Studies (WIIW).

Caloffi, A., Colovic, A., Rizzoli, V., & Rossi, F. (2023). Innovation intermediaries' types and functions: A computational analysis of the literature. *Technological Forecasting and Social Change, 189*, 122351.

de Quieiroz, S. R. R., Vonortas, N. S., & Canuto, O. (2025). *The challenge of fostering innovation and accelerating economic growth in Brazil* (RP-03/25). Policy Center for the New South.

Fujita, M., & Thisse, J. (2002). *Economics of agglomeration: Cities, industrial location and regional growth.* Cambridge University Press.

Gentile, E. (2020). Intellectual property rights and foreign technology licensing in developing countries: An empirical investigation. *Economic Development and Cultural Change, 68*(2), 655–698.

Gorg, H., & Greenaway, D. (2004). Much ado about nothing? Do domestic firms really benefit from foreign direct investment? *The World Bank Research Observer, 19*(2), 171–197.

Hyvarinen, A. M. J., Keskinen, M., & Levanen, J. (2024). Intermediaries as drivers of innovation development in resource-constrained environments: Insights from the Kenyan water sector. *Technovation, 131*, 102956.

ICTSD (2009). *The global debate on enforcement of intellectual property rights and developing countries* (Programme on IPRs and sustainable development, issue paper no. 22). International Centre for Trade and Sustainable Development.

Javorcik, B. (2004). Does foreign direct investment increase the productivity of domestic firms? In search of spillovers through backward linkages. *American Economic Review, 94*(3), 605–627.

Jiang, K., Keller, W., Qiu, L. D., & Ridley, W. (2024). International joint ventures and internal technology transfer vs. External technology spillovers: Evidence from China. *Journal of International Economics, 150*, 103939.

Kanwar, S. (2012). Intellectual property protection and technology licensing: The case of developing countries. *The Journal of Law and Economics, 55*(3), 539–564.

Lee, K., & Kim, Y. K. (2010). IPR and technological catch-up in Korea. In H. Odagiri, A. Goto, A. Sunami, & R. N. Richard (Eds.), *Intellectual property rights, development and catch-up: An international comparative study* (pp. 133–167). Oxford University Press.

Lee, K. (2016). *Economic catch-up and technological leapfrogging: The path to development and macroeconomic stability in Korea*. Edward Elgar.

Lee, K. (2019). *The art of economic catch-up: Barriers, detours and leapfrogging in innovation systems*. Cambridge University Press.

Lu, Y., Tao, Z., & Zhu, L. (2017). Identifying FDI spillovers. *Journal of International Economics, 107*, 75–90.

Markusen, J. R., & Trofimenko, N. (2009). Teaching locals new tricks: Foreign experts as a channel of knowledge transfers. *Journal of Development Economics, 88*(1), 120–131.

Martinez, C., & Zuniga, P. (2017). Contracting for technology transfer: Patent licensing and know-how in Brazil. *Industry and Innovation, 24*(6), 659–689.

Noviaristanti, S., Acur, N., & Mendibil, K. (2024). The different roles of innovation intermediaries to generate value. *Management Review Quarterly, 74*, 2545–2577.

Smeets, R. (2008). Collecting the pieces of the FDI knowledge spillovers puzzle. *World Bank Research Observer, 23*(2), 107–138.

Soh, H. S., Youngsun, K., & Aridi, A. (Eds.). (2023). *Innovative Korea: Leveraging innovation and technology for development*. World Bank.

Stojcic, N. (2021). Collaborative innovation in emerging innovation systems: Evidence from Central and Eastern Europe. *The Journal of Technology Transfer, 46*, 531–562.

Stojcic, N. (2024). Innovation failure, training for innovative activities and public support for innovation: Multi-annual evidence from emerging European innovation systems. *Research Policy, 53*, 105059.

Stojcic, N., & Orlic, E. (2020). Spatial dependence, foreign investment and productivity spillovers in new EU member states. *Regional Studies, 54*(8), 1057–1068.

Stojcic, N., Vujanovic, N., & Radosevic, S. (2025). Resource sharing in enterprise groups and innovation failure: Emerging innovation systems perspective. *The Journal of Technology Transfer*. Online first.

Stojcic, N., Pylak, K., & Jurlina Alibegovic, D. (2022). The spatial impact of entrepreneurial zones: Firm, city and inter-city evidence. *Regional Studies, 56*(12), 2164–2176.

Vujanovic, N., Radosevic, S., Stojcic, N., Hisarciklilar, M., & Hashi, I. (2022). FDI spillover effects on innovation activities of knowledge using and knowledge creating firms: Evidence from an emerging economy. *Technovation, 118*, 102512.

WHO. (2017). *Indian policies to promote local production of pharmaceutical products and protect public health*. World Health Organization.

Yang, L., & Maskus, K. E. (2009). Intellectual property rights, technology transfer and exports in developing countries. *Journal of Development Economics, 90*(2), 231–236.

Zhang, C., & Liu, N. (2024). Innovation intermediaries: A review, bibliometric analysis, and research agenda. *The Journal of Technology Transfer, 49*, 1113–1143.

Chapter 4
Weaknesses of Domestic Innovation Systems

A chain is only as strong as its weakest link. (Thomas Reid)

Abstract Every country aspires to build an innovation system that fuels growth, yet many find that the machinery sputters rather than accelerates. This chapter explores why domestic systems so often fall short of their promise. The narrative begins with the fragmented landscapes of science and industry, where universities, firms and policymakers operate in parallel but rarely in concert. Weak institutions and policy inconsistencies deepen these gaps, leaving strategies on paper that rarely translate in practice. In many transition economies, limited resources and unstable governance further constrain the ability to sustain long-term investments in knowledge and technology. The result is a system that looks complete in design but proves fragile in function. By weaving together examples of misaligned incentives, policy volatility and underdeveloped networks, the chapter reveals how domestic weaknesses are less about a lack of ambition than about structures that cannot support it, turning innovation systems into promises only partially fulfilled.

4.1 Introduction

By the late 2010s, many transition countries in Central and Eastern Europe had checked every box of modernisation. They had joined the European Union, reformed their institutions, liberalised trade and adapted to global intellectual property standards. Foreign investors arrived, research institutes were restructured, and EU funds flowed into newly established innovation agencies. On the surface, these systems seemed ready for innovation. But despite these efforts, innovation results remain to this day surprisingly weak. R&D intensity remains considerably lower than in Northern and Western Europe, business investment in innovation lagged behind, and high-growth domestic firms were rare. Although countries such as Slovakia, Hungary or Czechia became efficient manufacturing hubs within global value chains they struggle to achieve deeper technological upgrading or build home-grown innovation capacity. The pattern is widespread across the region. This paradox of strong inputs but weak performance is not unique to Central and Eastern Europe. In many

N. Stojčić, *Elusive Innovation*, Applied Innovation and Technology Management,
https://doi.org/10.1007/978-3-032-14900-8_4

emerging economies, foreign knowledge may be available, universities active, and policy frameworks in place, yet innovation remains fragmented or shallow. As this chapter argues, the core problem is not only external but lies in the structure of domestic innovation systems.

As we already argued, much of the discourse on innovation in emerging economies focuses on access to foreign knowledge through FDI, global value chains and international partnerships. This is not wrong, but it tells only part of the story. For knowledge to lead to innovation, it must land in an environment capable of absorbing, adapting and applying it. This process depends not only on openness, but also on the readiness of the system at home. In many emerging countries, innovation systems lack this readiness. Networks of firms, universities and public institutions do exist, but their links are weak, their goals misaligned and their processes too rigid to enable real learning. These internal weaknesses are less visible than external investment or the outcomes such as the number of patents, but they can be even more crucial. They are the reason why innovation strategies often fall short and why repeated policy efforts fail to achieve major or sustainable results. This chapter looks inward to examine the structural barriers, fragmentation, inertia, skills mismatches, weak demand and lack of feedback that undermine innovation potential from within.

One of the most damaging assumptions in innovation policy, as we pointed out in the previous chapter, is that knowledge can be absorbed passively. This belief has characterised, for example, much of early EU cohesion policy, in which countries are encouraged to invest in infrastructure, adopt innovation strategies and support SMEs with little regard for coordination, learning or system coherence. But knowledge is not a liquid that fills empty vessels. It is sticky, context-dependent and embedded in routines. If systems lack the mechanisms to adapt, exchange and apply knowledge, even cutting-edge technology remains inert. This can be seen in the Western Balkans, where donor-driven (mostly EU-funded) centres of excellence, equipped with advanced infrastructure, have often been unable to establish meaningful firm partnerships or commercialisation pipelines. The problem was not ambition, but the inadequacy of the institutional framework. Universities worked in isolation, firms lacked innovation experience and public bodies struggled to link knowledge with application. Without systems designed for dynamic absorption, technology becomes symbolic rather than transformative, reinforcing the illusion of progress while actual capabilities remain underdeveloped.

The cost of weak domestic innovation systems is threefold. First, it limits the potential for external engagement. Multinationals are less inclined to build local supply chains or invest in joint research and development if domestic firms lack basic technological or managerial capabilities. Second, it undermines the effectiveness of policy. Innovation vouchers, tax credits and grants do not produce lasting results if firms do not understand or trust the programmes, or if the institutions administering them are disconnected and only pay attention to compliance. Third, it creates a structural path dependency. Once actors become accustomed to a system where innovation is symbolic, collaboration is risky and failure is hidden, they stop evolving. Procurement avoids novel solutions, public institutions fear experimentation, and firms withdraw from partnerships. Over time, these behaviours become institutionalised. Instead of improving through learning and iteration, the innovation system becomes an echo chamber of safe, non-transformative practices. The result is not stagnation by neglect but stagnation by design, a system incapable of responding to new challenges or new opportunities.

All too often, innovation systems are judged by visible factors such as the number of labs, digital infrastructure or the number of PhD students. But these inputs are only part of the picture and what matters more is how the systems use them. This chapter proposes shifting the focus from inputs to capabilities. Effective innovation systems are characterised by the ability to learn from failure, connect different actors for common tasks, support experimentation and build trust across sectors. These capabilities are difficult to measure, but essential. They determine whether investments in research infrastructure or human capital translate into societal and economic benefits. They depend not only on funding, but also on feedback mechanisms, cultural norms and governance structures that reward learning rather than penalise risk. Without these deeper capabilities, even well-intentioned innovation policies fall short. Countries end up with islands of excellence that are disconnected from broader ecosystems and unable to catalyse systemic change.

In the further course of this chapter, these central weaknesses are elaborated. We begin with reflection on fragmentation and discuss how disconnected institutions and overlapping mandates create silos of innovation. The chapter then examines governance inertia, where outdated procedures and rigid hierarchies slow down adaptation. Next, it looks at the persistent mismatch between education systems and innovation needs, particularly in post-socialist contexts where universities often produce theoretical knowledge with limited practical relevance. The chapter also addresses the problem of weak demand for innovation. In many emerging economies, most firms remain low-tech, while public procurement rarely incentivises R&D or new solutions. Finally, we examine the lack of evaluation and feedback loops. Without systems that enable learning from policy failures or successes, innovation strategies become static. This is not a failure of ambition or investment, but a failure of institutional design and strategic direction.

This chapter offers no magical solutions. Rather, it argues that no amount of external integration or foreign knowledge can compensate for the weaknesses of the domestic system. Innovation is not simply about access to knowledge, but about the willingness to use it. The key challenge for emerging innovation systems is not to mimic the institutions of their advanced counterparts, but to build their own that reflect local needs, connect actors and enable learning. This requires a long-term commitment to building institutional coherence, stakeholder trust and adaptability. It also requires a cultural shift in which innovation is no longer understood as a series of programmes, but as a system of relationships and feedback loops. Until this change takes place, many emerging innovation systems risk to remain performative rather than transformative. As the next sections will show, internal alignment, not external access, is the true foundation for innovation success. Without it, the gap remains difficult to close, no matter how many boxes are ticked on the modernisation checklist.

4.2 Fragmentation and Disconnected Subsystems

In any innovation system, relationships are the connective tissue that transforms isolated efforts into collective progress. Innovation is not just about producing new knowledge, but also about how that knowledge circulates across institutions, sectors and disciplines. The most impactful ideas are rarely developed in isolation, they emerge through dialog, feedback and collaboration. Yet in many emerging economies, the institutions responsible for the production, application and regulation of knowledge remain disconnected (Intarakumnerd et al., 2002). Universities focus on academic publications, firms prioritise short-term market survival and public authorities implement policies without real coordination (Stojcic, 2024). These actors often function as isolated islands, each pursuing innovation according to its own logic and constraints. The result is fragmentation, a systemic state in which subsystems coexist but rarely interact (Koschatzky, 2024). This fragmentation weakens feedback loops, slows diffusion and makes transformative innovation the exception rather than the rule. Without targeted efforts to build bridges between these islands, even the best-funded innovation systems risk becoming archipelagos of potential rather than engines of shared progress.

One of the defining features of fragmented innovation systems is the persistent separation between key actors, particularly universities, research institutes and the private sector. Academic institutions often conduct research and train graduates with limited regard for industrial needs, while firms pursue innovation largely in isolation from the public knowledge base. Government support, though present, is typically channelled through separate, poorly coordinated ministries or agencies. As a result, the pathway from knowledge creation to application remains disjointed (Dabic et al., 2016). This structural disconnect is especially visible in parts of Central and Eastern Europe, where institutional legacies from the socialist era have preserved rigid disciplinary boundaries and vertical governance structures (Švarc & Dabić, 2019). Even with EU accession and increased investment in science, many systems continue to operate in silos. Researchers prioritise academic benchmarks, while firms remain hesitant to engage with slow and bureaucratic public institutions thus limiting the translation of research into commercially or socially useful innovation (Hillebrand, 2022).

Yet this challenge is far from unique to Europe. Across diverse regions, from Southeast Asia to Sub-Saharan Africa, innovation systems are undermined by institutional fragmentation. Despite investment in scientific infrastructure, collaboration between universities, firms and policymakers remains sporadic. National reports and policy reviews routinely point to a lack of inter-ministerial coordination, duplicative efforts, and weak incentives for cooperation (Intarakumnerd et al., 2002; Stojcic, 2024). These are not merely technical shortcomings, but reflections of deeper institutional and cultural divides (Havas et al., 2015). Public researchers often work towards long-term academic goals, firms seek near-term market solutions, and policymakers operate on political timeframes. These groups speak different languages, follow different metrics and rarely share platforms for alignment. Without proactive mechanisms, such as bridging institutions, shared funding instruments or integrated evaluation systems, collaboration remains the exception. Innovation, in turn, remains an episodic outcome rather than an embedded function of the system.

Effective governance in innovation systems depends not only on formal structures but also on trust, shared narratives and adaptive capabilities (Kuhlmann & Arnold, 2001). Without these relational elements, strategic frameworks remain symbolic and fail to foster meaningful collaboration. Many governments have introduced national innovation strategies, smart specialisation frameworks or inter-ministerial coordination bodies to align actors and streamline policy planning, yet their impact is often limited. In several Central and Eastern European countries, alignment with EU research and innovation agendas has brought little institutional change (Stojcic, 2024). Ministries, agencies and subnational authorities frequently operate in isolation, launching parallel instruments such as start-up grants, innovation hubs or SME schemes in pursuit of political visibility or budgetary relevance. This leads to duplication, policy confusion and limited system learning (Stojcic et al., 2020). Similar issues arise in other emerging regions, where coordinating bodies lack authority, capacity or sustained political backing, resulting in fragmented initiatives, high transaction costs for entrepreneurs and weak mechanisms for assessing cumulative impact.

Aside from implementation inefficiencies, fragmentation undermines the ability to learn within innovation systems. When institutions operate in silos, there are few mechanisms to gather, share and respond to feedback. Policies are often designed and evaluated in isolation, with success measured by budget disbursement or number of outcomes rather than long-term impact or behaviour change as we will discuss in detail in next sections. Ministries rarely compare results or jointly evaluate the synergistic effects of programmes. Public agencies focus on compliance rather than adaptation to new realities, while businesses and researchers receive little systematic feedback to drive continuous improvement. Without coordinated feedback loops such as joint monitoring systems, multi-stakeholder reviews or cross-sectoral learning platforms, innovation systems cannot evolve. Fragmentation therefore not only blocks the flow of knowledge but also disables the very mechanisms that would allow systems to recognise failure, correct course and build resilience over time.

Overcoming the fragmentation of innovation systems does not require centralisation or rigid conformity. Innovation thrives on diversity and experimentation, but these must be supported by connectivity mechanisms that enable collaboration across domains, sectors and disciplines. The connectivity of the system depends on shared problem definitions, joint agenda setting and learning platforms that bridge the gap between actors. Recent work on mission-oriented innovation policy (Mazzucato, 2018) emphasises that alignment around shared societal goals such as climate neutrality or digital inclusion can help create coherence without stifling diversity, another issue that will be revisited in more detail in following chapters. Missions can combine regulation with R&D, finance with societal needs and science with public value. The EU Smart Specialization Strategy (S3) was an attempt to move in this direction by requiring regions to identify local strengths and build inclusive innovation strategies. Although implementation varied, S3 showed how policy can promote ecosystem-level coordination rather than isolated projects. Such approaches point to a new generation of innovation policy that focuses on system architecture rather than just programme delivery.

Perhaps greatest problem with fragmentation is in the fact that its effects are deeply corrosive. Over time, it weakens the connective tissue of the innovation system. It makes it harder to disseminate knowledge, align funding with strategy, or spread breakthroughs beyond individual projects. Fragmentation turns innovation from a systemic process into a fragmented process driven by chance rather than planning. Solving this problem requires not only new strategies or programmes, but also the cultivation of relationships based on trust, a shared language and mutual accountability. Without this connective infrastructure, even the best-funded innovation initiatives risk becoming isolated islands of excellence disconnected from the broader system. A long-term commitment to integration through platforms, feedback mechanisms and joint governance structures is essential. To this end, the next section addresses another important internal barrier, the one of institutional inertia. If governance systems are unable to adapt, revise or learn, they can turn past successes into current obstacles and freeze innovation systems into outdated forms.

4.3 Institutional Inertia and the Absence of Adaptive Governance

Across Central and Eastern Europe, numerous innovation support programmes have been launched to encourage collaboration between firms and public research institutions. These initiatives typically aim to strengthen university–industry linkages, foster applied research and build domestic innovation capabilities in line with EU strategic objectives (Švarc & Dabić, 2019). Many are well funded and supported by national strategies, with clearly defined goals and active promotion. Yet in practice, their impact has often been short-lived. Participation tends to decline after initial enthusiasm, as firms encounter burdensome reporting requirements and universities struggle to align project timelines with academic procedures. In some cases, evaluation mechanisms were weak or absent, and follow-up collaboration between partners failed to materialise. Programmes have been discontinued with little institutional reflection, their lessons lost as quickly as the funding was spent. This recurring pattern highlights a deeper challenge. In many emerging economies, innovation policy is undermined not by lack of ambition, but by institutional inertia, the tendency of public organisations to resist adaptation even as their environments evolve.

Most public institutions involved in science, technology and innovation (STI) have evolved within bureaucratic structures designed for stability, compliance and control (Švarc & Dabić, 2021). While these characteristics are essential for legal and fiscal accountability, they are often at odds with the demands of innovation such as flexibility, responsiveness and risk-taking. In bureaucratic systems, formal rules and procedures often take precedence over learning outcomes or user experience. Programme managers become gatekeepers of compliance rather than enablers of experimentation. Risks are avoided even when they are necessary for breakthrough results. As a result, agencies tend to support incremental projects over ambitious or unproven ideas while rigid eligibility criteria and excessive paperwork discourage many high-potential firms from participating in public R&D calls. Moreover, the renewal of programmes is often driven by political timing rather than evidence of impact. The bureaucracy may excel at disbursing funds, but without adaptive mechanisms it finds it difficult to build dynamic innovation ecosystems.

Institutional inertia is also evident in the persistent gap between ambitious policy goals and outdated implementation mechanisms. Many national STI strategies embrace the language of transformation, emphasising digitalisation, green growth and collaboration but actual delivery remains tied to legacy routines. Calls for proposals are often narrowly framed, evaluations focus on formal compliance, and cross-sector engagement is minimal. Across Central and Eastern Europe, strategies are frequently developed to align with EU expectations, but implementation is fragmented, with limited coordination between ministries and weak institutional capacity at regional and operational levels. Funding remains discipline-bound, oversight is dispersed, and incentives for interdisciplinarity or private sector involvement are rarely embedded. The result is policy drift where objectives move in one direction, while everyday practices remain unchanged. This undermines trust across the system and leads to status quo bias (Samadi et al., 2024). Businesses become sceptical of public support, researchers retreat into familiar academic structures, and civil servants default to procedural checklists.

Effective innovation policy requires the ability to learn through insight, reflection and adaptation (Games et al., 2024). Yet many STI agencies in emerging economies lack functioning feedback loops. While monitoring and evaluation are in place, they are treated as administrative requirements rather than learning tools. Performance indicators emphasise disbursement or compliance, not impact. Final reports are written but rarely read and recommendations are filed rather than implemented. Without internal learning cultures, agencies repeat programmes with only superficial changes. There are few mechanisms to find out why a voucher programme worked in one sector but not another, or why college–industry collaboration disintegrated after funding ended. The lack of feedback means that the system cannot evolve. It becomes a cycle of repetition rather than innovation, a machine for managing grants rather than fostering a learning ecosystem.

Besides its structural dimension, institutional inertia can also be cultural (Kheiridoust, 2024). Managing innovation requires not only rules and funding, but also people with the skills and mindset to navigate complexity, foster collaboration and take calculated risks. Yet many agencies are underfunded and understaffed, particularly at the regional level. Officials often lack experience with best practices in innovation policy or experience working with start-ups, researchers or global trends. Promotions often reward process mastery rather than creativity or problem solving. This leads to a culture where "playing it safe" becomes the norm and where doing things differently is seen as dangerous rather than necessary. Too often innovation agencies struggle to retain experienced staff, leading to knowledge loss and inconsistent programme implementation. When institutional memory depends on a few individuals, resilience suffers. Changing this requires long-term investment in capacity building, not only in training programmes, but also in career paths, incentives and leadership development that rewards adaptive, entrepreneurial leadership.

Institutional inertia is also a matter of a deeper failure of reflexivity. Reflexivity means that institutions are able to critically examine their own assumptions, scan the horizon for new trends and adjust their goals accordingly. In fast-moving technological areas such as AI, synthetic biology or the green transition, this capability is essential. But in many emerging markets, STI agencies lack the tools for forward-looking governance. Few have foresight units, policy labs or iterative design processes that engage stakeholders in real time. Funding cycles remain rigid, instruments are rarely piloted, and course corrections are rare. This contrasts innovation agencies across advanced economies that have integrated learning and flexibility into their core activities by holistically assessing their portfolios, co-designing with users and dynamically updating their strategies. For emerging economies to develop this capacity, they need to invest not only in skills and data infrastructure, but also in political continuity and a culture that rewards long-term learning.

Institutional inertia is compounded by path dependency, the tendency for past decisions and structures to shape current options, even when they are no longer fit for purpose. Bureaucracies often replicate existing models because doing so is administratively simpler, politically less risky and legally embedded. In several Central and Eastern European countries, research systems remain heavily centred on legacy institutions dating back to the socialist period (Radošević, 2024; Švarc & Dabić, 2019). Despite policy shifts promoting competitive, collaborative and demand-driven research, institutional reform has been uneven. Established actors continue to wield disproportionate influence, while new entrants struggle to navigate rigid structures or access meaningful support. The result is a system where the outward form of innovation policy appears modern, but its underlying logic remains static. Similar dynamics are evident elsewhere with STI bodies operating under outdated administrative rules that do not reflect contemporary innovation needs. Without structural renewal, new policy tools risk being layered onto fragile institutional foundations.

A final irony of institutional inertia is the promotion of innovation without internal experimentation. Public institutions encourage firms, start-ups and universities to take risks, try new approaches and learn from failure. However, they rarely do this themselves. Most operate in a rigid administrative environment that offers little scope for testing new instruments or making adjustments based on user feedback. This gap between rhetoric and practice undermines credibility. If innovation agencies are risk averse, how can they ask others to be bold? Adaptive governance requires public institutions to embed experimentation into their core processes. They need to test programmes on a small scale, adjust them based on early signals and scale only what works. Instruments such as regulatory sandboxes, experimental procurement or innovation funds with flexible criteria are not a luxury, but essential tools for system learning. Without them, innovation policy becomes static and performative.

To close this gap, a cultural change is needed that involves a shift from control to learning and from command to co-creation.

Overall, institutional inertia is not the result of individual inadequacies, but of a systemic inability to adapt. It stems from entrenched routines, risk-averse cultures and the gap between policy ambition and operational capacity. Often invisible in the short term, inertia only becomes apparent when innovation strategies falter, partnerships weaken, or promising reforms quietly bob along. In the context of innovation systems, the effects of inertia are particularly corrosive as they cause feedback loops to break down, learning to stagnate and trust between stakeholders to dwindle. Well-intentioned strategies become empty slogans, and even well-funded programmes falter in execution. But this is not an irreversible situation. Through targeted investment in institutional reflexivity, smarter feedback mechanisms and adaptive governance capabilities, systems can evolve. Change requires not only a reform of policy instruments, but also a change in the way institutions learn, collaborate and make decisions. However, before we revisit that issue, the next section turns to another critical source of internal weakness that determines the future readiness of the innovation system, namely the persistent mismatch between skills supply and innovation demand.

4.4 Skills Mismatch and Weak Human Capital Linkages

As a premium Tier 1 supplier in the automotive industry, Matador Automotive represents the growing technological ambitions of advanced manufacturers in Central and Eastern Europe. Like many firms in the region, it has invested heavily in high-end equipment including robotics lines, precision tools and digital production systems often sourced from global technology leaders. Yet as companies like Matador move up the value chain, the limiting factor is increasingly not machinery, but people. Premium technology requires premium skills: technicians who can programme, troubleshoot, and adapt complex systems in real time. Across the Central East European region, this is a common bottleneck (Bykova et al., 2023). Vocational graduates often possess solid mechanical skills but little exposure to automation or system integration. University graduates bring theoretical knowledge but lack hands-on experience. The result is a persistent mismatch between skills supply and demand. The challenge is not the quantity of education, but its alignment with industrial needs. Bridging this gap is essential if innovation is to become embedded rather than episodic.

Across Central and Eastern Europe, higher education attainment has increased significantly since the early 2000s. In countries such as Poland, Lithuania and Estonia, the proportion of college graduates is now over 40%. However, this increase in graduates often masks a more worrying reality of the misalignment between education and innovation needs. In many parts of the region technical faculties are still popular, but their curricula are outdated and overly theoretical. Graduates have no experience with new technologies, interdisciplinary teamwork or real-world problem solving. High-tech firms often report a shortage of data scientists, systems integrators and product managers, not because of a lack of graduates, but because their education is not aligned with evolving market needs. This problem is also echoed in Latin America, where countries such as Brazil and Mexico are struggling with a shortage of STEM talent despite having large higher education sectors. Employers cite deficits in creativity, adaptability and soft skills, all of which are key to innovation. So education may be increasing in volume, but not necessarily in value.

Vocational education and training (VET) systems are essential to the implementation of innovation. Yet in many emerging economies, they are treated as second-tier education, underfunded, stigmatised and disconnected from the innovation agenda. As a result, VET is often a fallback option for students not attending college rather than a strategic pipeline for advanced manufacturing, ICT or green technologies. In contrast, countries such as Germany are an example of how dual education systems, which combine classroom teaching with on-the-job training, embed students in dynamic innovation environments (Kroll et al., 2012). Some Central and Eastern European countries, such as Estonia, have taken steps towards this model by investing in modernised vocational curricula and digital skills development. However, in much of the region, VET plays only a minor role in national innovation strategies. To close this gap, the status of VET needs to be upgraded and it needs to be more directly integrated into policy frameworks for innovation.

While universities are often seen as engines of innovation, their ability to make a meaningful contribution to resolving this issue depends on their links to practice. In many emerging economies, academic institutions operate in isolation from the labour market. Curricula are often rigid, discipline-bound and dominated by theoretical teaching. In Croatia, for example, universities maintain strong academic autonomy but rarely work systematically with industry to shape learning outcomes. Internships are inconsistent and joint curriculum design is rare and hampered with rigid and slowly adapting institutional support at national level. Career centres remain underdeveloped, so students lack structured experience with real-world applications. As a result, graduates are often not ready for the job market, even in high-growth sectors such as IT or biotechnology. Firms have to invest time and resources to retrain new employees, which reduces productivity and slows down the introduction of innovations. This discrepancy reflects a broader coordination failure where innovation policy treats universities as research producers but neglects their function as human capital. Without strategic efforts to link higher education with firm needs, the system produces credentials but not capabilities.

One of the most visible symptoms of the mismatch between education and innovation is the underemployment of college graduates. Across emerging economies many graduates are either unemployed or working in jobs that do not match their qualifications. This means not only a personal loss of potential, but also a systematic waste of investment in human capital. The innovation system loses twice: first, by not utilising the skills of its best-educated citizens and second, by weakening the talent base needed to absorb and apply new knowledge. Meanwhile, employers become sceptical of academic credentials, creating a vicious cycle in which degrees lose their signalling power and practical skills remain in short supply. Without stronger feedback loops between employers and educators through advisory boards, joint projects or tracer studies, curricula evolve slowly or not at all. Over time, the system moves further and further away from the needs of a knowledge-based economy, even if educational indicators continue to rise on paper.

Innovation depends not only on technical know-how, but also on a broader set of competencies, often referred to as "soft skills". These include critical thinking, teamwork, adaptability and communication, qualities that are essential for working in interdisciplinary teams, dealing with uncertainty and iterative learning. Unfortunately, most education systems in emerging countries still emphasise memorisation, standardised tests and individual performance. Employers across Central and Eastern Europe often report that even those graduates that have excellent technical skills lack confidence in public speaking, collaborating across disciplines or leading group projects. These shortcomings can hold back innovation, especially in start-up environments or in collaborative research and development. To tackle this problem, it is not enough to update curricula. Rather, it requires a pedagogical shift towards project-based learning, interdisciplinary teaching, revised assessments and a redesign of the incentive structures that guide teacher behaviour.

Even if countries succeed in producing highly qualified skilled workers, retaining them is another matter. The brain drain remains a critical issue in many emerging economies, particularly in Eastern Europe. Eurostat data shows that more and more adults with higher education degrees from countries of the region live abroad and often work in sectors where there is a shortage of skilled workers at home. But the challenge does not stop with emigration. Within national borders, many highly skilled people are being misplaced. R&D institutes can be overstaffed with researchers stuck in legacy projects just as public institutions can exclude technically competent staff due to rigid hierarchies and outdated procedures. In addition, top talents often seek stable, prestigious careers in law, finance or government rather than entrepreneurial or innovation-driven roles. The result is a double loss, one external and one internal, leading to underperforming innovation systems. As Hidalgo and Hausmann (2009) point out, innovation relies on assembling unique combinations of capabilities and when these are dispersed or underutilised, entire sectors stagnate.

Recognising that skills shortages directly hinder innovation, some countries have begun to link education and training more specifically to their innovation strategies. The Strategic Research and Innovation Partnerships (SRIPs) in Slovenia are a good example of this. These collaborative platforms bring together academia, industry and government to jointly define skills needs, develop curricula and support internships and PhD positions in strategic areas such as robotics, sustainable energy and health technologies. In Vietnam, national innovation centres are working with universities to introduce applied programmes in artificial intelligence, cybersecurity and advanced manufacturing, often co-funded by industry partners. These efforts reflect a growing awareness that R&D alone is not enough if there is no workforce capable of implementing, adapting and scaling innovation. At a European level, institutions such as the European Institute of Innovation and Technology (EIT) are leading the way in integrated approaches through Knowledge and Innovation Communities (KICs) that link research, education and business. Although such models are still mostly limited to Western Europe, they offer replicable frameworks for other countries.

The future of innovation in emerging economies depends not only on funding or infrastructure, but on building human capital systems aligned with innovation needs. This goes beyond simply raising education levels and requires a focus on relevance, adaptability and connectivity. Skills development must anticipate technological change, engage employers and adapt continuously to labour market feedback. The mismatch between skills supply and demand is not just a productivity issue but a structural barrier to innovation. Innovation systems rely on people who can understand, apply and reshape knowledge in new ways. Without such capabilities, even strong investment, research output or policy ambition will yield limited results. Education, vocational training, and lifelong learning must be treated as integral components of innovation policy, supported by cross-sectoral coordination, shared success metrics and investment in scalable models. Unless this shift occurs, many systems will remain stuck with impressive degree counts but limited capacity for innovation-driven transformation.

4.5 Weak Demand for Innovation

Across many emerging economies, promising innovations regularly fail to take of not due to technical shortcomings or lack of funding, but because of weak demand (Dabic et al., 2023; Stojcic et al., 2024). Start-ups develop scalable solutions aligned with national goals, yet public agencies hesitate to pilot them, large firms prefer established suppliers, and procurement systems remain risk averse and slow to adapt. Even when ideas are locally relevant and technically sound, they often struggle to find traction in environments where institutional incentives favour caution over experimentation. This dynamic reflects a broader systemic problem where innovation struggles not because ideas, talent or ambition are missing, but because the demand side is dormant (Arocena & Sutz, 2010). Firms seldom seek out new technologies, public institutions avoid unproven solutions, and regulators and consumers are often satisfied with the status quo. This section explores how weak and fragmented demand, both public and private, undermines innovation ecosystems, and why stimulating it is essential for unlocking transformative change.

Low demand for innovation becomes a self-reinforcing trap. When few firms innovate, there is little pressure on suppliers to improve, little incentive for universities to collaborate with industry and little attraction for public funding programmes. Policymakers struggle to find viable projects to fund and public-private partnerships lack momentum. Finally, institutions adapt not to promote innovation but to manage its absence. Over time, this undermines the entrepreneurial culture and deepens the mistrust between firms and the state. In some contexts, innovation policy becomes decoupled from economic reality and produces elaborate roadmaps that do not influence actual behaviour. This creates a vicious circle: Without active demand for new knowledge, the system loses the reflexes it needs to absorb, adapt and generate innovation. Ironically, the more complex and formalised the system becomes through strategic documents, agencies and metrics, the more vulnerable it can become if there is no real demand. Systems full of potential remain untapped and fail to develop into the dynamic ecosystems they aspire to be.

One potential escape from this low-demand trap lies in tapping external markets, where export-oriented firms can face stronger incentives to innovate due to exposure to international competition and evolving customer needs. Access to global value chains or niche foreign markets can create a demand pull that domestic environments fail to provide, pushing firms to upgrade processes, develop new products and meet higher standards. However, export markets are also more competitive and often dominated by incumbents with established brands, distribution channels and technological advantages. For early-stage innovators, these barriers can be formidable, especially when domestic capabilities and support systems are underdeveloped. Balanced strategies that stimulate domestic uptake through public procurement, lead markets or targeted sectoral programmes can provide innovators with the stability and feedback needed to refine products, build capabilities and establish trust with local partners before confronting the harsher conditions of global competition.

On the public side, procurement is one of the most powerful yet underutilised tools for stimulating innovation (Stojcic et al., 2020; Uyarra et al., 2020). As major purchasers of goods and services, governments have the capacity to create stable markets for novel solutions if procurement is designed with innovation in mind. Yet in many emerging and transition economies, procurement practices remain focused on cost minimisation and risk avoidance. Legal frameworks prioritise compliance, while officials are incentivised to play it safe. Pilot projects are rare, and procurement procedures are poorly adapted to the needs of start-ups and SMEs. A lack of alignment between innovation policy and procurement rules limits experimentation and adoption. Even where legal provisions for innovation-friendly procurement exist, implementation is hampered by unclear guidance, limited capacity and weak political commitment. As a result, procurement remains a bureaucratic function rather than a lever for transformation. Real change will require structural reform, inter-agency coordination and a broader redefinition of public value.

Complementary to the above, consumer behaviour plays a crucial role in shaping markets for innovation (von Hippel, 2005), especially in areas such as health, education, mobility and energy. But in many low- and middle-income economies, consumers are conservative (Radošević, 2017; Stojcic et al., 2024). They behave rationally and stick to what works as their incomes are low, risk tolerance is limited, and confidence in new products or services is often non-existent. Even in the digital sectors, where innovation is progressing rapidly, monetisation remains difficult as maintaining user engagement and revenue is a challenge and there is often a lack of education and support services. Cultural conservatism, limited marketing channels and fragmented after-sales services play a role here. Until consumer confidence and engagement improves many promising innovations struggle to gain traction, creating a bottleneck in the adoption cycle and weakening incentives for firms to take bold steps forward.

Many innovation policies are based on the idea that firms and universities should work together to share knowledge, solve problems and co-develop technologies. But collaboration rarely happens just because there are platforms or funding. There is often a lack of underlying demand. Firms may not see research as relevant. Universities may lack incentives to get involved. Government programmes that focus on top-down goals often fail to bridge this gap. Without demand signals from firms or co-creation processes to ensure alignment, collaboration becomes symbolic. A few pilot projects may be successful, but they cannot be scaled up. The real problem is not the infrastructure or even the policy design. It is the lack of genuine, active interest from firms and researchers to support the system.

The demand for innovation is not just a policy or economic problem, but also a cultural one. In many contexts, especially where failure is stigmatised and change is viewed with suspicion, actors avoid innovation not because they cannot do it but because it is safer not to. This is true for government officials who fear the consequences of an audit, for SMEs who shy away from risky investments and for consumers who distrust local products. In some parts of the world such as the Western Balkans, there is a cultural bias in favour of foreign technologies, even when local solutions exist. In the Gulf States, legacy rentier dynamic discourages private sector innovation despite massive public investment. Changing this requires more than money. It requires visible success stories, better communication of public benefits and the creation of safe spaces for experimentation. Innovation must be seen as a legitimate, even expected, form of problem solving, not a risky detour from the norm. Until then, demand will remain limited and many systems will not reach their potential.

Despite these obstacles, some countries have made progress in stimulating demand. Mission-oriented policy is one tool. South Korea's focus on semiconductors and green technology has led to steady public and private investment, aligning research, procurement and market creation. Finland's health innovation missions have brought hospitals, firms and universities to face common challenges. Another model is challenge-based funding. In Chile, public agencies pose concrete problems that university teams or start-ups try to solve. The winning ideas are supported, piloted and sometimes scaled up. In this way, clear pathways are created to bring innovation into the public domain. Procurement reforms are also important. The UK's Small Business Research Initiative (SBRI) and the US SBIR programme fund start-ups through government contracts to develop early-stage solutions. These models have been adopted in India, South Africa and across the EU. What unites them is the realisation that demand does not happen automatically, but needs to be shaped, structured and rewarded. Innovation systems don't just need more ideas. They need more people asking for them.

Innovation does not occur simply because resources are available or technologies exist, it happens because someone demands it (Fabrizio & Thomas, 2012). Firms seek better ways to compete, governments look for smarter solutions, and consumers pursue new forms of value. Yet in many emerging and transition economies, the focus of innovation policy remains overwhelmingly on the supply side building more universities, labs and incubators while the demand remains weak. When companies avoid experimentation, when public procurement favours the familiar, and when consumers distrust the new, the entire innovation chain stalls. Knowledge remains unused, entrepreneurs lose momentum, and funding instruments underperform. This failure is systemic but not inevitable. Creating demand means reshaping incentives, reforming procurement, building institutional trust and creating spaces for experimentation without fear of failure. Whether through challenge-based funding, mission-oriented policies or regulatory reform, demand activation is essential. Without it, even the best-designed supply-side efforts will struggle to gain traction. To make innovation matter, systems must generate not just ideas but the appetite for change.

4.6 Absence of Feedback, Evaluation and Iterative Learning

In many emerging countries, innovation programmes are launched with enthusiasm offering grants to start-ups, establishing new funds and promoting early-stage entrepreneurship. Initial uptake is often strong, and project-level documentation is usually submitted. Yet years later, when policymakers seek to understand what these programmes actually achieved, how many firms survived, what innovations reached the market, or what capabilities were built, the answers are elusive. System-wide evaluations are rare, impact tracking is weak, and institutional learning is limited. Too often, evaluation is treated as a bureaucratic formality rather than a strategic tool for reflection and course correction. Programmes are closed without serious review, while new ones are launched without learning from past experiences. This absence of feedback loops undermines adaptive governance and weakens the long-term effectiveness of innovation systems. As this section argues, the lack of structured, iterative learning is not a minor oversight but a central design failure that prevents systems from evolving and scaling what works.

Innovation is inherently uncertain. Unlike routine public services, innovation policy deals with unknowns: new technologies, unpredictable markets and new actors. No policy instrument can be perfectly designed in advance. Success depends on real-time adjustments, stakeholder input and adaptive management (Radosevic et al., 2023; Woolthuis et al., 2005). In this context, feedback is not only desirable but essential. It allows policymakers to see what works, understand why and adapt accordingly. It helps to avoid repeating mistakes, identify emerging bottlenecks and reallocate resources to more effective strategies. Feedback loops also create legitimacy. When beneficiaries see that their experiences are being incorporated into future programmes, they are more willing to participate, experiment and collaborate. When institutions acknowledge and learn from failures, trust in the system grows. Without feedback, innovation systems become rigid. Programmes are repeated out of habit. Failures are hidden or denied. And learning becomes anecdotal rather than systematic, preventing the kind of adaptation that innovation policy demands.

One of the reasons why feedback is weak in many innovation systems is that evaluation is driven by the logic of compliance (Havas et al., 2015; Hillebrand, 2022). Especially in systems that depend on donor funding or EU structural funds, the main objective of evaluation is to prove that the money has been spent according to the rules, rather than to understand whether it has served its purpose. This leads to several distortions. First, evaluations focus on inputs and outputs, on how many grants were awarded and how many projects were completed, rather than on outcomes and impact. Second, data collection is conducted retrospectively and disconnected from programme design. Thirdly, results are rarely openly discussed or used to inform future interventions. In Central and Eastern Europe, for example, ex-post evaluations of innovation programmes are often conducted by external consultants without the involvement of the agencies that managed the programmes. The reports are filed away but rarely translated into organisational learning. The result is a system in which evaluation exists but does not function as feedback. It closes the loop formally, but not in terms of content.

Feedback requires more than an occasional assessment. It requires institutionalised learning mechanisms of structures, routines and cultures that treat policy as an iterative process. Some countries have started to invest in such mechanisms. The Finnish innovation agency Business Finland uses portfolio-level evaluations to continuously adjust its instrument mix. Chile's CORFO conducts regular strategic reviews and incorporates learning into programme design. Singapore's A*STAR includes post-project dialogues and cross-sector future workshops to align innovation funding with emerging trends. In contrast, many emerging economies lack such mechanisms. Ministries operate in silos, agencies are under pressure to disburse their funds quickly, and staff turnover prevents knowledge retention. Lessons learned from previous programmes are not documented, shared or used. There are no feedback forums where policymakers, researchers, businesses and intermediaries can share their experiences. Even such basic practices as requiring funded projects to present a follow-up or funding pilot phases before scaling up are absent in most innovation systems, weakening their adaptability over time.

When feedback is absent or undervalued, innovation systems suffer from what might be called learning blindness. Programmes continue because they are politically visible or institutionally entrenched, not because they are effective. Agencies become risk averse and shun new models in favour of familiar instruments, regardless of their performance. Stakeholders lose confidence in public innovation efforts, viewing them as bureaucratic exercises rather than strategic investments. Most critically, systems lose the ability to evolve. They cannot respond to technological change, changing market demands or lessons learned. This rigidity undermines innovation at its core. In some countries, a decade of innovation funding has produced few breakthroughs, not because the money was misspent, but because it could never be adapted. Without systematic feedback, failures are repeated rather than remedied, and successes go unnoticed rather than scaled.

Promoting learning in innovation systems does not require wholesale reform but can start with practical design adjustments. Programmes can be fully tested before launch, with evaluation built into budgets from the start. Grant recipients can be asked to report not only on deliverables but also on what did not work to create a culture of reflection. Peer learning networks and cross-ministerial working groups can be established to promote knowledge sharing and identify common challenges.

Scenario planning and anticipatory exercises can help to anticipate disruptions and prepare adaptive responses. Some countries have already taken these steps. India's Atal Innovation Mission includes policy labs where new ideas can be tested in real time. Estonia's use of digital monitoring platforms enables ongoing adjustments to innovation support. In Canada, regulatory sandboxes in areas such as financial technology provide safe spaces for policy experimentation with built-in feedback loops. These cases show that iterative governance is not a luxury for high-performing states, but a matter of institutional intent and design.

Putting pieces together, the innovation systems that cannot learn cannot evolve. Without feedback, they remain trapped in cycles of repetition, scaling what is familiar rather than what works, funding what is safe rather than what is promising and ultimately losing the trust of those who want to support them. This is not a marginal flaw, but a fundamental weakness that undermines resilience, erodes effectiveness and limits a system's ability to respond to uncertainty. Yet of all the systemic failures we have examined, the lack of feedback and learning is perhaps the most solvable. Feedback is not a technology or a budget line, it is a habit, a mindset and a design principle. Even modest systems can begin to learn from themselves with the right incentives and culture. However, this requires seeing innovation not as a set of outcomes, but as a process of continuous improvement.

4.7 Conclusion

The innovation systems in emerging countries often give the impression of dynamism. Strategies are designed, agencies set up and funding programmes launched. But this visible activity masks deeper systemic weaknesses that quietly undermine performance. This chapter has examined these internal weaknesses not as isolated technical failings, but as structural constraints that affect the way knowledge is created, shared and applied. The first challenge examined was fragmentation, a condition in which institutions operate in silos, research is disconnected from application, and coordination between sectors is weak. Even strong ideas struggle to gain traction when the system lacks pathways for interaction. Innovation in this context remains limited to isolated initiatives that are unable to scale up or influence broader societal outcomes.

We then turned to institutional inertia, discussing how outdated governance structures and risk-averse cultures inhibit responsiveness and learning. In such environment, public agencies manage innovation programmes from a compliance rather than strategic adaptation perspective. This limits the ability to experiment, iterate or correct course. The chapter has also highlighted a persistent mismatch between the supply of skills and the needs of innovation-driven sectors. Education systems often produce formal credentials without fostering the applied, interdisciplinary and collaborative capabilities that innovation requires. At the same time, funding for vocational education and training remains inadequate, and coordination between education providers, businesses and policy agendas is weak or non-existent. These deficits affect the human capital base on which innovation systems rely.

In addition to these structural deficits, we examined two mutually reinforcing failures, the low demand for innovation and the lack of system-wide feedback. Without active interest from businesses, consumers or public agencies, innovative ideas struggle to find buyers or supporters. Even well-funded supply-side programmes falter when demand is lacking. At the same time, systems that do not learn cannot evolve. Evaluation is often treated as a bureaucratic formality, and failures are brushed aside rather than investigated. Taken together, these patterns create innovation systems that are diligent but brittle, that appear active on the surface but are unable to learn or transform. The conclusion is that many systems are underperforming not in spite of, but because of their structures. However, change is possible. The next chapter shifts from system-level challenges to examine a key set of actors within them, namely multinational corporations. It explores the dual role MNCs play in shaping innovation outcomes in emerging economies, both as potential enablers of learning and as sources of dependency and asks what conditions are needed to turn their presence into long-term developmental benefit.

References

Arocena, R., & Sutz, J. (2010). Weak knowledge demand in the South: Learning divides and innovation policies. *Science and Public Policy, 37*(8), 861137.

Bykova, A., Dobrinsky, R., Grieveson, R., Grodzicki, M. J., Hanzl-Weiss, D., Hunya, G., Korpar, N., Leitner, S., Moshammer, B., Sankot, O., Strohm, B. C., Tverdostup, M. & Zavarska, Z. (2023). *Industrial policy for a new growth model: A toolbox for EU-CEE countries.* (WIIW Research Report No. 469). The Vienna Institute for International Economic Studies (WIIW).

Dabic, M., Posinković, T., Vlačić, B., & Goncalves, R. (2023). A configurational approach to new product development performance: The role of open innovation, digital transformation and absorptive capacity. *Technological Forecasting and Social Change, 194*, 122720.

Dabic, M., Svarc, J., & Becic, E. (2016). Innovation in Central Europe. In J. Haar & R. Ernst (Eds.), *Innovation in emerging markets. International Political Economy Series* (pp. 102–120). Palgrave Macmillan.

Fabrizio, K. R., & Thomas, L. G. (2012). The impact of local demand on innovation in global industry. *Strategic Management Journal, 33*(1), 42–64.

Games, D., Amsal, A. A., Sari, D. K., Kartika, R., & Anggraini, D. Y. (2024). Inertia, innovation failures and learning from innovation failures: Some insights from MSEs in an emerging market economy. In N. Faghih & A. H. Samadi. (Eds.), *Institutional intertia: Theory and evidence* (pp. 339–350). Springer.

Havas, A., Izsak, K., Markianidou, P., & Radosevic, S. (2015). Comparative analysis of policy-mixes of research and innovation policies in central and eastern European countries. *GRINCOH Working Paper Series, Serie 3: Knowledge, Innovation, Technology.* Paper No. 3.12, Available at SSRN: https://ssrn.com/abstract=2577569 or https://doi.org/10.2139/ssrn.2577569

Hidalgo, C. A., & Hausmann, R. (2009). The building blocks of economic complexity. *Proceedings of the National Academy of Sciences, 106*(26), 10570–10575.

Hillebrand, E. (2022). *The second transition: Why Central and Eastern Europe needs proactive industrial and innovation policy now?* Friedrich Ebert Stiftung.

Intarakumnerd, P., Chairatana, P., & Tangchitpiboon, T. (2002). National innovation system in less successful developing countries: The case of Thailand. *Research Policy, 31*(8–9), 1445–1457.
Kheiridoust, Z. (2024). Inertia in informal institutions: Concepts and effects. In N. Faghih & A. H. Samadi (Eds.), *Institutional intertia: Theory and evidence.* Springer.
Koschatzky, K. (2024). Slovenia. A fragmented innovation system? In H.-J. Braczyk, P. Cooke, & M. Heidenreich (Eds.), *Regional innovation systems* (pp. 111–129). Routledge.
Kroll, H., Schricke, E. & Stahlecker, T. (2012). *Developing new roles for higher education institutions in structurally-fragmented regional innovation systems,* (Working Paper R2/2012). Fraunhofer-Institut für System- und Innovationsforschung ISI.
Kuhlmann, S. and Arnold, E. (2001). *RCN in the Norwegian research and innovation system.* (Background Report No 12. In the Evaluation of the Research Council of Norway). Technopolis.
Mazzucato, M. (2018). Mission-oriented innovation policies: Challenges and opportunities. *Industrial and Corporate Change, 27*(5), 803–815.
Radošević, S. (2017). Upgrading technology in Central and Eastern European Economies. *IZA World of Labor, 338.* https://wol.iza.org/articles/upgrading-technology-in-central-and-eastern-european-economies/long
Radošević, S. (2024). Performance of post-socialist innovation systems: Patterns of diversification, catching up and falling behind. In A. D. Gevorkyan (Ed.), *The Oxford handbook of post-socialist economies.* Oxford University Press.
Radosevic, S., Kanellou, D., & Tsekouras, G. (2023). The experimentation-accountability trade-off in innovation and industrial policy: Are learning networks the solution? *Science and Public Policy, 50*(4), 655–669.
Samadi, A. H., Panahi, M., & Raanaei, A. (2024). The roots of cognitive inertia: An introduction to institutional changes. In N. Faghih & A. H. Samadi. (Eds.), *Institutional intertia: Theory and evidence* (pp. 133–153). Springer.
Stojcic, N. (2024). Innovation failure, training for innovative activities and public support for innovation: Multi-annual evidence from emerging European innovation systems. *Research Policy, 53*, 105059.
Stojcic, N., Dabic, M., & Kraus, S. (2024). Customisation and co-creation revisited: Do user types and engagement strategies matter for product innovation success? *Technovation, 134*, 103045.
Stojcic, N., Srhoj, S., & Coad, A. (2020). Innovation procurement as capability-building: Evaluating innovation policies in eight Central and Eastern European countries. *European Economic Review, 121*, 103330.
Švarc, J., & Dabić, M. (2019). The Croatian path from socialism to European membership through the lens of technology transfer policies. *The Journal of Technology Transfer, 44*, 1476–1504.
Švarc, J., & Dabić, M. (2021). Transformative innovation policy or how to escape peripheral policy paradox in European research peripheral countries. *Technology in Society, 67*, 101705.
Uyarra, E., Zabala-Iturriaagaoitia, J. M., Flanagan, K., & Magro, E. (2020). Public procurement, innovation and industrial policy: Rationales, roles, capabilities and implementation. *Research Policy, 49*(1), 103844.
von Hippel, E. (2005). Democratizing innovation: The evolving phenomenon of user innovation. *Journal für Betriebswirtschaft, 55*, 63–78. https://doi.org/10.1007/s11301-004-0002-8
Woolthuis, R. K., Lankhuisen, M., & Gilsing, V. (2005). A system failure framework for innovation policy design. *Technovation, 25*, 609–619.

Chapter 5
The Role of Multinational Enterprises

He who controls the spice controls the universe. (Frank Herbert, *Dune*)

Abstract Multinational enterprises (MNEs) often arrive in emerging economies carrying the aura of modernity by bringing capital, technology and the promise of integration into global markets. Yet their presence is a double-edged sword. This chapter unpacks the complex role of MNEs as both engines of innovation and gatekeepers of knowledge. On the one hand, they can inject much-needed dynamism into host economies, introducing advanced practices and linking local firms to global value chains. On the other, their dominance often limits the diffusion of knowledge, creating dependencies rather than capabilities. Local firms may find themselves trapped as suppliers of low-value tasks, while strategic decision-making and core technologies remain tightly guarded within headquarters abroad. The narrative highlights how the contribution of MNEs depends on local absorptive capacities, institutional frameworks and policy choices. Ultimately, MNEs can be catalysts or constraints, transformative partners or monopolisers of opportunity, in the fragile balance of innovation systems.

5.1 Introduction

In 2004, Slovakia proudly announced the arrival of Kia Motors, a large South Korean multinational, as an anchor investor for a new manufacturing plant near Žilina. It was a groundbreaking moment, celebrated as proof of the country's successful post-socialist transformation and integration into the global economy. The plant brought thousands of jobs and increased exports, firmly integrating Slovakia into European value chains. But two decades later, the glamour of this initial success is overshadowed by a deeper question common to all emerging innovation systems: Did this kind of foreign investment make Slovakia more innovative or more dependent? This dilemma is the central concern of this chapter. While multinational enterprises (MNEs) often appear as engines of modernity, technology and opportunity, they also

N. Stojčić, *Elusive Innovation*, Applied Innovation and Technology Management,
https://doi.org/10.1007/978-3-032-14900-8_5

embody asymmetries of power and control. For countries seeking to build innovation systems, the presence of MNEs represents both an avenue and a potential trap, offering global connectivity on the one hand and structural dependency on the other.

MNEs are among the most powerful institutions in the global economy. They control technology, shape supply chains and influence innovation agendas across all industries. For emerging economies, they often promise a shortcut to modernity by providing capital, knowledge and market access in a bundled package. If successful, multinationals can drive local upgrading through technology transfer, supplier development and labour mobility. They introduce new standards and routines, increase productivity and stimulate institutional reform. However, this promise comes with risks. Many multinationals keep high-value activities such as R&D, strategic planning and product design in their home countries. Local operations are often limited to assembly, logistics or low-value services. Knowledge may be available but protected, production may be localised but learning is not guaranteed. In such contexts, multinational companies do not act as enablers of innovation, but monopolists of it, hoarding capabilities and limiting spillover effects. This duality of opportunity and constraint is not theoretical. It happens every day in regions from Central Europe to South East Asia.

This chapter argues that the impact of MNEs on domestic innovation is not determined by their presence alone, but also by how that presence is governed. The balance of power between foreign firms and host country institutions determines whether FDI becomes a catalyst for capability development or a mechanism of dependency. We analyse both sides of this equation. First, we discuss how MNEs can serve as drivers of innovation through supply chain spillovers, knowledge diffusion and talent circulation. We then examine the structural and strategic barriers that limit these effects, namely the opacity of corporate knowledge, the use of restrictive contracts and the systemic weakness of domestic absorptive institutions. In particular, we highlight how multinationals can inadvertently suppress local learning by dominating ecosystems, crowding out local firms or creating shallow subcontracting relationships. These effects are particularly pronounced when domestic firms, universities or public institutions lack the capacity or leverage to capitalise on the engagement.

The rest of the chapter deals with three interrelated questions: Under what conditions do multinational companies promote domestic innovation capacity? When do they inhibit it? And what can policymakers do to reshape the relationship? Using examples from Slovakia, Hungary, Malaysia, Mexico and Vietnam, we examine how domestic policies, institutional readiness and strategic coordination influence outcomes. We show that MNEs are not inherently good or bad actors, but rational actors that respond to incentives and constraints. Whether they become bridges or barriers to innovation does not depend on their intentions, but on the strategic capabilities of the host country. MNEs can accelerate the catching-up process, but only if they are embedded in a broader system that supports learning, fosters linkages and builds bargaining power. In this sense, innovation policy is not just about attracting investment. It is about shaping its trajectory. The rest of the chapter provides a roadmap for how this can be done.

5.2 MNEs as Drivers of Innovation

MNEs are among the most powerful vectors of technological change in today's economy. Their influence goes far beyond the products they produce or the services they offer. MNEs set the agenda: Their research and development (R&D) budgets often exceed those of national science systems, their supply chain strategies dictate how and where technologies are implemented, and their operating standards become de facto benchmarks for entire industries. For emerging economies, securing the presence of such firms is often seen as a milestone in development. MNEs are expected not only to create jobs and increase exports, but also to transfer knowledge, develop skills and modernise domestic industries (Aitken & Harrison, 1999; Findlay, 1978). In this narrative, foreign firms are more than just investors, they are partners on the path of transition from production-driven to innovation-driven growth.

In many cases, this partnership has proven successful. The multinationals have helped local firms meet international standards, they have pushed their suppliers to improve technologically, and they have trained local workers in advanced production methods. But these positive spillover effects do not occur automatically (Orlic et al., 2018). They depend on sectoral dynamics, as some sectors such as the automotive or electronics industries have greater potential for upgrading than others. They also depend on local conditions: Whether domestic firms have the capabilities to absorb knowledge, whether universities and training institutions can adapt, and whether public policy encourages deeper integration rather than shallow subcontracting. This section examines the mechanisms by which MNEs can support innovation in host countries, through supply chain linkages, labour mobility and demonstration effects, and explores the institutional conditions that determine whether these opportunities are seized or squandered.

One of the most consistent and well-documented mechanisms through which MNEs contribute to domestic innovation is labour mobility (Markusen & Trofimenko, 2009; Stojcic & Orlic, 2020). Workers trained in the subsidiaries of MNCs are often familiar with advanced processes, management systems and quality standards that can become vectors of tacit knowledge transfer when they move to domestic firms or start their own businesses. This is a characteristic feature of innovation ecosystems in the Chinese ICT sector, where entrepreneurs and engineers who have returned from abroad and gained experience in foreign firms have played a catalytic role in the growth of domestic capabilities in software, hardware and e-commerce (Liu et al., 2010). These individuals not only imported knowledge but also introduced global norms of agility, efficiency and product orientation. Their contribution shows that innovation spillovers depend not only on the presence of knowledge, but also on its movement across firms, sectors and institutions, as well as the conditions under which this movement takes place.

Vietnam's experience with labour mobility in the electronics sector is similar to the Chinese case, albeit on a smaller scale (ILO, 2022). Although initial evidence suggested prevailing negative labour mobility effects of MNCs (Phi et al., 2024), there is also evidence that in some regions former employees of foreign giants such as Samsung and Intel have started to move to local firms or found start-ups and to reshape the local innovation landscape, particularly in niche areas such as mobile applications, hardware prototyping and embedded software. The value of these spillovers lies not only in technological know-how but also in softer skills such as project management, quality assurance and business process design. By bringing the skills acquired in MNEs to local companies, these individuals build institutional bridges between foreign knowledge ecosystems and the emerging domestic ones. This type of learning-by-hiring or learning-by-doing leads to cumulative effects that increase the innovation potential of host countries over time.

Similar effects of labour mobility have been observed in Central and Eastern Europe, particularly in countries such as Poland and the Czech Republic, where multinational companies in the automotive and aerospace industries have established a significant presence. Engineers and technicians trained in foreign subsidiaries have occasionally moved to local SMEs, sometimes setting up their own companies or contributing to technology adoption in existing firms. However, such spillover effects depend on the broader ecosystem. In much of the region, the scale and impact of labour mobility is limited by structural challenges such as low rates of entrepreneurship, wage differentials between foreign and domestic firms and weak support for risk-taking (Stojcic & Orlic, 2020). Without an environment that supports experimentation, such as accessible funding, innovation intermediaries and mentoring networks, even highly skilled individuals may struggle to translate their experience into businesses.

Supplier development is another channel through which multinationals can drive innovation (Mariotti et al., 2015). In global sectors such as automotive or electronics, leading firms often invest in the technical upgrading of their suppliers by enforcing quality standards, providing training and sometimes even sharing process innovations. Mexico's integration into the North American automotive value chains is a good example of this: Suppliers' capabilities have improved significantly through collaboration with US firms (Vidal & Gonzalez Pandiella, 2024). A similar dynamic played out in Thailand, where Japanese automakers helped local parts manufacturers meet global benchmarks. However, such upgrading is not automatic. MNCs often prefer to source from global suppliers they already trust or internalise production within their own networks. As long as there are no targeted policy measures to incentivise local sourcing and help SMEs to meet the demanding standards, the potential for supplier-led innovation remains underutilised.

Malaysia's experience, particularly in Penang's electronics sector, shows how proactive institutional design can lead to successful supplier development (Eltgen et al., 2021; UNCTAD, 2011). Early investment in technical training, infrastructure and local coordination centres helped local suppliers not only to participate in the value chains of multinational companies, but also to improve their processes and move up the value chain ladder. These firms benefited not only from contracts but also from embedded learning. Over time, some of them evolved into technology partners and not just component suppliers. This transformation was possible because the region was treated not only as a production site but also as a learning space. The contrast with many post-socialist economies is remarkable: Where local institutions are weak or fragmented, and where policies emphasise attraction over integration, multinationals tend to operate in enclaves. Supplier development then becomes a missed opportunity and domestic firms remain stuck in low-value roles, with limited scope for innovation or strategic autonomy.

R&D spillovers are one of the most advanced and valuable forms of knowledge transfer that MNEs can offer their host countries. When multinationals localise parts of their R&D operations by hiring local engineers, opening innovation labs or entering research partnerships, the potential for deep and sustainable learning increases significantly. Countries such as Israel and India have demonstrated this with remarkable success. IBM, Microsoft and Google have set up R&D centres in Israel, tapping into the country's strong talent pool and contributing to its rise as a global innovation hotspot (Business Insider, 2016). Similarly, GE's R&D investments in India, particularly in frugal healthcare innovation, have contributed to both product development and the training of local talent (MTPConnect, 2019). In Central and Eastern Europe, firms such as Honeywell and Siemens have embedded their R&D activities in local ecosystems, working with technical universities in Prague and Brno (Aridi & Querejazu, 2019). These efforts illustrate how local R&D can help build capabilities when multinationals are willing to invest beyond production and when host countries have the talent and institutions to engage.

But such high-value R&D investments remain the exception rather than the rule. Most multinationals keep their core innovation functions at their headquarters or global tech hubs, where strategic design, intellectual property and cutting-edge research are tightly controlled (Stojcic et al., 2025b). The R&D activities they outsource abroad are often limited to late-stage development, customisation for local markets or support services. This limits the scope of spillover effects and increases dependency on foreign technology pipelines. Collaboration with domestic universities, research institutes or start-ups is also limited, unless there are political incentives, intermediary institutions and absorption capacities. In Costa Rica, for example, Intel's early commitment to invest in research partnerships only materialised because the government actively supported university reforms, facilitated connections and co-financed the innovation infrastructure (World Bank, 2006). Without such government efforts to align interests and reduce transaction costs, multinationals rarely engage in deep innovation collaboration. This suggests that R&D spillovers are possible, but they require a conscious design of the ecosystem.

Finally, multinational companies play a key role in disseminating global standards for production, quality and safety, providing a pathway for domestic firms to integrate into international value chains (Stojcic & Orlic, 2020). Compliance with certifications such as ISO 9001, environmental audits or lean manufacturing protocols is often a prerequisite for working with global buyers or entering export markets. In sectors such as automotive, pharmaceuticals, electronics and food processing, these standards are not optional, but the ticket to entry. In Tunisia, for example, European automotive and electronics firms have worked with local suppliers to meet EU technical and environmental standards, allowing these firms to become more integrated into regional production networks (OECD, 2024). But setting standards alone is not enough. When multinational companies set requirements without providing training, technical assistance or progressive adaptation, they can inadvertently exclude local firms that lack the resources or knowledge to comply. Successful transfer of standards requires institutional facilitation through industry associations, public funding agencies or supplier development programmes to turn compliance into capacity building.

Putting pieces of this puzzle together, it is evident that MNEs can serve as powerful engines for innovation diffusion and capability building in emerging economies. Their presence enables knowledge transfer through various channels such as labour mobility, supplier development, competitive pressure, localised R&D and the diffusion of global standards. When these mechanisms work well, domestic firms and institutions can learn, adapt and improve, contributing to the long-term strengthening of national innovation systems. However, this potential is not automatically realised. For the spillover effects from multinationals to materialise, domestic firms must have sufficient absorptive capacity, institutions must be able to broker effective partnerships, and public policies must be strategically designed to translate foreign presence into local change. Where these conditions are not met, opportunities are lost and foreign knowledge remains isolated. In the next section, we move from enabling mechanisms to constraining forces, examining how multinationals sometimes limit spillover effects, protect proprietary technologies and maintain control over high-value activities, thereby reinforcing structural dependency rather than enabling technological upgrading.

5.3 MNEs as Knowledge Gatekeepers

MNEs are often portrayed as agents of modernisation and technological upgrading, and in many cases they are. But MNEs are also strategic players operating in highly competitive global markets where the protection of proprietary knowledge is not just a business preference but a necessity. Their technologies, processes and know-how are key assets that are protected by intellectual property rights, internal confidentiality and strict control of supply chains. As a result, while multinational companies can create productivity gains and jobs, they often keep critical knowledge within the firm, limiting the potential for spillovers to local partners, suppliers or institutions. This restriction of knowledge is particularly evident in high-value activities such as design, software development or advanced engineering, functions that remain concentrated in headquarters or selected global innovation centres (Stojcic et al., 2025b).

This dual role of multinationals, both as knowledge brokers and as gatekeepers, requires policymakers to take a more careful view. It is not enough to welcome foreign investment. What matters is the nature of the engagement: the depth of integration, the strategic intentions of the firm and the institutional arrangements that determine how and whether knowledge circulates beyond corporate boundaries. Some governments have responded by promoting collaborative research programmes, enforcing local content rules or negotiating technology sharing agreements. Others have been passive, hoping that proximity to foreign firms will be enough to trigger learning. As this section shows, relying on the goodwill of global actors is rarely enough. Instead, host countries must actively shape the terms of engagement if they want MNEs to act as innovation partners rather than just producers in enclaves.

One of the most common ways in which MNEs restrict knowledge spillovers is by fragmenting their global operations. Strategic functions such as research and development, design and decision-making tend to be centralised in a handful of high-capability innovation hubs such as those in United States, Germany or South Korea. In contrast, subsidiaries in emerging markets are usually entrusted with low-value activities such as assembly, logistics or routine services. These local operations are often tightly controlled, have limited autonomy, minimal involvement in innovation processes and have little familiarity with the core technologies or management systems that make the multinational competitive (Stojcic & Matic, 2024). Even when subsidiaries operate with advanced equipment, the work is usually highly codified and detached from the kind of learning-by-doing that fosters local capabilities. This structure reflects a conscious strategic decision by multinationals to protect intellectual property, minimise coordination costs and retain control over the most valuable parts of their business models.

This dynamic has led scholars to characterise many foreign-led industrial companies in emerging economies as examples of "enclave economies" (Gallagher & Zarsky, 2007). These are technologically advanced companies that are embedded in domestic economies, but only physically, not institutionally. They do not interact meaningfully with local firms, research organisations or policy actors, which limits their contribution to national innovation systems. In Romania, for example, global manufacturers in the automotive and electronics sectors operate high-tech plants that produce for Western European markets. However, only a few of these companies conduct local research and development (e.g. Porsche in Timisoara), support the development of suppliers or collaborate with universities. The result is a dual economy where a globally networked manufacturing enclave operates surrounded by a domestic system that remains underdeveloped and disconnected. Without targeted policy measures that promote integration, such as incentives for joint innovation, local content rules or joint research platforms, these multinationals risk reinforcing dependency rather than catalysing structural change.

MNEs are increasingly relying on intellectual property rights (IPRs) discussed in Chapter 3 to safeguard their competitive advantage in global markets. Patents, trade secrets, software licences and copyrights serve not only as incentives for innovation, but also as strategic tools to limit knowledge diffusion. Since the enforcement of the WTO's TRIPS agreement, the global IPR regime has limited the scope for imitation, adaptation and reverse engineering, mechanisms that were crucial in earlier waves of industrial catch-up (Canavire-Bacarreza & Castro Peñarrieta, 2021; Stojcic et al., 2025a). In sectors such as electronics or machinery, reverse engineering once enabled firms in East Asia and Southern Europe to understand and build on foreign technologies. Today, legal barriers and a complex patent thicket make such informal learning considerably more difficult. This affects not only private firms but also public organisations, which often find themselves excluded from the frontier of technological knowledge. The result is a landscape in which access to knowledge is legally restricted and the risks of violating intellectual property laws prevent experimentation and adaptation.

This dynamic is particularly acute in knowledge-intensive sectors such as pharmaceuticals and agricultural biotechnology, where tacit knowledge is closely guarded alongside formal intellectual property rights. Pharmaceutical MNEs control not only the patent claims, but also the clinical data, manufacturing processes and quality standards required to produce generic drugs, making it difficult for latecomers to compete even after the patent expires. In the field of agricultural technology, a handful of MNEs hold patents on genetically modified seeds, limiting the ability of national research institutes to experiment or develop alternatives. Some countries have fought back, India with strict patentability criteria, Brazil with compulsory licences, but these strategies often trigger international disputes, diplomatic pressure or retaliatory trade measures. In this context, intellectual property rights function not only as legal instruments, but also as instruments of geopolitical control that determine who can learn and who can innovate, and under what conditions. The barriers to learning are therefore both formal and deeply political.

In many sectors, multinational companies rely on "black box" production systems that deliberately restrict knowledge transfer. Local partners receive pre-assembled modules, proprietary equipment or embedded software with minimal technical disclosure. Workers and engineers are trained to operate these systems according to rigid procedures but are rarely given access to the underlying designs or principles. This approach is particularly evident in high-tech manufacturing. In the Malaysian electronics industry, for example, local firms often act as contract manufacturers, assembling imported components under tight specifications without understanding the product architecture. The result is a form of shallow learning where local firms acquire operational routines but not the ability to design or solve problems. Even engineers can become highly qualified testers but are not able to develop or adapt technologies independently. This makes innovation marginalised and confines local firms to low-value tasks.

The multinationals exercise strategic control over their supply chains and determine not only what is produced, but also who is authorised to produce it and under what conditions. They often rely on a small pool of certified global suppliers that fulfil precise technical and operational standards, excluding many local firms. Even when local firms are involved, the collaboration can be transactional and rigid, focusing on cost, volume and compliance rather than innovation or co-development. These suppliers are expected to adhere to detailed blueprints, with little room for deviation or suggestions for improvement. In the automotive clusters in Hungary and Slovakia, for example, local firms are often confined to low value-added tasks such as packaging, tooling or the production of smaller parts, while critical systems remain under the control of foreign Tier 1 suppliers. Moving up the value chain requires not only financial investment but also trust and partnership on the part of multinational companies, which are rarely granted without long-term relationships or policy incentives.

Equally problematic is the weak anchoring of MNEs in local innovation ecosystems. They may employ thousands of people and operate sophisticated facilities, but their interaction with local knowledge institutions is often minimal. Many multinationals bypass local universities, avoid collaborating with start-ups and rarely collaborate with public research institutes. Training of local staff tends to focus on firm-specific protocols rather than broader skills that promote mobility or innovation. As a result, co-creation, where local and foreign actors jointly develop new solutions, is rare. Cases such as Intel in Costa Rica or Samsung in South Korea show that meaningful integration is possible but usually requires proactive government policies and a mature ecosystem. In many emerging markets, however, public authorities have limited influence to demand such partnerships. Research centres report few enquiries from foreign firms, and domestic innovators find the barriers to accessing global value chains almost insurmountable. Without deeper institutional relationships, the transformative potential of multinationals' presence often remains untapped.

As we already argued, multinationals rarely delegate strategic innovation functions such as core R&D, product design or budgeting to subsidiaries in emerging or transition economies. Instead, these tasks remain centralised at headquarters in global innovation centres. Even if promising ideas come from local operations, they are scrutinised internally at multiple layers of internal review, with decision-making authority far removed from the context in which the innovation originated. This structure reinforces a pattern of institutional dependency: Local subsidiaries may be technologically advanced in execution but have no influence over strategic direction. As a result, domestic firms and institutions are often positioned as followers rather than leaders, reacting to global priorities rather than shaping them. Over time, this undermines entrepreneurship and reduces the scope for local experimentation. Innovation systems become compliant rather than creative, and actors learn to act efficiently rather than explore new opportunities. Strategic centralisation thus not only limits spillovers, but also the development of autonomous innovation trajectories.

Overall, MNEs are not designed to build indigenous innovation systems. They are driven by shareholder value, global market positioning and the protection of proprietary knowledge. Their ability to create jobs, exports and even some learning should not obscure the deeper risks they pose. MNEs often act as knowledge gatekeepers, selectively sharing information and maintaining control over high-value activities. This is not malicious per se but rather reflects a rational corporate strategy in a competitive global economy. However, the consequences for host countries can be profound. Without targeted policies and strong institutions, the presence of multinationals can reinforce existing hierarchies, leaving local firms technologically dependent and innovation ecosystems underdeveloped. In the next section, we examine what happens when this asymmetry becomes embedded in the system. We examine the long-term effects of dependence on foreign firms for innovation and argue that meaningful transformation requires more than attracting higher quality investors. It demands a reconfiguration of the innovation system itself, its incentives, institutions and underlying logic.

5.4 Dependence on Foreign Firms for Innovation

In the years following EU accession, Hungary became a magnet for foreign direct investment, securing major commitments from global giants such as Audi, Mercedes-Benz, Bosch and GE. These investments transformed Hungary into a manufacturing powerhouse, dramatically boosting the country's export performance and positioning it as a major player in European supply chains. But beneath the surface, concerns began to grow. By the late 2010s, policymakers realised that Hungary's innovation capacity remained weak. Domestic R&D spending was low, local firms played only a limited role in technology development, and innovation leadership continued to be concentrated in foreign-owned companies. The country had integrated into global production networks but had not developed a robust, independent innovation system. This pattern reflects the deeper risk associated with reliance on multinationals for growth, the one of being trapped in a model that delivers jobs and production without building learning capacity. This section examines how such dependency arises, why it persists and what is needed to escape its structural grip.

Dependency is not the result of a single decision, but arises cumulatively through structural conditions, policy choices and institutional design. It typically begins with the attraction of foreign direct investment as an instrument of modernisation. MNEs bring with them what domestic players often lack: capital, global networks, management experience and technological expertise (Stojcic & Matic, 2024; Stojcic et al., 2025b). Eager for rapid gains, governments put together generous incentive packages such as tax exemptions, fast-track approvals, infrastructure investment, often without requiring local integration, technology transfer or collaborative R&D. Over time, these incentives become entrenched. National innovation strategies begin to revolve around the priorities of foreign firms. Local suppliers become dependent on individual customers. Research agendas at universities become orientated around the needs of multinationals, especially where foreign funding or partnerships dominate. Policymakers can link economic growth to technological upgrading, even if most of the value added remains external. This dependence increases in smaller economies with limited industrial depth. In such an environment, it seems pragmatic to let multinational companies take the lead. But the result is often a system that performs yet does not evolve.

As MNEs expand, they increasingly dominate sectors that are critical to national development, squeezing domestic companies out of high value-added segments. These global firms come with economies of scale, control over the supply chain and access to proprietary technologies. In contrast, local SMEs often do not have access to finance, skilled labour or certifications required to meet multinational standards. The result is a two-tier system with globally networked foreign firms at the centre and domestically oriented SMEs on the periphery. In Latin America, this dynamic has hindered local industrial deepening. Argentina and Mexico have succeeded in attracting multinationals in the automotive and electronics industries but have struggled to foster local firms capable of climbing the value chain. The Brazilian innovation system remains unbalanced despite public support with large foreign firms dominating research and development, while most domestic firms operate in low-technology, commodity-based sector. A similar pattern has emerged in Central and Eastern Europe. Foreign firms anchor production networks, but domestic firms rarely influence standards or strategies. Even when spillovers do occur, they are often only superficial and have nothing to do with systemic upgrading.

Over time, dependence on multinational companies reshapes the innovation ecosystem from within. Public research organisations begin to align their activities with multinational priorities, either to obtain funding or to remain relevant. Talent is migrating to foreign firms for better pay, prestige or career development, leaving domestic firms and public institutions understaffed. Education systems are slow to adapt, if they adapt at all, and focus on meeting the immediate needs of the labour market rather than fostering long-term innovation capability. This erosion is subtle but corrosive. The appearance of an active innovation system remains as there are labs, programmes and incubators but these often operate in isolation, have no long-term focus or serve to support foreign-led production networks. If high-value functions such as R&D, design or strategic planning remain centralised in foreign headquarters, local ecosystems become implementers rather than initiators of innovation.

Once foreign-led production and innovation systems become dominant, they tend to become deeply embedded in the technological and institutional architecture of the host economy. The multinationals bring with them their own machinery, production systems, quality standards and digital platforms that local firms and workers must learn to deal with. Skills development is increasingly tailored to these imported systems, often at the expense of building broader or more adaptable competences. Even public innovation policies are beginning to reflect the operational needs of MNEs by emphasising applied research, efficiency improvement or export support rather than generic innovation capacity. This leads to a kind of technological lock-in, with domestic firms and institutions constantly adapting to foreign templates rather than creating their own. The scope for alternative innovation paths is shrinking as both financial and cognitive resources are channelled into maintaining existing models.

As multinationals become pillars of economic performance, contributing to GDP, exports and employment, they often gain an outsized influence on national innovation policy. Governments are reluctant to introduce regulatory conditions such as mandatory R&D spending, skills transfer obligations or quotas for domestic suppliers for fear of discouraging investment. This leads to a distorted policy landscape in which incentives, infrastructure and even education reforms are designed to meet the preferences of multinationals rather than national innovation needs. In parts of Eastern Europe, this dynamic has led to industrial parks, R&D centres and vocational training programmes that serve the operational needs of foreign automotive and electronics firms, while the development of a broader innovation system is neglected. In South Africa, similar patterns can be observed in the extractive sectors, where R&D priorities are dictated by global corporations with little long-term commitment to local knowledge systems. Even inclusive measures such as tax credits or grants often favour large, well-resourced firms, so that local SMEs are not adequately supported and the two-track nature of innovation systems is reinforced.

A subtle but profound consequence of long-term dependence on MNEs is the erosion of entrepreneurial culture. When the economic and innovation landscape is dominated by foreign firms, domestic entrepreneurship is often suppressed not by regulation, but by perception and aspiration. Talented graduates prefer the higher salaries and prestige of working for a multinational company to starting their own. Public officials see foreign firms as the default engines of progress. Universities teach their students to implement rather than invent. This psychological shift is gradually undermining the belief that domestic players can lead innovation. In Malaysia and Thailand, despite their impressive industrial capabilities, start-up ecosystems remain underdeveloped. In contrast, in Vietnam and Indonesia, stronger government support for local entrepreneurship and the visibility of home-grown success stories have led to a more vibrant start-up culture. Once entrepreneurial momentum is lost, it is difficult to restore as it depends not only on policies or funding, but also on mindset and shared ambition.

However, not all systems dominated by MNEs are excluded from learning processes. In fact, many domestic players come into contact with new technologies, standards and processes. Engineers working in foreign subsidiaries acquire valuable skills. Universities co-operate in research. Suppliers improve their quality management systems. However, this learning often does not translate into systemic progress. Employees remain in subordinate roles and are unable to apply their skills in start-ups. Research partnerships produce papers but not products. Suppliers fulfil requirements but remain locked into low margin contracts. This is the dilemma of learning without leverage, where knowledge is accumulated but structural barriers prevent its transformation into autonomy. Public policy plays a key role here. Without instruments aimed at domestic value creation, such as public procurement for innovation, SME support programmes or coordinated cluster strategies, learning remains atomised. The Polish aerospace sector is a good example of this as individual firms have developed world-class capabilities through long-term contracts with multinationals, but these gains have not reshaped the innovation landscape in general.

Dependence on foreign firms for innovation capacity is not only an economic burden but also a strategic risk, an issue that we touch in greater detail in next chapter. A country that is unable to independently design technologies, control its supply chains or respond to new challenges is vulnerable to external shocks. This became painfully clear during the COVID-19 pandemic, when the disruption to global supply chains left many countries without access to essential goods such as medical devices, semiconductors and vaccines. These shortages highlighted the cost of outsourcing not only production but also innovation. The same vulnerability looms in sectors critical to national security and long-term resilience such as green energy, cybersecurity and defence manufacturing. Countries that fail to build domestic innovation capacity risk becoming technologically dependent in areas where autonomy is essential. In a multipolar and increasingly insecure world, innovation is no longer just an instrument of competitiveness, but a pillar of sovereignty. Reducing dependence on multinationals is not about rejecting globalisation, but about regaining the strategic flexibility that innovation makes possible.

Foreign firms can play an important role as a catalyst for learning and upgrading in emerging innovation systems but without careful management they can also become crutches that hinder long-term development. What begins as a beneficial partnership can gradually evolve into a dependency in which domestic firms and institutions lose the initiative to innovate independently. While integration into global value chains is often celebrated, it can sometimes mask a deeper subordination when local actors are limited to low-value roles. The key challenge is therefore not to reject multinationals, but to reshape the conditions for their engagement. Host countries must move from being passive recipients of foreign investment to active shapers of innovation relationships. This requires building systems that absorb, adapt and ultimately transform external knowledge into domestic capabilities. In the next section, we examine the precise conditions under which this is possible: What policies and institutional structures enable capability building? When does foreign presence become learning? And how can dependency be transformed into co-creation?

5.5 When Multinationals Contribute to Domestic Technological Capacity

Despite the risks and asymmetries analysed in the previous sections, MNEs are not inherently agents of dependency. Under the right institutional and policy conditions, MNEs can become partners in building domestic innovation capacity. Their contribution can go beyond capital and technology transfer to include the dissemination of routines, standards and organisational cultures that enhance local practices. They can partner with local companies to develop new products, invest in talent development, fund applied research and help anchor vibrant innovation ecosystems. However, such results are never automatic. They require a combination of incentives, robust local institutions and clear strategic intentions on the part of the host countries. Rather than simply integrating into global value chains, countries need to pursue a logic of co-creation in which domestic and foreign actors are not only involved in market transactions but work together to transform the innovation system itself. This section examines how and when MNEs can support technological upgrading, drawing on international examples to identify practical lessons and policy principles.

A strong absorptive capacity of domestic firms and institutions is the first essential condition for the presence of MNEs to lead to innovation gains as we already argued in Chapter 3. Absorptive capacity, as defined by Cohen and Levinthal (1990), includes the ability to recognise, assimilate and apply external knowledge. This requires not only a skilled labour force, but also a supportive ecosystem, technological infrastructure, R&D expertise, managerial capabilities and institutional routines that promote learning. In South Korea, for example, early technology transfers from American and Japanese firms were absorbed through active domestic investment in in-house R&D, vocational training and public intermediaries such as KITECH. Taiwan followed a similar path, combining the attraction of foreign direct investment with public investment in higher education and indigenous research. In both cases, multinationals were embedded in a broader system of national learning in which domestic actors had the capacity and mandate to adapt, localise and build on imported technologies, rather than simply passively using them.

In contrast, weak absorptive capacity has proven to be a bottleneck in many Central and Eastern European countries. Despite high levels of foreign investment, domestic firms, especially SMEs, often lack the technical, financial and organisational capacity to benefit from proximity to multinationals. These firms can participate in supply chains, but their tasks are typically low value and highly standardised. Public institutions are also often focused on compliance rather than learning. Innovation agencies prioritise the disbursement of funds over development, and research institutions often lack strong links to domestic industry. As a result, foreign subsidiaries operate like enclaves with limited interaction with the surrounding innovation system. Even where formal links exist, such as university partnerships, they often lack depth or strategic intent. The knowledge may be there, but the system cannot absorb it. Without targeted investment in skills, infrastructure and coordination, absorptive capacity remains an obstacle and potential spillovers remain untapped.

This is where policy comes into play, not as a passive mediator, but as an active architect of incentive structures that influence the behaviour of multinational companies. The governments must use policy tools to harmonise the interests of multinational companies with national innovation goals. These instruments range from domestic content requirements that encourage domestic sourcing to mandates for R&D investment that make market access contingent on the contribution of knowledge. Malaysia's experience in Penang shows what is possible when foreign investment is coupled with targeted public efforts. Initially dependent on multinational companies for basic assembly, Penang has gradually moved up the value chain through coordinated efforts by state and federal actors. Universities have been involved, co-funded training programmes have been developed and multinational companies have been encouraged to deepen their local engagement through recognition, incentives and peer pressure. Crucially, these measures were not counterproductive but co-operative, creating a shared vision between public authorities and private investors. In this way, Malaysia transformed the foreign presence from a transactional relationship into a platform for the country's transformation.

An important difference between transformative and superficial MNE engagement lies in the degree of embeddedness, i.e. how well the foreign firm is connected to local institutions, talent and problem-solving networks. Embedded MNEs go beyond transactional relationships. They participate in innovation platforms, collaborate with universities, customise products to local needs and invest in the development of local suppliers. A good example of this is the southern Polish aviation cluster. The region, which is led by global players such as Pratt & Whitney and Safran, has developed from a low-cost production location into a place of co-innovation. The Aviation Valley association, the engineering programmes of the University of Rzeszów and the support of the regional authorities played a role in this. These connections enabled the development of trust and long-term cooperation, with local firms gradually upgrading their capabilities. This is in stark contrast to the enclave models more common in Central and Eastern Europe, where multinational companies have their managers abroad, maintain limited local connections and have minimal knowledge transfer beyond production routines.

The state is a key player in determining whether the presence of multinationals promotes or hinders domestic innovation. Effective states not only incentivise investment, but they also set conditions, monitor commitments and build institutions that facilitate learning and co-creation of innovation. Strategic governance combines technical expertise with relational capacity, i.e. the ability to negotiate with foreign firms, incentivise and adapt policies over time. Singapore's Economic Development Board (EDB) is an example of this approach. It actively manages the composition of foreign direct investment, ensures partnerships with local institutions and invests in the infrastructure needed for long-term upgrading. In contrast, weak or fragmented public institutions often fail to move beyond rhetoric. When there is no oversight and expectations are vague, multinationals adhere to minimal standards and remain disconnected from domestic ecosystems. Innovation becomes an imported feature of production rather than an embedded function of the economy. Ultimately, the role of the state is not only to attract MNCs, but also to manage their participation in a way that fosters national capabilities.

The successful integration of MNEs into domestic innovation systems depends on a long-term orientation and a genuine culture of co-creation. Innovation does not happen overnight, but develops gradually through relationship building, risk-taking and joint problem solving. However, short political cycles and a preference for quick wins often disrupt this process and lead to missed opportunities for deeper collaboration. A culture of co-creation requires a shift from transactional interactions to shared missions, where multinational companies and local actors partner to shape solutions to national challenges. Mission-oriented approaches provide a powerful framework for this, as can be seen in sectors such as renewable energy, smart mobility and public health. Rwanda's collaboration with Zipline is a compelling example. The company not only provided drone delivery services but became part of a broader national strategy to improve health logistics. This embedding facilitated the learning process in terms of the local regulatory frameworks, data systems and operational infrastructure. This shows that when multinational companies co-create rather than just operate, the innovation ecosystem matures for all stakeholders.

MNEs are neither inherently engines of innovation nor automatic sources of dependency, and their influence is determined by the strategic choices of host countries. Whether MNEs act as catalysts for capability building or as barriers to learning at home depends on the quality of institutions, the alignment of incentives and the absorptive capacity of local actors. If managed effectively, multinationals can support co-creation of innovation, invest in local ecosystems and partner in national innovation strategies. To realise this potential, however, it is necessary to move beyond passive attraction to active governance, where countries compete not only on costs but also on capabilities, and where policies are designed to encourage, not just expect, spillovers. As this section shows, the challenge is not to choose between openness and autonomy, but to design systems that can learn, adapt and grow in the presence of global corporate power.

5.6 Conclusion

Multinational companies are among the most powerful players in the global economy and among the most influential forces influencing the development of innovation in emerging economies. They bring not only capital and technology, but also practices, routines, standards and connections that can profoundly reshape domestic economic systems. For policymakers in emerging economies, the arrival of multinationals is often a milestone, a vote of confidence in national reform, an opportunity to accelerate modernisation and a bridge to global markets. But as this chapter has shown, the role of multinationals is very ambivalent. Their contribution to capability building is real, but it is never guaranteed or evenly distributed. How much domestic value results from foreign presence depends not only on goodwill or technical aptitude, but also on power, policy and preparedness. In this sense, MNEs are not development actors in their own right, but instruments that need to be strategically managed within a broader national innovation framework.

On the one hand, MNEs can be catalysts of innovation. Through labour mobility, supplier upgrading, demonstration effects and collaboration, they can bring domestic actors to the frontiers of global knowledge. They can raise standards, create demand for advanced skills and serve as anchors for industry clusters. Case studies from the Malaysian electronics sector, the Polish aviation industry and the Vietnamese technology ecosystem show that the presence of foreign companies can boost domestic learning if local firms, institutions and governments are proactive. However, this requires strong absorptive capacity, effective incentives and institutions capable of brokering long-term partnerships. Without these elements, spillovers are shallow, learning is limited and the domestic innovation system remains reactive. The challenge is therefore not to attract MNCs, but to ensure that their activities are in line with national development goals.

On the other hand, MNCs can act as gatekeepers and monopolisers of knowledge by isolating the core functions of innovation at headquarters, tightly controlling intellectual property and relegating host countries to low value-added tasks. Their strategic interest in protecting competitive advantage often limits the depth of local integration. And without a targeted policy, their presence can reinforce dependency, undermine local entrepreneurship and stifle the emergence of indigenous innovators. Black-box production, shallow supplier contracts and weak links to universities are common in CEE countries and beyond. In such contexts, innovation is imported rather than built, replicated rather than reimagined. This undermines long-term technological sovereignty and forces countries into a subordinate role within global value chains, even if their export figures and industrial production appear strong on paper.

Whether multinationals drive or hinder innovation depends less on their intentions than on the structure of the systems they penetrate. In weak ecosystems with low absorptive capacity, shallow institutions and fragmented governance, multinationals tend to replicate global hierarchies. They work efficiently, but not transformatively. In stronger systems, where domestic actors are capable, incentives are well aligned and the state plays a strategic coordinating role, MNCs can make a significant contribution to building capabilities and upgrading. Overall, the presence of multinationals is not enough and what matters is how they are embedded, how they are governed and whether domestic systems are prepared to deal with them not as customers, but as co-creators of innovation. This raises a deeper and more provocative question, which will be the focus of the next chapter: Can emerging economies ever build autonomous innovation capacity while remaining deeply embedded in global systems?

References

Aitken, B. J., & Harrison, A. E. (1999). Do domestic firms benefit from direct foreign investment? Evidence from Venezuela. *American Economic Review, 89*(3), 605–618.

Aridi, A., & Querejazu, D. (2019). *Manufacturing a startup: A case study of Industry 4.0 development in the Czech Republic.* World Bank.

Business Insider (2016). *Execs from Facebook, Google, and Microsoft explain why they use Israel for their R&D.* Retrieved on 11.1.2026. https://www.businessinsider.com/facebook-google-microsoft-israel-rd-2016-10

Canavire-Bacarreza, G., & Castro Peñarrieta, L. (2021). Can licensing induce productivity? Exploring the IPR effect. *Empirical Economics, 61*, 549–586.

Cohen, W., & Levinthal, M. (1990). Absorptive capacity: A new perspective on learning and innovation. *Administrative Science Quarterly, 35*, 128–152.

Eltgen, M. P., Liu, Y., & Chong, Y. K. (2021). Malaysia—Attracting superstar firms in the electrical and electronics industry through investment promotion. In C. Z. Qiang, Y. Liu, & V. Steenbergen (Eds.), *An investment perspective on global value chains* (pp. 276–298). World Bank.

Findlay, R. (1978). Relative backwardness, direct foreign investment, and the transfer of technology: A simple dynamic model. *Quarterly Journal of Economics, 92*(1), 1–16.

Gallagher, K. P., & Zarsky, L. (2007). *The enclave economy: Foreign investment and sustainable development in Mexico's silicon valley*. The MIT Press.

ILO, International Labour Organization. (2022). *Viet Nam's electronics supply chain: Decent work challenges and opportunities.* International Labour Office.

Liu, X., Wright, M., Filatotchev, I., Dai, O., & Lu, Y. (2010). Human mobility and international knowledge spillovers: Evidence from high-tech small and medium enterprises in an emerging market. *Strategic Entrepreneurship Journal, 4*(4), 340–355.

Mariotti, S., Mutinelli, M., Nicolini, M., & Piscitello, L. (2015). Productivity spillovers from foreign multinational enterprises to domestic manufacturing firms: To what extent does spatial proximity matter? *Regional Studies, 49*(10), 1639–1653.

Markusen, J. R., & Trofimenko, N. (2009). Teaching locals new tricks: Foreign experts as a channel of knowledge transfers. *Journal of Development Economics, 88*(1), 120–131.

MTPConnect. (2019). Frugal innovation in medical devices and technologies: The India opportunity. *Asialink Business.*

OECD. (2024). *FDI qualities review of Tunisia: Boosting productivity and creating better jobs.* OECD Publishing.

Orlic, E., Hashi, I., & Hisarciklilar, M. (2018). Cross-sectoral FDI spillovers and their impact on manufacturing productivity. *International Business Review, 27*(4), 777–796.

Phi, V. T., Tran, K. H., Hoang, V. H., & Dong, V. C. (2024). The role of foreign direct investment in technology development in Vietnam. *Cogent Social Sciences, 10*(1). Article 2300514.

Stojcic, N., & Matic, M. (2024). A journey toward global value chain upgrading: Exploring the transition from backward to forward integration. *Technology in Society, 76*, 102435.

Stojcic, N., & Orlic, E. (2020). Spatial dependence, foreign investment and productivity spillovers in new EU member states. *Regional Studies, 54*(8), 1057–1068.

Stojcic, N., Vujanovic, N., & Baum, C. F. (2025a). Breaking or making futures: How laws and regulations shape innovation in emerging innovation systems. *Review of Managerial Science, 19*, 1743–1782.

Stojcic, N., Vujanovic, N., & Radosevic, S. (2025b). Resource sharing in enterprise groups and innovation failure: Emerging innovation systems perspective. *The Journal of Technology Transfer*. Online first.

UNCTAD (United Nations Conference on Trade and Development). (2011). *Best practices in investment for development: How to create and benefit from FDI-SME linkages—Lessons from Malaysia and Singapore* (Investment Advisory Series B, No. 4). United Nations.

Vidal, E., & Gonzalez Pandiella, A. (2024). *A review of Mexico's participation in global value chains* (OECD economics department working paper no. 1802).

World Bank. (2006). *The impact of Intel in Costa Rica: Nine years after the decision to invest.* World Bank.

Chapter 6
Towards Innovation Sovereignty

Freedom is nothing else but a chance to be better. (Albert Camus)

Abstract For many countries, the pursuit of innovation is not just a matter of growth but also one of sovereignty. This chapter explores how the ability to generate, control and apply knowledge becomes a question of independence in a world shaped by global value chains, digital platforms and shifting geopolitics. It traces how reliance on foreign technology and multinational enterprises can leave economies vulnerable, dependent on decisions made elsewhere and unable to chart their own development paths. At the same time, it examines how building domestic capabilities through investment in research, strong institutions and inclusive policies can create the foundations for greater autonomy. Yet sovereignty in innovation is never absolute; it requires balancing openness with resilience, integration with self-reliance. The chapter argues that the challenge for emerging innovation systems is not to isolate themselves, but to secure enough strategic capacity to ensure that innovation serves their societies, rather than leaving them perpetually at the margins.

6.1 Introduction

In 2021, a global shortage of microchips highlighted the fragility of modern production systems. Assembly lines halted, delivery times lengthened, and prices rose, not because of a lack of labour or capital, but because a few firms in East Asia held the keys to critical components. For many governments, this was a wake-up call. The crisis meant that innovation was no longer just a tool for growth, but a question of national resilience. European leaders began to advocate for "technological sovereignty". The United States passed the CHIPS and Science Act to bring semiconductor manufacturing back into the country. India and other emerging economies rushed to offer incentives for domestic chip production. While semiconductors dominated the headlines, the underlying message was broader, and it argued that the dependence on strategic technologies, whether in health, energy or communications, has become a

N. Stojčić, *Elusive Innovation*, Applied Innovation and Technology Management,
https://doi.org/10.1007/978-3-032-14900-8_6

geopolitical liability. The ability to produce, adapt and secure access to key technologies is now central to sovereignty in the twenty-first century (Gereffi et al., 2025).

The implications of above go far beyond a single sector. Innovation sovereignty is not just about reshoring manufacturing or shielding against future disruption. It is about ensuring that countries, particularly emerging economies, retain the ability to determine their own development paths in an increasingly complex and uneven technological landscape. It is about whether societies can determine the direction of their innovation systems themselves, rather than simply adapting to decisions made elsewhere. In an era characterised by multinational platforms, global power shifts and existential risks such as climate change, technological dependence is more at stake than ever. This chapter argues that innovation sovereignty offers a new framework for thinking about development not as a race to catch up with the frontier, but as a process of building strategic autonomy, resilience and purpose in national innovation systems.

Innovation sovereignty refers to a country's ability to chart its own course in science, technology and innovation without becoming structurally dependent on foreign actors. It is not about isolation or rejection of global co-operation (Edler et al., 2023). Rather, it is about ensuring that participation in global systems enhances domestic capabilities rather than replacing them. It means being able to identify national or regional priorities in health, agriculture, energy or digital infrastructure and mobilising resources, institutions and policies to pursue them. It means retaining authority over the standards, platforms and institutions that determine how innovation unfolds (Blind, 2025). And it means developing the ability to adapt and respond to global technological change on one's own terms. In practice, innovation sovereignty means a combination of strategic foresight, investment in domestic knowledge systems, institutional reform and policy adaptation that ensures that global engagement serves, rather than hinders, national objectives. It is a balancing act: openness with purpose, interdependence without subordination.

This idea is not entirely new. In recent decades, it has appeared under terms such as "technological self-reliance" in literature on developing countries (Sharif, 1999; UNIDO, 1981) or "appropriate technology" in debates on indigenous innovation (Patnaik & Tarei, 2022; Shin et al., 2019). In the European Union, the term has recently evolved into "open strategic autonomy" (European Commission, 2024) reflecting concerns about digital dependency and geopolitical vulnerability. In the Global South, the movements for "knowledge sovereignty" and local innovation ecosystems reflect similar impulses. What has changed today is the context as digital platforms are consolidating power over data and infrastructure, intellectual property is increasingly concentrated in global consortia, and cloud services, AI models and payment systems are often controlled from abroad. This creates new layers of dependency not just on physical production, but on the entire architecture of technological systems. For emerging economies, the danger is no longer just technological lag, but epistemic subordination, where what is developed, known and valued is decided elsewhere. Innovation sovereignty therefore requires a more comprehensive approach that includes governance, ownership and the power to define what innovation means in a given context.

For emerging innovation systems, innovation sovereignty has become more important than ever due to three accelerating structural changes. Firstly, technological concentration has reached unprecedented levels, with a handful of firms and countries controlling foundational sectors such as AI, semiconductors and biotechnology (Khanal et al., 2025; LSEG, 2024). This dominance is creating bottlenecks in global value chains and narrowing technological opportunities for latecomers. Secondly, geopolitical fragmentation has intensified. Innovation is no longer governed solely by markets, but by power blocs that manifest themselves through export bans, investment screening and strategic decoupling (Tung et al., 2023). Thirdly, dependence on platforms is increasing. In finance, health, media and logistics, many domestic innovations are dependent on foreign-owned digital platforms that determine data access, standards and algorithms (Han et al., 2024; Wang et al., 2023). As a result, countries may appear integrated into the global economy but remain on the periphery in terms of value capture and strategic control. In this environment, innovation sovereignty is not about rejecting global connections but renegotiating them to protect national interests and enable autonomous, inclusive innovation pathways.

Innovation sovereignty requires a different kind of capability that goes beyond traditional innovation metrics such as R&D spending, patent numbers or the number of STEM graduates. While these factors are still important, the real test lies in a system's ability to adapt, manage and protect its own innovation trajectory. Can a country reconfigure its supply chains in times of crisis? Can it define and enforce its own standards for data governance, AI ethics or sustainability? Can it maintain and expand its knowledge base in critical sectors? And can it align the fragmented efforts of different ministries, regions and sectors to fulfil nationally relevant missions? These are not just technical questions, but the ones that require institutional maturity, strategic foresight and a culture of learning. Sovereignty in this sense means not only what a country produces, but also what it can control and shape. It requires an indigenous, mission-oriented innovation policy and agile public institutions that are capable of both coordination and long-term commitment.

Chapter 5 has emphasised the complex role that multinational companies play in shaping innovation outcomes. While they bring knowledge, capital and connections, they can also create dependencies that force countries into the role of assembly centres or service providers without promoting innovation leadership at home. Innovation sovereignty is a response to this structural trap. It marks the transition from reacting to external forces to actively designing national innovation systems. This means developing institutions capable of absorbing and upgrading knowledge, forming partnerships that go beyond cost arbitrage and building resilience to external shocks or corporate leverage. The goal is not to reject foreign engagement, but to shape it on terms that support the building of national capabilities and societal priorities. In short, the transition from dependency to design is about asserting agency by constructing systems that are integrated but not subordinate and open but not vulnerable.

This chapter examines what it means for emerging economies to pursue innovation sovereignty in today's highly interconnected but increasingly fragmented world.

It begins by unpacking the various dimensions of innovation dependency, technological reliance on imported machinery or software, institutional dependence on external funding or consultancy models and cognitive dependence on foreign benchmarks and policy paradigms. These forms of dependency are not just outcomes, but are embedded in the way policies are designed, how firms compete and how the flow of knowledge is structured. The chapter then outlines four pillars of a sovereign innovation strategy: building domestic technological capacity, expanding institutional policy space, designing integration strategies that are selective and strategic, and investing in long-term learning infrastructures such as public R&D institutions, vocational training systems and mission-oriented programmes. Sovereignty, it argues, is not a static end goal, but a dynamic process of learning, negotiation and institution building. Ultimately, innovation sovereignty means reclaiming the right to define and pursue innovation not just for growth, but for the broader goals of national development.

6.2 Rethinking Dependency in a Globalised Innovation System

As we argued in the second chapter, in the traditional globalisation narrative, innovation is portrayed as a fluid and inclusive process where knowledge crosses borders, technology trickles down, and integration into global markets naturally drives development. In reality, however, the global innovation system is highly stratified, with power, infrastructure and decision-making concentrated in a handful of countries and corporations (Schot & Steinmueller, 2018; Von Hippel, 1994). For many emerging economies, integration has not meant equal participation, but functional subordination within global value chains (Gereffi et al., 2025). What is different with contemporary dependency over its predecessors is its nature, which has changed from overt colonial control to more complicated systems of technological dependency, institutional emulation and cognitive subjugation. These dependencies are not simply inherited, but reproduced through policy choices, market incentives and the architecture of global governance. As a result, even well-intentioned efforts to build innovation capacity often fail because of the rules and norms established elsewhere. This section examines the three core dimensions of modern dependency, technological (Patel, 1974), institutional (Acemoglu & Robinson, 2012; Di Maggio & Powell, 1983; Dos Santos, 1970; Frank, 1966) and cognitive dependence (Fredin, 2016; Schot & Steinmueller, 2018), and how they quietly shape the limits of innovation sovereignty.

For decades, the central goal of innovation policy in emerging economies was to "catch up", close productivity gaps, move up the value chain and increase R&D spending. However, in an era of profound global interdependence, catching up is no longer just a race against benchmarks, but a question of action. Is a country really innovative or is it merely implementing the plans of others? Is it adopting global models or developing its own innovation paths? Are its capabilities geared towards long-term transformation or towards fulfilling the roadmaps of multinational firms and foreign agendas? These questions highlight the strategic limits of the catch-up paradigm. The challenge is not just to grow faster, but to grow differently, under conditions that reflect national priorities and resilience. Sovereignty is therefore not a retreat from openness, but a recalibration of it. It means ensuring that integration into global systems enhances, rather than undermines, a country's ability to shape its own innovation future.

Technological dependency is perhaps the most visible and entrenched form of innovation asymmetry in the global economy. While many emerging economies have become indispensable nodes in global value chains (GVCs), they typically do so by inserting themselves into segments that offer limited control over technology development or strategic choices (Stojcic & Matic, 2024). Countries such as Mexico, Vietnam and Slovakia manufacture complex goods, cars, electronics, medical devices, but the design blueprints, software and core intellectual property are often located in foreign headquarters. This division of labour is efficient but restrictive. Local firms become specialists in execution, not in direction. The modular structure of GVCs, as described by Gereffi et al. (2005), allows participation without empowerment. And once a firm or sector becomes embedded in a low-value function, upgrading is difficult. Even national innovation systems designed to support local firms often end up reinforcing this hierarchy by focusing on supporting subcontractors rather than building independent design and innovation capabilities (Stojcic, 2024).

The rise of the digital economy has added a new layer to this dependency. In Africa, Southeast Asia and parts of Latin America, foreign-owned digital platforms, mostly based in the United States or China, dominate critical infrastructure. From payment systems to cloud services to e-commerce logistics, indigenous innovations are increasingly mediated by foreign APIs, app stores and terms of service. This not only limits economic capture, but also the space for local experimentation and regulation. For example, domestic start-ups may grow, but their ability to scale is often constrained by platform rules or algorithmic visibility determined elsewhere. In these environments, national innovation trajectories become reactive, chasing compliance, compatibility or integration, rather than proactive and sovereign. Without the capacity to shape the standards, tools and architectures of innovation, even vibrant ecosystems can be cornered by the invisible architecture of technological dependency.

Institutional dependency arises when countries adopt external innovation models, frameworks and governance templates without tailoring them to their specific development context. In many emerging economies, innovation policy is heavily influenced by international donors, multilateral development banks and policy advisors who promote "best practices", including concepts such as smart specialisation, triple helix collaboration and the development of start-up ecosystems. While these concepts can be valuable, their implementation is often performative and focused on ticking boxes rather than transforming systems. In the Western Balkans, for example, national innovation strategies often reflect EU priorities without taking into account related industrial capabilities or workforce preparedness. The result is a set of policy instruments that look modern on paper but are not rooted in local needs or institutions.

This kind of institutional isomorphism can stifle creativity and reduce ownership. Ministries and agencies become implementers of donor agendas rather than stewards of national innovation visions. Across emerging innovation systems donor-funded innovation initiatives have led to a proliferation of underused incubators, fragmented support schemes and overlapping governance bodies, each with its own reporting logic but no clear coordination. Over time, this leads to a cycle of dependency on external expertise, foreign evaluation standards and temporary project funding. Crucially, this undermines the development of institutions that can learn, adapt and govern over the long term. Innovation becomes a procedural and externally driven affair that is more about meeting donor milestones than enabling transformation. Without targeted efforts to build context-sensitive, mission-oriented institutions, there is a risk that innovation governance becomes a shadow system, legible to outsiders but disconnected from domestic innovation actors and aspirations.

Cognitive dependency shapes the way innovation is imagined, valued and pursued in emerging economies. This often begins subtly through exposure to global discourse, policy benchmarking and participation in international forums, but over time it restructures the way domestic actors perceive their own capabilities and opportunities. Silicon Valley becomes not just a reference, but a gold standard. Innovation is equated with venture capital, start-ups and technological disruption, even if the local context requires a focus on incremental improvements, public sector innovation or informal economy solutions. This leads to a strong mismatch between the problems countries face and the instruments they choose to solve them. Countries with urgent needs in agriculture, health systems or climate resilience may instead prioritise AI accelerators or blockchain sandboxes because they appear globally legitimised. The risk is that innovation becomes an aesthetic, something to be showcased in reports and rankings, rather than a grounded, problem-solving process shaped by local needs and institutions.

This kind of cognitive dependency can also encourage policy inertia. Governments may be reluctant to explore more adaptive, experimental or mission-oriented approaches because they do not fit into the established global script. When international agencies and donors prioritise narrow definitions of innovation as measured by the number of patents, venture capital deals or high-tech exports, national systems follow suit, often at the expense of neglecting broader forms of knowledge production and social innovation. In some cases, locally rooted solutions such as frugal medical devices, grassroots energy co-operatives or innovations in the informal economy are dismissed as non-innovative because they do not fit into the prevailing paradigms. This reinforces a cycle of dependency in which countries become reluctant to innovate in a way that already works for them. Breaking the cognitive dependency means not only changing policy, but also broadening the collective imagination of what innovation can be, who it serves, where it happens and what counts as success. It is a shift from imitation to authorship.

Technological, institutional and cognitive dependencies can rarely be considered in isolation. They interact and reinforce each other, creating a systemic form of fragility. Technological dependency discourages sustained investment in domestic research and development, institutional dependency reduces the flexibility of national innovation policy while cognitive dependency limits the imagination required to pursue alternative models. Together, they lead to innovation systems that appear active by issuing strategic documents, organising start-up events and attracting some foreign investment, but remain reactive, externally driven and unable to evolve on their own. This vulnerability became clearly visible during the COVID-19 pandemic. Many countries struggled to produce essential medical supplies, reconfigure data systems or localise digital tools, not because they lacked ingenuity, but because platforms, standards and supply chains were under foreign control. Systems that were optimised for global integration were not efficient when autonomy was required. Against this backdrop, innovation sovereignty is not a luxury or an ideal, but a necessity for resilience to shocks and structural constraints.

Dependency is woven into the current architecture of global innovation systems. It determines what countries can build, what they can imagine and how they structure their institutions. So the challenge is not simply to escape dependency, but to redesign systems so that they are less vulnerable to it. This means that we see dependency not just as a constraint, but as a design problem that requires building stronger institutions, fostering adaptive capacities and cultivating cultures of innovation rooted in domestic priorities. The goal is not autarky, but engagement on better terms. It is about moving from passive integration to active negotiation, from alignment to co-creation. The next section examines what this change can look like in practice. The question is what institutional arrangements, governance capabilities and strategic instruments need to be developed so that countries move from being innovation followers to becoming shapers of their own futures?

6.3 Policy Space and Institutional Capabilities for Innovation Sovereignty

Innovation sovereignty is not just a rhetorical ideal, but a practical outcome shaped by institutional architecture, strategic governance and policy capability. In a world characterised by interdependence, reclaiming innovation sovereignty does not mean cutting ties with global systems (Blind, 2025; March & Schieferdecker, 2023). Rather, it is about developing a domestic legal, financial, administrative and knowledge-based infrastructure that enables autonomous decision-making. Sovereignty does not come from isolation, but from the ability to select, adapt and steer innovation in line with national goals (Edler et al., 2023). This requires institutions that are not only technically competent, but also strategically agile and able to anticipate, coordinate and learn. In addition, policy space must be expanded to enable the freedom and legitimacy to shape innovation agendas without being unduly constrained by external models, donor conditions or multinational interests. This section explores how countries can institutionalise innovation sovereignty by strengthening governance capacity, promoting cross-sectoral coordination, aligning innovation with development missions and establishing learning mechanisms that help systems evolve in response to new challenges and opportunities.

The assumption that emerging economies suffer primarily from institutional weakness, discussed in previous chapters, oversimplifies the more complex reality. Certainly, there are problems such as limited capacity, fragmented mandates and politicisation, but the core problem is often one of misalignment, where institutions are not serving the strategic goals of innovation (Stojcic, 2024). In many countries, there is a plethora of innovation-related institutions: ministries, agencies, councils and committees that publish strategies, manage funds and organise events. But these institutions often operate in isolation, follow outdated or donor-imposed templates, and lack the mandate or coordination mechanisms to drive systemic transformation. The problem is not the absence of institutions, but their inability to function as an integrated, adaptive system. Reclaiming innovation sovereignty means reshaping this architecture, not necessarily by creating new institutions, but by ensuring that existing institutions are empowered, aligned and responsive. Institutions need to evolve from passive administrators of projects to strategic orchestrators of innovation, capable of steering national trajectories in a rapidly changing and uncertain world.

Policy space refers to a country's ability to design and implement innovation policies that serve its development goals (Mayer, 2009), even if those goals diverge from global market pressures, donor preferences or international norms. Traditionally, debates on policy space have focused on trade protection, subsidies or tariff regimes. In the context of innovation sovereignty, however, policy space is broader and more strategic. It includes the ability to prioritise emerging technologies without waiting for global demand signals, structure public procurement to build domestic capabilities, design intellectual property laws to allow learning and adaptation, and regulate digital platforms and data governance in the national interest. Importantly, policy space is not about rejecting globalisation but about shaping the conditions for engagement. Reclaiming policy space requires institutional capacity, legal skill and a willingness to resist political orthodoxy when it is not conducive to long-term technological transformation.

Several countries have already begun to experiment with expanding their innovation policy space. India has used TRIPS flexibilities to grant compulsory licences for essential medicines, challenged global technology firms through data localisation laws and launched mission-oriented innovation programmes in health, space and digital infrastructure. Brazil has used public procurement in its health sector to develop domestic production of vaccines and diagnostics, while South Africa has trialled regulatory sandboxes to enable controlled experimentation in fintech. These endeavours illustrate an important principle that sovereignty does not mean isolation, but strategic flexibility. However, asserting this flexibility often requires dealing with strong political and economic pressures. Global corporations and trading partners may oppose local content mandates or data regulations. Donors may favour market-friendly solutions over state-led experimentation. Therefore, innovation sovereignty depends not only on having the legal instruments, but also on the institutional courage and coordination to use them. Countries must be prepared to negotiate sovereignty across borders, sectors and power asymmetries.

The realisation of innovation sovereignty requires institutions that are embedded across sectors and equipped with forward-looking capabilities. Innovation does not belong in a single ministry, as it touches on the areas of industry, education, health and digital policy. Strategic institutions must be coordinated horizontally and vertically to ensure the coherence of fragmented governance systems. The Economic Development Board (EDB) in Singapore, mentioned previously, is a good example of this. Much more than an investment agency, the EDB steers long-term industrial strategy by aligning priorities in skills development, infrastructure and technology in the public and private sectors. Equally important is the capacity to anticipate. Institutions need to anticipate change, not just react to it. Sweden's Vinnova and South Korea's KISTEP are examples of this approach. They use scenario planning and technology roadmapping to guide national R&D strategy. These organisations not only fund innovation but also give it direction by proactively identifying where future capabilities are needed. Without such intelligence and embedding, innovation systems remain reactive, fragmented and vulnerable to external shocks or technological dependencies.

Innovation governance must be flexible and adaptive. Sovereign systems should treat policies as iterative instruments that can be trialled, tested and revised based on what works (Radosevic et al., 2023). Institutions that are experimental and reflexive are better able to respond to uncertainty and evolving challenges. Chile's Laboratorio de Gobierno has institutionalised experimentation in the public sector and uses pilot projects to test innovations before rolling them out to all ministries. Canada's Impact Canada uses results-based funding to promote cross-sector learning and experimentation. These models show that learning, not just implementing, institutions are essential to building innovation sovereignty. Equally important is the focus on the mission orientation. Generic R&D grants alone cannot influence national trajectories. Funding should be designed to fulfil societal missions such as clean energy, health resilience or digital inclusion through multi-stakeholder collaboration. The EU's Horizon Europe programme and the German High-Tech Strategy 2025 illustrate this principle. But resource-constrained countries like Rwanda also show that it is possible: by jointly developing public service pilot projects with start-ups, the Rwandan Ministry of ICT combines procurement, experimentation and capacity building.

In the digital age, innovation sovereignty increasingly depends on who controls platforms, standards and data infrastructure. Strategic innovation institutions must be capable of governing not just research pipelines but digital ecosystems. This includes regulating large platforms, setting standards for AI and data ethics and managing public data as a national asset. Estonia's Information System Authority provides an advanced model for overseeing digital identity, cybersecurity and cross-government e-governance systems. Its work ensures digital sovereignty while enabling efficiency. India's Digital Public Goods approach also offers an instructive case. By building foundational platforms such as Aadhaar for digital identity and UPI for financial infrastructure, India maintains control over core digital systems while enabling innovation by public and private players. These models show a new frontier of innovation governance, the one where countries must not only fund research and development, but also build, regulate and maintain the infrastructure through which innovation takes place. Otherwise, digital sovereignty will remain elusive and innovation paths will be dictated from abroad.

Dealing with institutional constraints has as much to do with politics as it is about policy. Building capability within innovation systems cannot be reduced to hiring staff or drafting mandates, but requires securing political capital, aligning interests and embedding institutions within broader governance frameworks (Radosevic et al., 2023; Stojcic, 2024). Institutions are effective when they are backed by laws or high-level political authority, staffed by qualified professionals who are shielded from patronage, have stable funding and enjoy the trust of public and private actors. However, in many emerging economies, innovation agencies face chronic instability, which manifests itself in frequent leadership changes, limited budgetary control and fragmented mandates that isolate them from broader development planning. They are expected to deliver transformative results without having the authority to steer agendas or mobilise resources. Despite these challenges, reforms are possible. Countries such as Vietnam offer new examples of institutional strengthening, whether through empowered innovation councils, increased public R&D budgets or new foresight and intelligence units within ministries. The goal is not to create new institutions, but to rewire existing ones for strategic coordination, cross-sectoral engagement and adaptive learning.

Innovation sovereignty rests on the foundation of capable institutions that do more than administer grants or host conferences. It requires institutions that can think strategically, coordinate across fragmented governance structures, adapt in real time and lead long-term transformation. Expanding policy space is not just about resisting external constraints, but also about cultivating internally the capacity to harmonise public and private actors, set coherent agendas and experiment without fear of failure. Innovation systems need agencies that combine technical expertise with political backing, strategic foresight and relational legitimacy. As this section has shown, building such institutions is possible even with scarce resources if there is a commitment to governance that enables learning, cross-sectoral engagement and long-term vision. In the next section, we turn from architecture to substance. We explore how countries can develop the technological capabilities they need to not only absorb global innovation, but to create, adapt and lead their own innovation trajectories from within.

6.4 Building Domestic Technological Capabilities

One of the most persistent challenges for emerging economies is the gap between strategic ambition and technological reality. National plans often refer to frontier areas such as artificial intelligence, biotechnology and clean energy, but the foundational infrastructure to support such ambitions is often thin. Research laboratories lack stable funding, engineering and design capabilities are fragmented and prototyping facilities are scarce. Universities are often disconnected from industry, while firms, especially SMEs, invest too little in R&D due to risks, costs or lack of incentives. As a result, these countries are still primarily consumers or adaptors of technology, but not producers (Radošević, 2017). However, innovation sovereignty requires more than just the pursuit of it; it requires indigenous technological capabilities embedded in institutions, companies and talent pipelines. These capabilities enable countries to generate and shape knowledge rather than merely absorb it. They enable innovation to be aligned with national priorities, anchored in local contexts and aligned with public values rather than just global market trends. Without them, autonomy in innovation remains an illusion.

Much of the innovation policy literature emphasises absorptive capacity, i.e. the ability of firms and institutions to learn from foreign technologies and integrate them into local processes. While this is an important basis for catching-up economies, it is not sufficient to achieve innovation sovereignty. The danger lies in what Lall (1992) termed "passive absorption", where firms master the use of imported machinery or compliance with international standards, but fail to internalise the deeper design, engineering and R&D skills required for independent innovation. This dynamic can be seen in parts of Eastern Europe, where rising high-tech exports are accompanied by low R&D investment and minimal patent activity. Foreign firms are setting up production facilities, but the core knowledge remains abroad. Universities focus on academic publications, but their research rarely translates into the development or commercialisation of technologies. Integration is not synonymous with autonomy in this context. Without building capabilities to experiment, adapt and invent, countries remain dependent, even if they appear globally competitive.

Technological capability goes far beyond publishing scientific papers or attracting foreign direct investment. It refers to a country's internal capacity to develop, adapt and apply technology at different stages of the innovation process. This includes technical capacity, i.e. the ability to design and refine products and not just assemble them, scientific infrastructure such as test labs and research centres, and manufacturing know-how, in particular the ability to scale prototypes into commercially viable products. This also includes system integration, in which hardware, software and services are brought together to create complete, context-specific solutions. Crucially, technological capability depends on organisational learning of the routines that firms use to manage knowledge, improve quality and deal with uncertainty. These capabilities are difficult to acquire quickly or through market mechanisms alone. They require long-term public and private investment, institutional coordination and support structures such as technical universities, technology transfer offices, applied research institutes and development banks. Without this foundation, countries run the risk of becoming technologically dependent, even if they are superficially innovative.

There is no single path to achieve technological depth, but experience in different regions shows that some policy levers work consistently. Central to this is the creation of a strong, problem-orientated public R&D infrastructure. Successful latecomer countries have invested in applied research institutes that address real-world problems rather than doing research for its own sake. Brazil's EMBRAPA, for example, has played a critical role in transforming the country into a global agricultural powerhouse by combining cutting-edge biotechnology with regionally anchored agronomic solutions. Similarly, India's CSIR and ISRO have developed sophisticated technological capabilities under conditions of scarcity thanks to long-term government support and a focus on indigenous innovation. These institutions were successful because they were autonomous, mission-driven and well integrated with both local needs and the industrial ecosystem. The key lesson is that public research organisations need to be more than bureaucratic shells. They need to be adaptive, collaborative and embedded in national development goals, with stable funding and performance-based accountability.

Another powerful but under-utilised tool for capability development is public procurement (Stojcic et al., 2020) mentioned several times in previous chapters. When governments act as lead customers for innovative solutions, they can create stable, early-stage demand and encourage firms to invest in learning and R&D. Historically, the US defence sector has supported entire innovation ecosystems, from aerospace to computing, by procuring from domestic firms with stringent technical requirements. In India, government procurement has strengthened indigenous capabilities in renewable energy and public digital infrastructure. A compelling example from Africa is Rwanda's partnership with Zipline, which has used medical drone deliveries not only to improve healthcare logistics, but also to build indigenous technical expertise in drone management and data analytics. Procurement policies must go beyond selecting the lowest-cost supplier and should include innovation criteria, co-development clauses and support for local suppliers. Done right, procurement becomes a tool for fostering technology ecosystems, de-risking investment in new sectors and accelerating the diffusion of innovation through supply chains and public services.

Universities are key to long-term technological sovereignty, but they need to be restructured to serve as innovation centres rather than ivory towers. This means aligning academic research with the needs of industry and society, encouraging interdisciplinary thinking and creating spaces where applied problem solving can flourish. The reform should focus on modernising curricula, incentivising applied research and institutionalising collaboration with industry. Previously mentioned Poland's Aviation Valley, for example, has developed into a globally competitive aerospace cluster due in part to the close partnerships between technical universities and local firms supported by national and EU funding. These collaborations have enabled workforce development and the joint development of technical solutions that are relevant to both industry and academia. To expand this, universities need a supportive infrastructure such as incubators, technology transfer offices and translational research centres. Incentives for faculty need to shift to engagement and innovation, not just publications. When universities are embedded in a local ecosystem, they ultimately help produce not only talent, but also technologies and ventures that drive sovereign innovation.

While digital services and app-based start-ups often dominate the entrepreneurial landscape in emerging markets, these models rarely build foundational technological capabilities. Deep tech entrepreneurship centred on sectors such as advanced materials, robotics, clean energy or healthcare technology is critical for technological sovereignty, but it requires specific forms of support. This includes access to R&D infrastructure, prototyping labs, specialised mentors and a regulatory environment that allows for risk and iteration. Governments can support this through public VC funds, mission-driven accelerators and co-investment platforms. Israel's Yozma programme is a notable example where public capital has been strategically deployed to create a high-tech venture ecosystem focused on deep areas of innovation. Similarly, Block 71 in Singapore has created a curated environment that connects start-ups with labs, investors and policymakers, reducing friction in deep tech innovation. The goal is to make it possible and attractive for local entrepreneurs to build businesses on the technology frontier. With the right support, these firms can become an anchor for indigenous capabilities and long-term resilience.

Strengthening the engineering and maker culture is critical to building the human infrastructure behind innovation sovereignty. It is not enough to train STEM graduates. Countries need to encourage practical problem solving, curiosity and collaboration from an early age. This means embedding hands-on creativity into the education system through initiatives such as school-based makerspaces, community tinkering labs and vocational training programmes that address real-world challenges. Project-based learning and hackathons that address political or industrial problems help to bridge the gap between theory and application. Estonia's digital education reforms, India's Atal Tinkering Labs and Brazil's SENAI innovation centres are examples of how grassroots skills development can feed into national capability building. However, strengthening technological capabilities is not only a technical task, but also a political one. Structural barriers such as short-term public investment, risk-averse bureaucracies, brain drain and donor-driven agendas need to be addressed. Countries that make progress often do so through long-term commitment, inter-institutional coordination and a culture that values learning through experimentation.

No country achieves innovation sovereignty simply by purchasing technology alone. True sovereignty lies in the ability to build, adapt and recombine knowledge in a way that reflects national priorities and addresses local challenges. This requires more than just investment in R&D, but a broader ecosystem of institutions, funding mechanisms, talent pipelines and learning infrastructures that translate knowledge into impact. Indigenous technological capabilities are not a luxury for the wealthy, but the foundation for national resilience, economic flexibility and long-term autonomy. Without them, even the best thought-out innovation strategies risk becoming symbolic exercises disconnected from actual transformation. Countries therefore need to invest in both hard infrastructure, labs, tools, production facilities, and soft infrastructure, skills, trust, coordination and experimentation. In the next section, we look at how countries can strike a balance between this imperative and continued openness. The challenge is not whether to engage globally, but how to engage strategically to ensure that participation in global innovation ecosystems does not come at the expense of national control.

6.5 Selective Integration: Balancing Openness and Control

No country innovates in isolation (Edler et al., 2023). The cross-border flow of knowledge, people, capital and standards drives technological progress and enables faster discoveries, deeper specialisation and greater market reach. International scientific co-operation accelerates breakthroughs (Stojcic, 2021). Integration into global value chains enables firms to scale and specialise. Digital platforms provide access to new consumers, whilst foreign investment can bring in much-needed expertise and funding. In this sense, openness is not the enemy of innovation, but often its driver. But for emerging innovation systems openness also means vulnerability. It can increase technological dependence, shift strategic decisions abroad and leave domestic actors without control over critical infrastructure or standards. As the previous sections have shown, this leads to a fundamental policy tension of how to reap the benefits of global engagement whilst maintaining the capacity to act. This section proposes a way forward through selective integration, a strategy that avoids the false dichotomy between protectionism and liberalisation by developing mechanisms for engagement that promote domestic learning, resilience and innovation sovereignty.

All too often, innovation policy debates are trapped in binary thinking between free trade and protectionism, global integration and local control, open innovation and technological sovereignty. But the reality of governance is more complex. Countries can, and often do, combine different approaches depending on sectoral needs and strategic priorities. A country can be open to international academic exchange while strictly regulating digital infrastructure. It can welcome foreign investment but impose local requirements on training or R&D. This notion of calibrated openness distinguishes strategic integration from passive liberalisation. Rather than viewing openness and control as mutually exclusive, this approach treats them as points on a spectrum. The challenge for policymakers is to identify where to draw the line, what to share and what to regulate, and where to build independent capacity. In this way, emerging innovation systems can pursue global engagement on terms that promote learning, local value creation and long-term resilience without cutting themselves off from global flows of ideas and capital.

An important instrument of selective integration is the use of joint ventures and technology partnerships discussed in previous chapters. Rather than allowing foreign firms to operate completely independently, governments can mandate or incentivise collaboration with domestic players, be they firms, universities or public R&D institutes. This model has already been used with varying degrees of success. China required joint ventures in the automotive and telecoms sectors to enable technology diffusion and industrial learning. Malaysia promoted technology partnerships in the aerospace sector through its National Aerospace Blueprint and more recently Malaysian Aerospace Industry Blueprint 2030. Brazil encouraged its energy firms to co-develop technologies with state research institutions. While such agreements require strong governance to enforce and monitor knowledge transfer, they remain a viable method of gaining access to core competences. They work best when the local partners have a certain absorptive capacity and when the partnership is long term and strategic. Without these prerequisites, there is a risk that joint ventures will become vehicles for market access without any meaningful learning taking place. With these prerequisites, however, they can create the basis for deeper technological capabilities.

Local content and knowledge transfer requirements are another policy lever to shape the conditions for global engagement. Governments can require foreign firms to source some of their inputs, services or R&D activities domestically. This can include hiring local engineers, setting up in-country research facilities or jointly developing training programmes. Although often criticised by international institutions as distorting trade, such measures, if carefully designed and transparently enforced, can promote learning rather than just distort markets. A good example of this is South Africa's renewable energy independent power producer procurement programme (REIPPPP), which links public procurement with local content, skills development and business support. This strategy has helped to build an indigenous base in an industry that was previously dominated by imports. The key is to ensure that these requirements are not rigid quotas, but dynamic incentives that encourage capability development. When embedded in broader industrial strategies and coupled with support for domestic actors, these policies can help rebalance global relations and harness integration for national development.

Governments are often the largest buyers of technology and services in an economy. By including innovation criteria in tenders, for example, requiring functionality rather than branding, or working with firms to develop specifications, they can steer markets in a direction that encourages the development of indigenous capabilities. This does not mean excluding foreign firms, but shaping procurement in a way that encourages localisation, adaptation and learning. The UK's Small Business Research Initiative (SBRI) and Chile's Desafíos Públicos platform exemplify this approach. Both allow public bodies to pose real-world challenges and fund the development of innovative solutions by start-ups or research institutions. Importantly, these programmes include mechanisms to ensure that knowledge stays and grows locally, even if the original expertise is imported. Strategic procurement transforms public spending from a passive exercise into an active policy instrument that stimulates demand for innovation and connects global knowledge to local problems and opportunities.

In the digital economy, control over standards and platforms is crucial for innovation sovereignty. Countries that fail to effectively regulate platforms risk losing control over data governance, algorithmic accountability, digital identity and even national security. Selective integration in this area means setting clear national rules for the operation of global platforms, mandating the localisation of data in sensitive sectors, requiring transparency in algorithmic decisions or insisting on interoperability to reduce dependence on individual providers. The Digital Markets Act and the European Union's AI Act are compelling examples of how regulation can enforce sovereignty over dominant technology platforms. Even if emerging economies do not have the market power of the EU, they can shape digital infrastructure through coalitions, regional frameworks or by investing in public digital goods. India's approach, previously mentioned initiatives such as Aadhaar for digital IDs, UPI for payments and open health data standards, shows how countries can combine openness with institutional control. These systems support inclusive innovation while retaining national authority over key infrastructure.

Some technologies are simply too strategic to be left to market forces alone. This includes sectors with national security implications (e.g. cybersecurity, defence), systemic importance (e.g. AI, semiconductors) or profound impact on public welfare (e.g. energy, health). In these areas, selective integration requires proactive state engagement. Countries must be willing to maintain domestic capabilities even if they are not globally competitive, support public or mixed-ownership firms and invest in local alternatives to foreign platforms. Finland maintains national firms in the digital infrastructure sector. South Korea has supported domestic champions in AI and search technologies while engaging globally. This policy is not about isolation but about ensuring that critical systems can function independently in times of crisis. Strategic sectors need long-term planning, protected markets where appropriate and mission-driven investment. Sovereignty in these areas is not about resisting global participation but about ensuring one's own resilience and ability to manage development independently and in the national interest.

Finally, selective integration can be strengthened by a strategic internationalism that works through regional alliances and global coalitions. Countries do not have to choose between self-sufficiency and dependence. They can pool resources, harmonise standards and cooperate on innovation missions. The African Continental Free Trade Area (AfCFTA), for example, is working on common rules for intellectual property and digital regulations to support intra-African innovation. The Global Partnership on Artificial Intelligence (GPAI) enables countries to jointly shape responsible AI governance. And the EU's Horizon Europe programmes provide a model for how cross-border research funding can be reconciled with social missions. These partnerships show that sovereignty and solidarity are not opposing forces but can be mutually reinforcing. When countries agree on common principles such as open science, ethical standards and regional resilience, they gain bargaining power and reduce dependence on external monopolies. Innovation sovereignty is therefore not about closing borders but about opening them on fairer and more strategic terms.

In a world where technology is both global and geopolitical, innovation sovereignty is not achieved by closing borders, but by reshaping the way countries engage with the global system. Selective integration is a pragmatic way that allows countries to remain open to ideas, talent and investment while retaining the ability to develop, adapt and control the technologies most important to their future development. It is not about isolation, but about asserting agency, ensuring that global participation strengthens local capabilities rather than exacerbating dependency. It is a strategy of deliberate adaptation, using openness as a means to strengthen agency rather than as a source of vulnerability. As we move into the final section of this chapter, the focus shifts from individual instruments to a broader vision of innovation sovereignty as an evolving practice. It is not a status once achieved, but a continuous process of learning, negotiation and strategic engagement in an unequal but shared world.

6.6 Conclusion

Innovation sovereignty is not a final goal, but a continuous process of negotiation, learning and recalibration. For emerging innovation systems this means striking a balance between openness and control, global integration and local resilience. The challenge is not only to gain access to foreign knowledge, but to create the institutional and technological capacity to shape and redirect this knowledge in the service of national development. Innovation sovereignty requires agency, the ability to define strategic priorities, build and protect critical capabilities and maintain influence over key technologies and platforms. This requires systems that not only work but must evolve. They need to embed learning, foster cross-sector collaboration and respond to societal needs rather than just chasing market signals. As global uncertainties increase, innovation systems must move from being reactive recipients to strategic architects of their own future. Sovereignty in this sense does not mean isolation, but the freedom to participate globally on nationally defined terms.

This chapter has traced the architecture of dependency and the contours of sovereignty. It has shown how technological dependence, institutional imitation and cognitive subordination can quietly undermine a country's ability to innovate for itself. Escaping these traps requires both ambition and a conscious system design. Sovereign innovation is based on a foundation of capable institutions, long-term investment in domestic technological capacity and policy frameworks that balance openness with strategic selectivity. It means using instruments such as procurement, regulation and public–private partnerships to promote not only innovation performance but also the infrastructure of learning itself. Above all, it means reimagining innovation as a collective national endeavour and not just a competition. Sovereignty is not created by resisting globalisation, but by engaging with it on an equal footing. Countries must be able to say not just "yes" or "no" to global forces, but "this is how it works".

As global power dynamics shift and crises from climate change to technological monopolies intensify, innovation sovereignty becomes a core requirement for development rather than a luxury. The ability to chart own innovation path will increasingly determine which countries flourish and which remain reactive. Sovereignty offers an opportunity to protect strategic interests while building systems that are inclusive, resilient and aligned with societal goals. However, this requires a rethinking of policy architectures. The next chapter turns to that challenge: how to design innovation and industrial policies that are not only technically sound, but also politically durable, socially legitimate and economically transformative. If innovation sovereignty is the goal, what new institutional roles, funding models and regulatory strategies are needed to support it? How can we move beyond old paradigms of state versus market and instead build coalitions that align public purpose with technological change? Chapter 7 begins that conversation by addressing a forward-looking, mission-oriented approach.

References

Acemoglu, D., & Robinson, J. A. (2012). *Why nations fail: The origins of power, prosperity and poverty*. Crown Business.

Blind, K. (2025). Standardization and Standards: Safeguards of technological sovereignty? *Technological Forecasting and Social Change, 210*, 123873.

Di Maggio, P. J., & Powell, W. W. (1983). The iron cage revisited: Institutional isomorphism and collective rationality in organizational fields. *American Sociological Review, 48*(2), 147–160.

Dos Santos, T. (1970). The structure of dependence. *American Economic Review, 60*(2), 231–236.

Edler, J., Blind, K., Kroll, H., & Schubert, T. (2023). Technology sovereignty as an emerging frame for innovation policy. Defining rationales, ends and means. *Research Policy, 52*(6), 104765.

European Commission. (2024). *Assessing open strategic autonomy: A two dimensional index to quantify EU-27 autonomy in industrial ecosystems and strategic technologies* (JRC External Study Report) (H. Kroll).

Frank, A. G. (1966). The development of underdevelopment. *Monthly Review, 18*(4), 17–30.

Fredin, S. (2016). Breaking the cognitive dimension of local path dependence: An entrepreneurial perspective. *Geografiska Annaler: Series B, Human Geography, 98*(3), 239–253.

Gereffi, G., Humphrey, J., & Sturgeon, T. (2005). The governance of global value chains. *Review of International Political Economy, 12*(1), 78–104.

Gereffi, G., Pananond, P., Tell, F., & Fang, T. (2025). Navigating industrial policy and global value chains in an era of disruptions. *Journal of International Business Policy, 8*(3), 207–223.

Han, B., Li, M., Diao, Y., & Han, D. (2024). Assessing the effect of digital platforms on innovation quality: Mechanism identification and threshold characteristics. *Humanities and Social Sciences Communication, 11*, 951.

Khanal, S., Zhang, H., & Taeihagh, A. (2025). Why and how is the power of Big Tech increasing in the policy process? The case of generative AI. *Policy and Society, 44*(1), 52–69.

Lall, S. (1992). Technological capabilities and industrialization. *World Development, 20*(2), 165–186.

LSEG. (2024). *Tech concentration: A global phenomenon*. FTSE Russell Insights.

March, C., & Schieferdecker, I. K. (2023). Technological sovereignty as ability, not autarky. *International Studies Review, 25*(2), viad012.

Mayer, J. (2009). Policy space: What, for what and where? *Development Policy Review, 27*(4), 373–395.

Patel, S. J. (1974). The technological dependence of developing countries. *The Journal of Modern African Studies, 12*(1), 1–18.

Patnaik, J., & Tarei, P. D. (2022). Analysing appropriateness in appropriate technology for achieving sustainability: A multi-sectorial examination in a developing economy. *Journal of Cleaner Production, 349*(15), 131204.

Radošević, S. (2017). *Upgrading technology in Central and Eastern European economies* (p. 338). IZA World of Labor.

Radosevic, S., Kanellou, D., & Tsekouras, G. (2023). The experimentation-accountability trade-off in innovation and industrial policy: Are learning networks the solution? *Science and Public Policy, 50*(4), 655–669.

Schot, J., & Steinmueller, W. E. (2018). Three frames for innovation policy: R&D, systems of innovation and transformative change. *Research Policy, 47*(9), 1554–1567.

Sharif, N. (1999). Strategic role of technological self-reliance in development management. *Technological Forecasting and Social Change, 62*(3), 219–238.

Shin, H., Hwang, J., & Kim, H. (2019). Appropriate technology for grassroots innovation in developing countries for sustainable development: The case of Laos. *Journal of Cleaner Production, 232*(20), 1167–1175.

Stojcic, N. (2021). Collaborative innovation in emerging innovation systems: Evidence from Central and Eastern Europe. *The Journal of Technology Transfer, 46*(2), 531–562.

Stojcic, N. (2024). Innovation failure, training for innovative activities and public support for innovation: Multi-annual evidence from emerging European innovation systems. *Research Policy, 53*(8), 105059.

Stojcic, N., & Matic, M. (2024). A journey toward global value chain upgrading: Exploring the transition from backward to forward integration. *Technology in Society, 76*, 102435.

Stojcic, N., Srhoj, S., & Coad, A. (2020). Innovation procurement as capability-building: Evaluating innovation policies in eight Central and Eastern European countries. *European Economic Review, 121*, 103330.

Tung, R. L., Zander, I., & Fang, T. (2023). The tech cold war, the multipolarization of the world economy, and IB research. *International Business Review, 32*(6), 102195.

UNIDO. (1981). *Technological self-reliance of the developing countries: Towards operational strategies*. United Nations Industrial Development Organization.

Von Hippel, E. (1994). "Sticky information" and the locus of problem solving: Implications for innovation. *Management Science, 40*(4), 429–439.

Wang, N., Wan, J., Ma, Z., Zhou, Y., & Chen, J. (2023). How digital platform capabilities improve sustainable innovation performance of firms: The mediating role of open innovation. *Journal of Business Research, 167*, 114080.

Chapter 7
Rethinking Industrial and Innovation Policy for the Twenty-First Century

We cannot solve our problems with the same thinking we used when we created them. (Albert Einstein)

Abstract Industrial and innovation policy once evoked images of governments picking winners or protecting national champions. Today, the challenges are far more complex as climate change, digital disruption and geopolitical fragmentation demand new forms of statecraft. This chapter argues that policies of the twenty-first century must move beyond static blueprints and embrace adaptability, inclusivity and resilience. It explores how traditional tools such as subsidies, procurement and regulation are being reshaped into mission-oriented strategies that link technological progress to societal goals. At the same time, it warns of the risks of overreach, capture and widening inequalities if policies ignore institutional and systemic weaknesses. Through the lens of emerging economies, the chapter shows that rethinking policy is not only about catching up with advanced countries but about crafting development pathways that reflect local strengths while responding to global transformations.

7.1 Introduction

For decades, industrial policy was treated as a relic of a discredited past, too risky, too political and too easily captured by vested interests (Millot & Rawdanowicz, 2024). The prevailing wisdom of the 1980s and 1990s, characterised by the failure of state planning and the ideological rise of market fundamentalism, was clear: governments should create enabling environments, not pick winners (Gereffi et al., 2025). Policymakers were encouraged to liberalise trade, privatise state-owned enterprises and let comparative advantage determine industrial structure. The role of the state was limited to ensuring stable macroeconomic conditions, investing in basic research and occasionally correcting market failures. Any more proactive role in shaping economic development was dismissed as distortive. But this orthodoxy has not led to robust structural change in much of the world. Even in advanced economies, decades of deindustrialisation and growing inequality have raised doubts. The return

N. Stojčić, *Elusive Innovation*, Applied Innovation and Technology Management,
https://doi.org/10.1007/978-3-032-14900-8_7

of industrial policy is not just a political shift, but a response to deep economic and development disillusionment.

Today, the conversation has changed decisively. From the US's CHIPS and Science Act to the EU's Net-Zero Industry Act and from India's Production-Linked Incentive schemes to South Korea's national strategy for semiconductor innovation, governments are reclaiming a central role in shaping industrial development. However, this is not a simple return to old-style protectionism or planned economies. Industrial policy in the twenty-first century is being reimagined as a strategic tool to manage the transitions that are taking place: digitalisation, decarbonisation, demographic ageing and changing geopolitical alliances (Hauge et al., 2025; Juhasz et al., 2023; Terzi et al., 2022). These transitions are too complex, too capital intensive and too uncertain to be left to market forces alone. They require coordinated investment in infrastructure, research, skills and institutions. In this emerging consensus, industrial policy is about steering transformation not with rigid plans, but with agile, adaptable strategies that harmonise innovation with collective missions and long-term societal goals.

However, while industrial policy has gained traction in high-income countries, its revival in emerging economies remains fraught with complexity (Juhasz et al., 2023) and even resistance. These economies face what could be called a policy double bind. On the one hand, they are under intense pressure to accelerate structural transformation in order to escape the middle-income trap and avoid marginalisation in emerging reconfiguration of global value chains. On the other hand, they must do so under the constraints of limited fiscal capacity, inherited industrial weaknesses, fragmented institutional frameworks and policy models that are often shaped by external donors or conditionalities. For many, policy space has been narrowed by decades of liberalisation, the dismantling of the public sector and dependence on foreign capital. But there is arguably more at stake as failure to act now risks permanent exclusion from the green and digital revolutions that are redefining competitiveness and value creation in the global economy.

Three developments have been particularly important in rehabilitating industrial policy in the global discourse. First, the 2008 financial crisis shattered the illusion of self-correcting markets and re-legitimised state intervention. Governments around the world intervened with stimulus packages, bailouts and support for industry, measures that closely resembled industrial policy in substance if not in name (Gereffi et al., 2025). Second, the climate crisis has made it clear that markets alone are not capable of driving the scale and speed of change required for a net-zero transition. Decarbonisation requires coordinated investment in green infrastructure, clean technologies and innovation ecosystems, goals that only mission-orientated policies can deliver (Mazzucato, 2018). Third, rising geopolitical tensions and technological rivalry, particularly between the United States and China, have made industrial capacity a national security issue (Tung et al., 2023). Supply chain shocks, strategic decoupling and renewed efforts towards technological self-reliance have further reinforced the case for active state leadership. In this new context, industrial policy is no longer optional, but a prerequisite for navigating the twenty-first century.

For all these reasons, the emerging paradigm of industrial policy departs significantly from the models of import substitution or the promotion of heavy industry from the twentieth century (Juhasz et al., 2023). Today's industrial policy is mission oriented and geared towards tackling major societal challenges. Rather than targeting individual firms or sectors, it pursues a system-oriented approach that aims to strengthen entire ecosystems and value chains (Mazzucato, 2018). Implementation is based on collaborative governance in which public, private and civil society actors co-develop strategies and share responsibility for implementation. Crucially, the new policy model accepts uncertainty and complexity. It is experimental, iterative and adaptive and emphasises learning and institutional evolution (Radosevic et al., 2023). It is also underpinned by a normative shift: Industrial policy is increasingly being judged not just on its contribution to growth or exports, but on its ability to promote inclusion, resilience and sustainability. To achieve these goals, policymakers need to draw on an expanded innovation toolkit that utilises instruments such as public procurement, mission finance, digital regulation and skill-building frameworks.

For emerging economies, this makes industrial and innovation policies not optional instruments, but strategic prerequisites for long-term development. The era of passive integration, in which countries competed through low wages, generous tax systems or as low-cost assembly hubs, has largely run its course. In Eastern Europe, parts of Latin America and many sub-Saharan African economies, productivity growth has stalled despite deepening globalisation and increasing trade openness. At the same time, the requirements for participation in global value chains are increasing. Automation undermines the competitive advantage of cheap labour, while evolving environmental standards impose complex compliance requirements. Data-driven business models dominated by a handful of platform giants are creating new layers of exclusion. In this context, latecomer economies must actively build productive and technological capabilities. This requires not only market liberalisation but also coherent, long-term strategies to promote innovation, modernise industries and maintain competitiveness.

However, many emerging economies remain trapped in outdated policy paradigms. The frameworks they rely on, often developed in the 1990s, are rooted in a horizontal, market-friendly logic that neglects structural transformation. These policies are usually underfunded, fragmented and focus on generalised reforms of the business environment rather than targeted interventions. External pressures exacerbate the problem. Donor agendas, austerity measures and the continued influence of neoliberal ideology have limited policy imagination and discouraged ambitious industrial strategies. As a result, capability-building efforts are either sporadic or symbolic and unable to mobilise the institutional support and strategic focus required for genuine transformation. This chapter argues for a different path based on experimentation, strategic learning and systemic coherence. The aim is not to imitate Silicon Valley or import ready-made models, but to design context-specific strategies that respond to local development needs, capitalise on indigenous strengths and promote inclusive, sustainable innovation systems.

The remainder of this chapter examines how industrial and innovation policy can be redesigned to meet the challenges of the twenty-first century. It begins by questioning the long-standing distinction between horizontal and vertical policies and instead argues in favour of ecosystem-based, problem-oriented approaches that are tailored to real development bottlenecks. It then explores how innovation systems can become more adaptive and self-correcting by embedding mechanisms for learning, feedback and course correction, before examining the strategic use of missions, platforms and place-based innovation ecosystems to mobilise diverse actors around shared goals. From there we turn to the question of financing, asking how public and private investment can be channelled towards long-term transformation rather than short-term returns. The next section looks at governance and coordination and emphasises the need for strong institutions that are both effective and accountable. The concluding section calls for a new political ethos that focuses on transformation rather than transactional growth and rejects both market fundamentalism and state romanticism in favour of pragmatic ambition.

7.2 Beyond Horizontal vs Vertical: Reframing the Policy Toolkit

For much of the late twentieth century, policy debates were shaped by a rigid distinction between horizontal and vertical approaches (Shih, 2023). Horizontal policies, generic support measures such as improving education, research infrastructure, competition law or macroeconomic stability, were widely propagated as neutral and non-distortionary. Vertical interventions, on the other hand, were treated with suspicion, especially if they were targeted at specific sectors or firms. Critics argued that they invited political favouritism, distorted market signals and risked locking countries into inefficient industrial paths. This scepticism was reinforced by the legacy of failed state-led industrialisation in many countries and the dominance of neoliberal economic thinking, which favoured minimal state intervention. As a result, most emerging economies were advised to focus on the "basics" and invest in broad capabilities rather than concentrating resources on specific industries (Stojcic & Aralica, 2018). However, this dichotomy offered an oversimplified and static view of how innovation actually unfolds in practice and ignored the dynamic, systemic and often non-linear nature of technological development.

The traditional attraction of horizontal policies was its perceived neutrality and efficiency. Governments were expected to provide public goods such as education, infrastructure and macroeconomic stability without interfering in the functioning of the market. This policy framework was presented as generally beneficial and non-distortionary, especially suitable for emerging economies, which were wary of repeating the mistakes of the past. However, experience shows that horizontal measures alone are not enough to promote structural change. Without targeting industry's strategic priorities, increased R&D funding or broader access, education can only have a limited impact. This is particularly true in contexts with profound lack of coordination, firm capabilities and fragmented demand which, as we already established, are common traits of emerging innovation systems. As can be seen in cases such as South Korea, Taiwan or Finland, horizontal investments only lead to transformative results if they are embedded in broader national strategies that link education, technology and industrial development. In catch-up contexts, the lack of such coordination often leads to underutilised resources and missed opportunities.

Conversely, vertical policies have long been criticised for fostering rent-seeking, politicisation or inefficient subsidy allocation. However, this view overlooks the many successful examples of targeted industrial support that have led to genuine upgrading. The Brazilian aerospace industry, the Indian pharmaceutical sector and the Malaysian electronics clusters have all benefited from strategic government interventions targeting specific technologies, value chains or capabilities. These cases show that verticality itself is not the problem, but that the real problem lies in the design and implementation of policy. Effective interventions today are those that focus not just on sectors, but on solving specific challenges, enabling system transitions and building learning infrastructures. They rely on data, stakeholder engagement, iterative feedback and building complementary capabilities in public and private institutions. Successful policy is not characterised by whether it is vertical or horizontal, but whether it is passive or transformative. This calls for a move away from rigid categorisation and adoption of a smarter, challenge-driven approach to innovation and industrial transformation.

In the context of today's global challenges, climate change, digital transformation, supply chain disruption and geopolitical fragmentation, this binary framework is no longer valid. Structural change and innovation are not the automatic outcomes of well-functioning markets, but the result of coordinated action between actors, institutions and sectors (Mukherjee et al., 2021; van Dam & Frenken, 2020). The most effective policies bridge the old vertical and horizontal divide. They are inherently problem -solving and structured around missions that address pressing societal needs while serving as a catalyst for industrial upgrading and innovation. They are also ecosystemic, targeting not only firms or sectors, but also the linkages between them, including skills systems, finance, regulations and demand creation (Mazzucato, 2018). Moreover, they are experimental, designed with feedback loops and adaptive governance to respond to uncertainty (Radosevic et al., 2023). In this new paradigm, success depends less on whether a policy is vertical or horizontal and more on whether it creates system coherence, fosters learning and aligns innovation with inclusive and sustainable development.

However, despite the fact that the horizontal–vertical dichotomy no longer reflects the complexity of today's innovation challenges, its narrative still dominates policy discourse of many emerging economies. Clinging to this outdated framework means missing opportunities to drive meaningful change. What we need instead is a shift towards problem-solving and mission-oriented approaches that focus on purpose, learning and systemic coherence. This requires us to move beyond generic capacity building or narrowly focused subsidies. It requires tools that anchor innovation in societal needs, build collaborative platforms and ecosystems and enable institutions to adapt to changing conditions. Policies must become both more ambitious and more reflexive and be able to bring together different actors while remaining open to course corrections. In this context, the success of industrial and innovation policy can be judged not only by growth or export metrics, but also by its ability to catalyse inclusive, resilient and forward-looking development. The following section explores how such change can be made operational by embedding feedback, evaluation and learning into the structure of innovation systems themselves.

7.3 Building Innovation Systems that Learn

As we explained in the previous chapters, the concept of the innovation system has profoundly changed the way policymakers understand economic and technological development. Rather than viewing innovation as the outcome of individual firms or research laboratories, the innovation systems perspective emphasises the interdependencies between a variety of actors: businesses, universities, public research institutes, financial intermediaries, regulators and even end users. This framework has encouraged a move away from simplistic measures of R&D intensity towards a more holistic understanding of innovation as a collective, institutionalised process. It has also emphasised the importance of framework conditions such as regulatory frameworks, education systems and infrastructures that influence how knowledge is created, disseminated and applied. While this perspective has enriched the policy discourse, it has also led to overly static and technocratic interpretations. Innovation systems are often mapped, scrutinised and benchmarked, but rarely treated as dynamic, evolving entities. The danger is that we end up diagnosing structures without cultivating the learning processes that actually make them effective.

To move from structure to transformation, innovation systems need to be understood as learning entities that are able to adapt, evolve and improve in response to experience (Radosevic et al., 2023). This is particularly important in emerging economies where innovation systems are often fragmented, under-resourced and path-dependent (Stojcic, 2024). While these systems can generate projects and initiatives, they lack the necessary reflexivity to evaluate results, learn lessons and reshape policies accordingly. All too often, policy remains trapped in a logic of one-off programmes and static indicators, with little institutional memory or adaptability. A true learning system involves feedback loops not only within individual organisations, but across the entire system. It supports iterative policymaking, incentivises collaboration and fosters trust between actors. This requires not only technical adjustments, but also a cultural shift in the way innovation policy is designed, implemented and evaluated. The rest of this section looks at some of the mechanisms for fostering such systems, namely adaptive governance, experimental instruments and institutional arrangements that reward curiosity, not just compliance.

Learning is not an incidental feature of innovation systems as innovation is an inherently uncertain, non-linear process characterised by frequent failure, changing technologies and contextual factors. What succeeds in one instance may fail in another, and yesterday's solution may not meet tomorrow's challenge. The systems that stand the test of time are those that are able to reflect on their actions, adapt their course and develop institutional memory. This is particularly important in emerging economies, where the stakes are higher and the margin for error is smaller. Here, policymakers face institutional volatility caused by short political cycles, capability gaps between business and government, and a rapidly changing global landscape characterised by technological disruption, trade realignments and climatic uncertainties. These environments also face competing demands from international donors, foreign investors and local constituencies. In such complex and volatile contexts, rigid plans and imported blueprints are fragile. What matters most is a system's ability to learn, adapt and evolve in real time (D'Este et al., 2016; Metcalfe, 1995).

A cornerstone of learning innovation systems is the presence of robust feedback loops mentioned in first chapters of this book. These are the mechanisms through which insights from implementation, both successes and failures, are systematically fed back into policy and programme design (Leutert, 2021; Sewerin et al., 2020). Without such mechanisms, innovation systems become unresponsive and tend to repeat avoidable mistakes. Feedback loops take many forms as independent evaluations of innovation programmes that focus not only on compliance but also on generating actionable insights, structured follow-ups of failed projects to learn from them rather than assign blame or regular stakeholder consultations that genuinely influence ongoing priorities and instruments. User feedback in areas such as education technology or digital health can also reveal unexpected outcomes or bottlenecks. A good example is the Swedish innovation agency Vinnova, which funds "learning networks" and integrates continuous evaluation into all phases of project cycles. These practices embed learning in the DNA of the system and allow for gradual refinement rather than rigid adherence to outdated plans.

Learning systems must go beyond static planning and create institutional space for experimentation. This involves piloting new ideas, testing them in a controlled environment and scaling up what works. In terms of policy, this means creating mechanisms that tolerate failure and reward iteration. Innovation policy labs embedded in ministries can prototype new instruments before they are fully rolled out. Regulatory sandboxes allow emerging sectors such as fintech or AI to test solutions under relaxed rules and recognise pitfalls early. Challenge-based funding shifts the focus from predetermined solutions to clearly defined problems and demands creative responses from different players. Similarly, experimental procurement allows governments to act as early adopters and de-risk new technologies. The Canadian platform Impact Canada is an example of this logic, using behavioural science and co-creation approaches to address issues such as climate resilience or Indigenous health. Crucially, the lessons learnt from these experiments are codified and disseminated to create an institutional memory. This transforms policy from a one-off bet to a process of continuous improvement.

Another challenge stems from the fact that many public funding programmes are designed for predictability. Calls for proposals are rigid, eligibility rules are tight, and performance is measured by outcomes such as the number of patents or job creation. Such models miss the iterative nature of true innovation. Learning innovation systems embrace adaptive programme design as calls for proposals evolve based on learnings from previous funding rounds, different panels review proposals from different perspectives, technical, social and political, and grantees are encouraged to reorient themselves when new data reveal a better path. Monitoring frameworks track the milestones of learning and systemic impact, not just the outcomes achieved. Innovate UK has used this approach in its Future Mobility and Clean Growth programmes. By working with businesses, universities and users, the funding criteria are regularly updated. This flexibility allows public support to remain relevant in fast-changing sectors while strengthening the innovation system's ability to course-correct and improve over time.

In addition to programmes and instruments, innovation systems also need institutions that are able to learn about themselves (Beers & van Mierlo, 2017; Grimpe et al., 2020). Institutional reflexivity refers to the ability of public organisations to question their own assumptions, update mental models and accept discomfort when necessary. It manifests itself in internal reviews of existing policy portfolios, scenario planning and learning forums that cut across ministries and agencies. It is also crucial for reflexivity that dissenting voices from civil society, marginalised communities and independent experts are included in decision-making processes. This protects against blind spots and policy capture. The Chilean development agency CORFO is a good example of this. Over the past two decades, it has evolved from a narrowly focused grantmaker to a platform that promotes collective learning through ecosystem-level interventions. Rather than clinging to old tools, CORFO has restructured its internal departments and priorities to respond to external changes from commodity dependency to technological upgrading.

Building emerging innovation systems that learn is a compelling goal, but implementing such systems is fraught with institutional and political challenges (Intarakumnerd et al., 2002; Rodrik, 2007). In many emerging economies, policymakers are under immense pressure to deliver short-term results, which can discourage iterative, long-term approaches. Political cycles often prioritise visibility over learning, while donor funding typically focuses on rigid project timelines and predefined outcomes, leaving little room for endogenous experimentation. In addition, many public institutions lack analytical capacity for foresight, monitoring and systems thinking, all of which are core competences for adaptive governance. Even where these capacities are present, organisational cultures of risk aversion and blame can stifle openness to failure and learning (Stojcic, 2024). In such contexts, admitting that a policy needs revision is seen as a weakness rather than a strength, reinforcing inertia and stifling innovation.

Overcoming these obstacles requires technical solutions, but also institutional reform and cultural change. Stable, long-term mandates for innovation agencies are essential to insulate learning processes from short-term political volatility. Equally important is the promotion of a culture of trust and psychological safety within public institutions, where experimentation is encouraged and failure is seen as a source of insight rather than blame. This ethos must be fostered by political leaders who understand that complex societal changes such as the green transformation or digital inclusion cannot be managed with linear plans. They need to support iterative processes that respond to feedback and new conditions. Partnerships with universities, think tanks and civil society can help to strengthen the knowledge infrastructure around public learning and embed research and critical reflection into the innovation system itself.

For catching-up economies, this challenge extends beyond increasing investment in innovation, a commonly applied recipe, to fundamental change in the way this investment is conceptualised and deployed. Rather than replicating models from advanced economies, these countries need to prioritise learning-oriented approaches that emphasise adaptation and local relevance. This means funding pilot initiatives before they are fully implemented to allow for iterative learning, supporting cross-sector dialogue to align fragmented systems and focusing evaluation on building long-term capabilities and solving urgent problems rather than on superficial metrics such as patents or the number of start-ups. Traditional policy transfer often leads to what scholars call isomorphic mimicry (Andrews et al., 2017), the systems that appear advanced in form but have no functional impact. Learning systems offer a way out of this trap by institutionalising strategic modesty. They accept uncertainty, incorporate feedback mechanisms and continuously refine policies through experience. For countries facing resource constraints and complex development challenges, this approach offers a more realistic and resilient path to innovation-driven change.

Innovation systems that do not learn tend to stagnate, regardless of how much funding they receive or how many actors they involve. Activity without reflection can lead to repeating the same mistakes, fragmentation of initiatives and policy fatigue. In the twenty-first century, the real challenge for policymakers is not only to find the right sectors or technologies to support, but to foster systems that are able to adapt to complexity, uncertainty and changing needs. This requires a new mindset that sees policy as an iterative, learning-orientated process rather than a static set of tools. Strategic experimentation, feedback loops, institutional reflexivity and cross-sectoral coordination must become central features of innovation policy design and governance. Only in this way can innovation systems develop from output-driven to a result-driven performance. Building on this foundation, the next section turns to the mechanisms through which such learning can be anchored in the real world, namely missions, platforms and place-based innovation ecosystems.

7.4 Missions, Platforms and Ecosystems

In the last two decades, innovation policy has undergone a profound transformation. It is no longer defined solely by how much is spent on research and development or how many start-ups are founded. Instead, the central question has become how innovation can be geared towards solving complex, urgent social problems. Challenges such as climate change, digital inequality, pandemic preparedness or food security cannot be solved by technological breakthroughs alone. Nor can they be solved by fragmented market incentives or isolated government initiatives. These are systemic problems that are deeply embedded in specific political, social and environmental contexts. Tackling them requires coordinated, cross-sectoral action and long-term institutional commitment. In this changing landscape, innovation policy needs to evolve from a focus on inputs and outputs to an emphasis on outcomes and transformation. This section explores how three interlinked concepts, missions, platforms and ecosystems can serve as building blocks for such a reorientation, helping to align actors, mobilise resources and enable continuous learning and adaptation.

The concept of mission-oriented innovation has evolved considerably since its origins in the Cold War. While the Apollo programme was an example of a top-down, technology-driven mission with clear national prestige, today's missions focus more on solving urgent societal challenges such as decarbonising transport, tackling food insecurity or combating antimicrobial resistance (Mazzucato, 2018; Schot & Steinmueller, 2018). These new missions are not just about advancing specific technologies, but about achieving broad, transformative goals that require the coordination of multiple sectors, institutions and actors. Unlike traditional sectoral strategies, missions are defined by clear public outcomes, transcend disciplinary and institutional boundaries, and are inherently directional, focusing innovation on solving collective problems rather than leaving outcomes to market forces. Crucially, missions accept uncertainty and allow multiple paths to success by encouraging experimentation and iterative learning. They mobilise not only governments and businesses, but also civil society, recognising that legitimacy, participation and context-sensitive design are essential for lasting impact and systemic change.

In emerging economies, mission-oriented approaches offer a powerful way to anchor innovation policy in pressing local challenges rather than abstract aspirations for global competitiveness. Rather than measuring success by the number of patents or start-ups, missions can focus on concrete goals such as reducing urban air pollution, improving rural healthcare or ensuring climate-resilient agriculture. These place-based missions can foster collaboration between local SMEs, universities, government agencies and civil society, creating a sense of shared purpose and building domestic capability. This emerging mission orientation is not about prestige or mimicking high-income models but about aligning innovation with the real needs of citizens and communities. When done well, such missions can transform fragmented efforts into coordinated learning systems that provide both relevance and resilience.

Platforms are the connective tissue of innovation systems, spaces where ideas, actors and capabilities converge to enable experimentation and scale (Addo, 2022; Davies et al., 2018; Elzinga et al., 2023; Quan et al., 2021; Reike et al., 2023; Ritala, 2024; Sobota et al., 2025; Wiarda et al., 2024). They are gaining rising prominence in the context of mission-driven policies. While missions set the direction, platforms provide the enabling infrastructure: physical, digital, legal and organisational. In contrast to traditional policies that emphasise isolated inputs such as R&D grants or outputs such as patents, platform thinking focuses on the relational space in between. It recognises that innovation is a collective process shaped by collaboration, trust and access to tools and information. A well-designed platform, be it a prototyping facility, a regulatory sandbox or a standards-setting consortium, can lower costs, reduce risk and shorten time to impact. Crucially, platforms do not pre-determine the winners but broaden the base of stakeholders who can participate in solving complex challenges. This middle layer of policy is where the innovation system comes to life, not through top-down control, but through dynamic interplay between different institutions working towards common transformation goals.

In high-income countries, platforms have become a central feature of mission-oriented policies. The Dutch top-sector model or European Commission's NetZeroCities are examples of how thematic platforms focusing on areas such as sustainable food, smart mobility or energy can align government, industry and academia around a common agenda. These platforms enable not only the development of technologies, but also collaborative learning, co-creation of regulations and training of the labour force. Their strength lies in their modularity and scalability as successful pilot projects in one region can be adapted elsewhere, creating a distributed architecture of innovation. In contrast to isolated programmes, platforms promote ecosystems in which ideas and actors circulate continuously. They also help governments to move from passive funding to active orchestration, shaping markets, mobilising demand and enabling feedback loops. In this sense, platforms are not a policy add-on, but a governance tool that supports the flexibility and responsiveness needed for systemic innovation.

In emerging economies, platforms are not a luxury but a necessity. Many of these countries do not have the scale, capital or institutional depth to support full innovation pipelines in individual firms or universities. By pooling infrastructure and expertise, platforms reduce duplication of effort and strengthen local capabilities. For example, shared testing facilities or digital hubs can equip SMEs with tools they could never afford on their own. This democratises access to innovation and promotes broader participation. In addition, platforms create spaces for cross-sector dialogue and bring together stakeholders who would otherwise act in isolation. When platforms are developed with local needs in mind, they are more than just technical facilitators, they become institutions of collective learning and coordination. As such, they offer catching-up countries a realistic, scalable way to organise innovation based on public benefit, rather than simply following the templates of high-income countries.

Ecosystems represent the relational foundation of innovation, where direction (missions) and infrastructure (platforms) are animated by trust, collaboration and shared goals (Adner, 2017; Jacobides et al., 2018). Unlike clusters, which often refer to physical collections of firms in a particular sector, ecosystems emphasise the quality and density of interactions between different actors. These include universities, firms, start-ups, public institutions, investors and users. In a healthy ecosystem, innovation emerges through open communication, distributed capabilities, shared norms such as risk-sharing and openness, and institutional frameworks that enable flexibility and co-evolution. Crucially, ecosystems depend on feedback loops and intermediaries such as accelerators, incubators or development agencies that bridge institutional gaps and help turn ideas into action. Finland's shift from firm-centric to a place-based innovation policy illustrates this approach well with cities like Oulu and Espoo becoming innovation hubs, not through isolated funding, but through long-term collaboration between local actors based on mutual engagement and a culture of experimentation and shared learning.

National-level policies often focus resources on capital cities or established sectors, leaving large regional disparities in innovation capacity. Ecosystems, on the other hand, offer the opportunity to activate latent potential at the local level, be it in smaller cities, peripheral regions or post-industrial areas. If these ecosystems are rooted in specific resources such as a local university, natural resources or community networks, they can become engines for inclusive innovation. But building them takes time. Relationships must be cultivated, trust built and coordination maintained across electoral cycles and administrative changes. Ecosystems do not thrive on one-off grants or top-down mandates, but require ongoing investment in social capital, intermediary capacity and participatory governance. However, when nurtured effectively, they enable innovation systems to become resilient and adaptable, responding to both local needs and global change. They transform innovation from an abstract goal into a lived, collective process.

What gives missions, platforms and ecosystems their transformative power is not their isolated application, but their alignment. When a mission defines a clear societal goal, a platform provides the shared tools and infrastructure to achieve that goal, and an ecosystem ensures ongoing collaboration and learning, a system emerges that can produce not only innovation, but sustainable, comprehensive change. Denmark's green energy transition exemplifies this focus in practice. The national mission to achieve carbon neutrality sets the direction. Platforms such as GreenLab enable experimentation with renewable technologies. Local ecosystems in cities connect universities, public utilities, start-ups and citizens, creating a dynamic environment where feedback loops and trust accelerate change. The synergy between these elements enables innovation to be channelled, anchored and sustained. This is not just about installing solar panels or wind turbines, but also about building collective capacity to govern transitions, solve common problems and navigate complexity together.

For emerging innovation systems, coordination between missions, platforms and ecosystems is even more important given their limited resources and institutional fragmentation. The aim is not to copy institutional architecture of advanced economies, but to emulate the logic of purposeful coordination. For example, a country could define a mission to reduce maternal mortality. This mission could be supported by a health innovation platform that integrates digital health tools, mobile clinics and targeted procurement of diagnostics and care services. A broader ecosystem could form around this platform, connecting non-governmental organisations, health ministries, local governments and researchers through continuous feedback and adaptive learning. Such alignment leads not only to innovations in medical devices or service delivery, but also to systemic innovations in managing and improving health outcomes. This approach strengthens trust in institutions, builds indigenous capacity and ensures that innovation is not a technocratic exercise but a response to real human needs. For emerging economies, this type of adaptation can be key to transforming policy aspirations into tangible progress.

Missions, platforms and ecosystems invite us to rethink what it means to scale innovation. Rather than equating scaling with the expansion of a single firm or the widespread commercialisation of a single product, these approaches emphasise scaling as a process of institutional deepening and systemic replication. It is about embedding new ways of working, fostering lasting relationships and creating shared capabilities that can be adapted across contexts. Thus, the success of an urban mobility mission is measured not only by the launch of a new transport app, but also by how it reconfigures governance structures, reshapes citizen engagement with mobility and develops new models of public–private collaboration. In this sense, scaling is less about size and more about resilience, relevance and reach. It means transforming pilot initiatives into institutionalised routines, adapting successful platforms to new regions and enabling ecosystems to carry learning and innovation forward over time. This broader vision of scale makes transformation possible.

Innovation must become a central pillar of development strategy in emerging economies, not as an imitation, but as a mission. By anchoring innovation in shared societal challenges, building platforms that democratise access to tools and knowledge and fostering ecosystems that enable collaboration and learning, countries can move away from extractive growth models and forge their own paths to resilience and transformation. This approach requires a shift in mindset from fragmented projects to integrated systems, from short-term results to long-term capabilities and from isolated interventions to dynamic alignment. Missions provide direction, platforms provide capacity and ecosystems maintain momentum, but only if they are coordinated as part of a coherent whole. Scaling in this context is not about the size of organisations, but about the depth of institutional change. The following section addresses the question of how such change can be financed. It looks at the role of public capital, risk-taking and financial governance in building innovation systems for the twenty-first century.

7.5 Instruments that Align Finance, Risk and Purpose

Innovation is often described as a risky endeavour. Ideas fail, prototypes break, and markets change. Yet paradoxically, most public and private innovation funding mechanisms are designed to minimise risk rather than embrace it. Public grant programmes often emphasise predictability and predefined outcomes and discourage experimentation. Loan schemes demand guarantees, making them inaccessible to firms pursuing unconventional technologies or working in uncertain markets. Private venture capital typically seeks quick returns and favours digital platforms and consumer technologies over long-term societal missions. Even when funding science and research, conservative review processes often penalise bold or exploratory proposals. As a result, innovation systems in many countries produce safe, incremental improvements rather than the radical changes needed to address structural challenges such as climate change, technological sovereignty or health equity. This status quo penalises emerging economies in particular, which not only need to innovate but also develop new institutions, industries and capabilities in the face of limited resources and high global uncertainty.

To move beyond this incrementalism, emerging economies need a financial architecture that not only supports innovation, but fundamentally reshapes its direction, scope and inclusiveness. This means that financial instruments need to be focused on long-term, uncertain and transformative missions. It also requires public actors to move from passive funders or market correctors to active, entrepreneurial roles in shaping the allocation of capital. Rather than replicating Silicon Valley venture models, countries need to experiment with hybrid mechanisms such as public development banks that de-risk early-stage technologies, innovation funds that tolerate failure and support iteration, and procurement systems that create demand for socially valuable innovations. It is equally important to create governance structures around funding that encourage feedback, accountability and learning, and ensure that financial decisions are not static but evolve with evidence and need. This section explores how tools such as patient capital, mission-driven funding, challenge-driven procurement and blended funding models can be used to realign risk, purpose and innovation outcomes to create not just more innovation, but innovation that matters.

In many emerging innovation systems, public innovation finance has traditionally focused on addressing market failures by offering grants when private lenders pull out, providing tax incentives to attract foreign investment or subsidising R&D to stimulate innovation at the firm level. While these interventions are necessary, they are fundamentally reactive and risk reinforcing existing innovation patterns rather than transforming them. A more strategic approach to funding asks deeper questions: What problems are we trying to solve? What capabilities do we need to build? Who will be involved in the innovation process? Take, for example, a public fund that offers grants for research and development. If the funding criteria require prior intellectual property or demand short-term commercial returns, then socially important but uncertain innovations such as climate adaptation technologies or health diagnostics for remote areas may not qualify. Funding is not just about financing, it is also a form of governance. It shapes expectations, philtres opportunities and sets the boundaries of what is considered valuable or possible.

Transformative innovations do not follow linear timelines or deliver predictable returns. They require patient capital, public and private resources that are willing to absorb uncertainty, tolerate failure and invest over extended periods of time (Lazonick & Mazzucato, 2013; Mazzucato, 2013). This type of capital is essential for innovations with systemic impact, such as clean energy, cutting-edge medical technologies or inclusive digital infrastructure. In these areas, traditional market incentives are often insufficient as private investors are reluctant to fund projects that are risky, capital intensive or slow to commercialise. Patient capital bridges this gap by supporting early-stage experimentation, technology learning and the development of complementary capabilities. Without this capital, many promising solutions would never get beyond the lab or pilot phase.

History shows the power of strategic public risk-taking. The Internet, GPS and mRNA vaccines all emerged from publicly funded missions that supported high-risk, high-reward research (Mazzucato, 2013). Agencies such as DARPA in the United States, Sitra in Finland and InnovFin at the European Investment Bank have shown how flexible, mission-driven funding can unlock entire fields of innovation. These institutions have not only subsidised R&D. Rather, they have actively shaped technological directions and created new markets. This has a profound impact on emerging innovation systems as public finance must be enabled to act not just as a corrector of market failure, but as a co-creator of the future of innovation. This means accepting uncertainty as a necessary part of transformation, learning from failure, iterating financing strategies and sticking to long-term societal goals, even if the short-term returns are unclear.

Blended finance is a pragmatic response to the fact that neither governments nor markets alone can finance the scale of transformation needed to address urgent societal challenges (Convergence Blended Finance, 2025; OECD, 2018). By combining public, private and philanthropic capital, it spreads risk, incentivises and unlocks investment in areas of innovation that are typically underfunded, particularly in emerging economies. In innovation policy, this often means that public actors take on the risk in the early stages through first-loss guarantees, subordinated capital or preferential terms. Such instruments give private investors the confidence to participate in ventures that they might otherwise avoid. This approach has proven successful in de-risking emerging sectors such as clean energy, agri-tech and digital health, where technological and market uncertainty is still high. When designed strategically, blended finance can serve as both a catalyst for innovation and a mechanism to raise private capital for long-term development goals.

Real-life examples illustrate the potential. The Breakthrough Energy Catalyst initiative, supported by public funding and philanthropy, combines concessional and commercial finance to scale up key climate technologies. Similarly, the European Investment Fund (EIF) has provided capital to early-stage venture funds in under-capitalised regions of Europe, creating entry points for private finance that would not otherwise have flowed. However, the challenge for emerging economies is not to replicate these models across the board, but to adapt them to specific national and regional conditions. This requires the development of localised blended finance instruments, the strengthening of development banks and the promotion of partnerships with mission-oriented corporate actors and international donors. When such collaborations are embedded in a clear innovation strategy, they can channel capital towards national priorities, be it sustainable agriculture, inclusive digital infrastructure or affordable healthcare, while spreading the risk across a broader coalition of actors.

Public procurement, as we mentioned repeatedly throughout the book, holds untapped potential as a driver of innovation, especially in emerging economies where public spending accounts for a significant share of GDP. If procurement goes beyond routine purchases and becomes a strategic tool for solving societal challenges, it can generate strong demand signals for emerging technologies and services. Pre-commercial procurement, innovation-oriented tenders and competitions allow public bodies to act not only as regulators or funders, but also as early adopters and co-creators of innovation. Programmes such as the UK's SBRI and Chile's Desafíos Públicos show that by defining a problem rather than prescribing a solution, the public sector encourages the creativity of start-ups, SMEs and research institutions. These initiatives often support iterative development, provide feedback loops and help innovators refine their offerings while addressing unmet public needs. In this way, public procurement can simultaneously reduce the risk to innovation and accelerate adoption, particularly in sectors where private demand is weak or fragmented.

For emerging innovation systems, the strategic use of public procurement offers a triple benefit: fostering domestic innovation, strengthening local supply chains and demonstrating the viability of new technologies or services (Stojcic et al., 2020). Procurement initiatives can target critical sectors such as healthcare, education, mobility or digital services, areas where there is an urgent public need and where local solutions can create broad societal benefits. For example, sourcing affordable diagnostic tools from local firms can reduce dependence on imports and build local manufacturing capacity. Supporting grassroots innovation through community-driven tenders can lead to bottom-up solutions that are often more contextualised. However, structural reforms are needed to unlock this potential. Procurement laws need to shift from rigid compliance and cost minimisation to outcome-based and innovation-friendly criteria. Public buyers need to be trained to evaluate new solutions and deal with uncertainty. Most importantly, governments need to see procurement not as an administrative task, but as an investment in the country's problem-solving capabilities. When procurement is aligned with broader mission-oriented strategies, it becomes a foundational instrument for inclusive and sustainable innovation.

One of the hidden barriers to innovation funding is the way in which success is measured. All too often, funding is measured by short-term results such as the number of patents filed, the creation of start-ups or the volume of R&D expenditure mobilised. These indicators are easy to count, but miss what really matters, i.e. capability building, resilience, integration and system transformation. To fund transformative innovation, we need to broaden the definition of value. This means recognising not only commercial success, but also the learning impact. We need to value public outcomes such as health equity, decarbonisation or digital inclusion, track ecosystem effects such as the formation of new partnerships, skills development or the evolution of regulatory frameworks, and support innovations that serve marginalised communities, even if they don't scale quickly. Alternative models already exist. Finland's Sitra tracks social and environmental impact, Rwanda evaluates digital public goods based on reach and trust, and India includes gender, caste and regional equality in its innovation metrics. If funding is to match purpose, then accountability must match transformation.

Innovation funding is not just about how much is spent, but also about how capital is allocated, how risk is shared and how success is defined. For catching-up economies, building a resilient and sovereign innovation system requires more than just closing funding gaps, but also financial instruments that are aligned with national priorities and societal needs. This includes shifting from short-term gains to long-term transformation, from passive subsidisation to strategic focus and from narrow measures to broader measures of public benefit. It means prioritising purpose over scale, learning over speed and inclusion over efficiency. Public finance must act as a catalyst, not just a filler, determining the direction and quality of innovation through its terms and conditions. Financial reform is therefore not a technical issue, but a strategic imperative. The next section looks at the final part of this transformation, the one of governance. It explores how innovation policy can be steered, institutionalised and made adaptable in a world of uncertainty and competing interests.

7.6 Policy Capacity and Governance for Innovation

Innovation policy unfolds in the reality of public institutions, where it must be conceived, negotiated and executed often in the face of bureaucratic inertia, institutional fragmentation or unclear mandates. While much of the policy literature focuses on what innovation policies should be implemented, far less attention is paid to who implements them and how. In many emerging economies the obstacles to effective innovation policy are less a lack of ideas or funding than weak coordination, isolated governance structures and limited administrative capabilities. Promising initiatives often fail because they are not supported by the institutional capacity needed to guide them through complexity, adaptation and learning (Radosevic et al., 2023; Stojcic, 2024). As a result, innovation strategies often become performative, they are announced but not executed, funded but not monitored, aligned in rhetoric but not in reality.

This section looks in more detail at how innovation governance can work in practice. It begins with a fundamental but often overlooked question: How can countries develop institutional arrangements that not only manage innovation programmes but also enable transformative change? The most resilient and effective systems are those that combine a clear purpose with institutional flexibility and are not about rigid control, but about enabling collaboration, experimentation and adaptation. This requires mission-oriented agencies, empowered coordinators, trusted intermediaries and mechanisms for continuous learning. The goal is not simply to fix market failures, but to design innovation systems that are able to evolve with new challenges, align diverse stakeholders and create public value. These lessons are particularly urgent for emerging economies, where building policy capacity and institutional intelligence can be the determining factor in whether innovation leads to lasting transformation.

In many emerging economies, innovation policy remains focused on managing individual programmes, issuing calls, reviewing proposals, allocating funds and reporting on key metrics. While this model may work in high-performing environments with stable institutions and mature ecosystems, it often falls short in more volatile contexts. Here, innovation policy must operate in the midst of shifting political priorities, institutional fragmentation and pressing development challenges. Under such conditions, governance must evolve beyond technical project management to systemic orchestration. This means understanding innovation not as a linear process, but as a complex, adaptable system (Schot & Steinmueller, 2018). Effective governance must harmonise the various stakeholders, manage uncertainty, encourage feedback and change course when conditions change. It must move from reactive implementation to anticipatory coordination and build institutional capacity that not only delivers programmes but also shapes the conditions in which innovation can flourish (OECD, 2019). This requires a shift in mindset from compliance to curiosity, from routine management to active governance of the system.

Rwanda offers a compelling example of this shift. Over the years, the Rwandan Ministry of ICT and Innovation has evolved from a telecommunications regulator to a central orchestrator of the country's digital transformation. Instead of merely issuing licences or managing donor-funded projects, it is now engaged in cross-sector coordination, supporting experimental initiatives such as regulatory sandboxes and investing in digital public goods that serve long-term societal goals. This development was not achieved through structural reforms alone but required a strategic mandate from the highest levels of government and internal reforms that emphasised the ability to collaborate, learn and be flexible. The example shows how governance itself can become a lever for innovation not only by empowering others, but by actively shaping the development of the system. For other catching-up countries, the lesson is clear that innovation governance needs to be reconceptualised as a dynamic function that bridges policy domains, builds trust and supports purposeful experimentation.

One of the central challenges of innovation governance is to manage interdependence without fragmentation. Since innovation by its very nature spans sectors ranging from education and health to trade, environment and finance, no single ministry or agency can claim sole responsibility. However, without clear mandates and coordination structures, this complexity often leads to a dispersion of responsibility and policy incoherence. Successful innovation systems do not address this problem by concentrating power in a "super authority", but by creating institutional mechanisms for coordination and co-operation. This includes setting up formal bodies for inter-ministerial dialogue, empowering agencies with cross-sectoral convening powers and aligning innovation goals with broader national strategies. Coordination is not a bureaucratic add-on, but a core function of policy design. Without it, efforts become isolated, duplication of effort occurs and opportunities for synergies are lost. Innovation policy is not about who owns the agenda, but about how multiple actors can jointly own it and act together to drive systemic transformation.

Examples from both advanced and emerging economies show how this form of coordination can be institutionalised. In South Korea, inter-ministerial steering committees such as those linking the Ministry of Science and ICT with the Ministry of Trade, Industry and Energy enable strategic alignment on overarching innovation priorities, from digital transformation to green technology. These bodies are supported by strong policy intelligence units that enable forward-looking and informed decision-making. In South Africa, the Decadal Plan for Science, Technology and Innovation will introduce an Innovation Compact, an agreement that binds the various government departments to common goals, responsibilities and timelines. Importantly, these mechanisms are not just forums for discussion but create shared ownership of outcomes and embed collaboration into the budgeting and implementation process.

When it comes to policy capacity, the focus is often on staffing, i.e. how many civil servants an authority employs, how well trained they are and what technical skills they have. While these elements are important, they only scratch the surface of what constitutes real policy capacity. An effective innovation governance also requires room for experimentation, adaptation and course correction without fear of reprisals. It requires long-term time horizons that allow institutions to accompany complex, uncertain changes. It depends on access to knowledge, both internal analytical skills and the ability to draw on external expertise. Crucially, it depends on political cover, the mandate and support to take risks, learn from failures and try again. In many emerging economies, dedicated professionals work in innovation agencies, but their work is hampered by rigid bureaucracies, limited budgets and short political cycles. As a result, even the best-intentioned initiatives can stall, not because of weak ideas, but because of limited institutional conditions.

Moreover, capacity is not only a question of technical competence, but also of institutional design and political insulation. Agencies such as Finland's Vinnova are an example of this model; they operate independently of day-to-day political changes, have a clear mandate that focuses on system-level learning and manage a diverse portfolio of programmes that evolve over time. In Colombia, iNNpulsa began as a narrowly focused agency support for start-ups, but has evolved into a national innovation platform with a broader mission and deeper strategic focus. This expansion was not automatic but was made possible by consistent political support and the ability to demonstrate value across administrations. These examples illustrate an important realisation: Policy capacity is deeply political. It must be cultivated through institutional mandates that endure beyond electoral cycles, secured through governance mechanisms that protect discretionary power, and reinforced through long-term commitments to learning and systemic change.

Innovation systems must be capable of learning, just like the institutions that govern them. In a dynamic environment in which technologies, societal needs and risks evolve rapidly, static institutions with fixed mandates and rigid programme cycles become a burden. Learning governance systems are characterised by several key features: They build in feedback loops from users and stakeholders; they evaluate programmes in real time rather than waiting for final reviews; they allow for course corrections without political sanctions; and they are open to experimentation through pilot projects, regulatory sandboxes and adaptive rules. Singapore is often held up as a model of strategic foresight and coordination, but its real strength lies in how it develops policy prototypes, tests institutional innovations and scales up what proves effective. Agencies like the Economic Development Board and the Smart Nation Office operate with a level of agility and focus rarely found in traditional bureaucracies. Catching-up countries may not have the same resources, but they can still embrace the underlying principle to view governance itself as a process of continuous learning.

As innovation institutions gain strength, they also become more vulnerable to two major risks: capture and inertia. In some contexts, innovation policy is hijacked to serve narrow interests, the interests of large, established companies, politically connected actors or external donors with prescriptive agendas. While the rhetoric remains forward-looking, the actual outcomes entrench existing power structures and prevent broader participation. To prevent capture, institutions need to put safeguards in place such as transparent decision-making processes, independent oversight, stakeholder involvement and performance criteria that reflect societal outcomes and not just economic metrics. Meanwhile, institutional inertia is a quieter but equally damaging threat: Programmes are continued not because they are effective, but because they are familiar. Legacy initiatives absorb resources even when their relevance has faded. To combat both capture and inertia, governance structures that embed accountability and renewal are needed. These include time-limited mandates, sunset clauses, regular portfolio reviews and the institutional flexibility to reallocate resources to new challenges to ensure that innovation remains both effective and equitable.

Innovation governance extends beyond the state. While government institutions continue to play a central role in strategy and funding, effective governance increasingly depends on distributed models that involve a broader group of actors, universities, municipalities, business associations and civil society. These actors bring local knowledge, long-term commitment and the ability to anchor innovation in specific contexts. Austria's regional innovation systems are a good example of this. Multi-stakeholder governance platforms enable joint decision-making, prioritisation and performance monitoring with genuine local ownership. In contrast, many Central and Eastern European and Western Balkan countries have implemented smart specialisation strategies with significant donor support, but have struggled to establish sustained local engagement or decision-making power. Often these platforms invite participation without sharing authority. The challenge for the future is to create governance arrangements that are inclusive not only in form but also in function, replacing symbolic consultation with genuine co-creation and co-decision. Only then can innovation systems respond effectively to local needs while aligning with broader national or regional goals.

Innovation governance provides the invisible scaffolding that supports meaningful transformation. Without it, even well-designed policies risk fragmentation, delays or failure in implementation. With it, innovation becomes more than a policy objective and transforms into a strategic national capability that enables countries not only to respond to external change, but to actively shape their trajectories. For emerging economies, this requires a change of perspective. Governance should not be seen as a bureaucratic hurdle, but as an important prerequisite for experimentation, coordination and long-term learning. Investing in governance means strengthening institutions, nurturing talent and embedding processes that enable adaptation and resilience. Moreover, success needs to be redefined not only by achievements, but by strengthening systems and enabling future prospects. The conclusion of this chapter is that we need not just better tools or more funding, but a fundamentally new policy ethos based on transformation, learning and public purpose. Only then can innovation policy fulfil its promise to deliver inclusive and sustainable progress.

7.7 Conclusion

Innovation policy has traditionally followed a growth-oriented paradigm: fund R&D, stimulate entrepreneurship, attract investment and expect the economic benefits to cascade through the system. While this approach has delivered benefits, it is no longer sufficient in a world characterised by increasing inequality, environmental limits and technological disruption. The real challenge now is not simply to innovate more, but to innovate purposefully. To develop innovation systems that address urgent societal challenges, stay within planetary boundaries and promote inclusive prosperity. In this new context, it is not about catching up with yesterday's pioneers, but shaping a future that is sustainable, equitable and resilient. This requires a profound rethink of both the goals and methods of innovation policy. More funding or new institutions alone will not be enough. What we need is a change of ethos into the one that puts public value, learning and long-term transformation at the heart of innovation governance. In this chapter, we have identified five key transitions needed to support this change.

Innovation policy change starts with moving away from the rigid dichotomy between horizontal and vertical approaches. Instead, countries need to embrace problem-oriented policies that stimulate cross-sector collaboration through clear, ambitious missions. These missions should not just fund innovation in the abstract, but orientate it towards solving real societal challenges, be it climate adaptation, public health or digital inclusion. To achieve this, policymakers must mobilise stakeholders from government, industry, academia and civil society around common goals and create a sense of collective responsibility and purpose. But mobilisation for tasks alone is not enough. Innovation systems must also learn. They must become adaptive and reflexive and be able to admit failure, experiment with new models and evolve over time. This requires an institutional culture that tolerates uncertainty, values diverse feedback and avoids blind imitation. In such systems, learning is not a one-off event, but an ongoing process that strengthens local capabilities, influences policy iteration and embeds resilience into the structure of innovation governance.

Equally important is the use of structural instruments, missions, platforms and ecosystems, as interconnected pillars of transformation. Missions articulate purpose, platforms provide shared capabilities and tools, and ecosystems build the relationships and trust necessary for sustainable innovation. When aligned, they transform abstract ambitions into actionable strategies and lasting impact. Supporting this architecture requires a rethinking of financial instruments. Rather than chasing short-term gains or safe bets, public finance must align capital with public purpose through patient financing, risk-sharing instruments, innovation-friendly procurement and outcome-focused mechanisms. However, all of this will only be effective if metrics are reconceptualised into measures that prioritise learning, inclusiveness and long-term societal impact over immediate economic returns. Finally, transformative innovation depends on governance. This means building institutions that not only manage programmes but orchestrate change, ministries that break down silos, agencies that bring actors together and bureaucracies that value experimentation. Governance must shift from compliance to coordination, from rigidity to learning and from control to strategic empowerment.

For emerging economies, embracing these changes is not a matter of choice, but a matter of necessity. The old ways of development, relying on cheap labour, passive integration into global value chains or emulating Silicon Valley, are increasingly constrained by geopolitical shifts, technological concentration and environmental limits. Instead, these countries need to cultivate the ability to shape their own innovation pathways that are rooted in local realities, driven by societal needs and aligned with long-term development goals. This does not mean turning away from global integration or external knowledge flows. Rather, it requires a more strategic engagement with stronger institutions, clearer priorities and governance frameworks capable of managing complexity. As we have seen, transformation requires direction, collaboration and learning. But it also requires inclusion. In the next chapter, we ask: Who gets to participate in innovation? Who sets the priorities? Who gets the credit? Because if innovation is to truly serve the public good, it must serve everyone.

References

Addo, A. (2022). Orchestrating a digital platform ecosystem to address societal challenges: A robust action perspective. *Journal of Information Technology, 37*(4), 359–386.

Adner, R. (2017). Ecosystem as structure: An actionable construct for strategy. *Journal of Management, 43*(1), 39–58.

Andrews, M., Pritchett, L., & Woolcock, M. (2017). *Building state capability: Evidence, analysis, action.* Oxford University Press.

Beers, P. J., & van Mierlo, B. (2017). Reflexivity and learning in system innovation processes. *Sociologia Ruralis, 57*(3), 415–436.

Convergence Blended Finance. (2025). *State of blended finance 2025.* Convergence Report.

D'Este, P., Namara, A., & Olmos-Penuela, J. (2016). Fostering novelty while reducing failure: Balancing the twin challenges of product innovation. *Technological Forecasting & Social Change, 113*(B), 280–292.

Davies, J., Maru, Y., Hall, A., Abdourhamane, I. K., Adegbidi, A., Carberry, P., Dorai, K., Ennin, S. A., Etwire, P. M., McMillan, L., Njoya, A., Ouedraogo, S., Traore, A., Traore-Gue, N. J., & Watson, I. (2018). Understanding innovation platform effectiveness through experiences from west and central Africa. *Agricultural Systems, 165*, 321–334.

Elzinga, R., Janssen, M. J., Wesseling, J., Negro, S. O., & Hekkert, M. P. (2023). Assessing mission-specific innovation systems: Towards an analytical framework. *Environmental Innovation and Societal Transitions, 48*, 100745.

Gereffi, G., Pananond, P., Tell, F., & Fang, T. (2025). Navigating industrial policy and global value chains in an era of disruptions. *Journal of International Business Policy, 8*(3), 207–223. Online First.

Grimpe, B., Stahl, B. C., Holter, C. T., Inglesant, P., Eden, G., Patel, M., & Jirotka, M. (2020). From collaborative to institutional reflexivity: Calibrating responsibility in the funding process. *Science and Public Policy, 47*(5), 720–732.

Hauge, J., Chan, K., Donnelly, C., Haraguchi, N., & Lavopa, A. (2025). *The future of industrialization: Harnessing megatrends for sustainable growth* (UNIDO Policy Brief no. 21). United Nations Industrial Development Organization.

Intarakumnerd, P., Chairatana, P., & Tangchitpiboon, T. (2002). National innovation system in less successful developing countries: the case of Thailand. *Research Policy, 31*(8-9), 1445–1457.

Jacobides, M. G., Cennamo, C., & Gawer, A. (2018). Towards a theory of ecosystems. *Strategic Management Journal, 39*(8), 2255–2276.

Juhasz, R., Lane, N. J., & Rodrik, D. (2023). *The new economics of industrial policy* (NBER Working Paper 31538). https://doi.org/10.3386/w31538

Lazonick, W., & Mazzucato, M. (2013). The risk-reward nexus in the innovation-inequality relationship: Who takes the risks? Who gets the rewards? *Industrial and Corporate Change, 22*(4), 1093–1128.

Leutert, W. (2021). Innovation through iteration: Policy feedback loops in China's economic reform. *World Development, 138*, 105173.

Mazzucato, M. (2013). *The entrepreneurial state: Debunking public vs. private sector myths.* Anthem press.

Mazzucato, M. (2018). Mission-oriented innovation policies: challenges and opportunities. *Industrial and Corporate Change, 27*(5), 803–815.

Metcalfe, J. S. (1995). Technology systems and technology policy in an evolutionary framework. *Cambridge Journal of Economics, 19*, 25–46.

Millot, V., & Rawdanowicz, L. (2024). *The return of industrial policies: Policy considerations in the current context* (OECD Economic Policy Papers No. 34). OECD Publishing.

Mukherjee, I., Coban, M. K., & Bali, A. Z. (2021). Policy capacities and effective policy design: A review. *Policy Sciences, 54*, 243–268.

OECD. (2018). *OECD DAC blended finance principles: For unlocking commercial finance for the sustainable development goals, best practices in development co-operation.* OECD Publishing.

OECD. (2019). *Declaration on public sector innovation* (OECD/LEGAL/0450). OECD.

Quan, X., Xiao, H., Ji, Q., & Zhang, J. (2021). Can innovative knowledge management platforms lead to corporate innovation? Evidence from academician workstations in China. *Journal of Knowledge Management, 25*(1), 117–135.

Radosevic, S., Kanellou, D., & Tsekouras, G. (2023). The experimentation-accountability trade-off in innovation and industrial policy: Are learning networks the solution? *Science and Public Policy, 50*(4), 655–669.

Reike, D., Hekkert, M. P., & Negro, S. O. (2023). Understanding circular economy transitions. The case of circular textiles. *Business Strategy and the Environment, 32*(3), 1032–1058.

Ritala, P. (2024). Grand challenges and platform ecosystems: Scaling solutions for wicked ecological and societal problems. *Journal of Product Innovation Management, 41*(2), 168–183.

Rodrik, D. (2007). *One economics, many recipes: Globalisation, institutions and economic growth.* Princeton University Press.

Schot, J., & Steinmueller, W. E. (2018). Three frames for innovation policy: R&D, systems of innovation and transformative change. *Research Policy, 47*(9), 1554–1567.

Sewerin, S., Beland, D., & Cashore, B. (2020). Designing policy for the long term: Agency, policy feedback and policy change. *Policy Sciences, 53*, 243–252.

Shih, W. C. (2023, September–October). The new era of industrial policy is here. *Harvard Business Review.*

Sobota, V. C. M., Wiarda, M., Coenen, T. B. J., & Ortt, J. R. (2025). How can platform ecosystems support mission-specific innovation systems? In *Proceedings of the 58th Hawaii International Conference on System Sciences* (pp. 6236–6246). HICSS.

Stojcic, N. (2024). Innovation failure, training for innovative activities and public support for innovation: Multi-annual evidence from emerging European innovation systems. *Research Policy, 53*(8), 105059.

Stojcic, N., & Aralica, Z. (2018). (De)industrialization and lessons for industrial policy in Central and Eastern Europe. *Post-Communist Economies, 30*(6), 713–734.

Stojcic, N., Srhoj, S., & Coad, A. (2020). Innovation procurement as capability-building: Evaluating innovation policies in eight Central and Eastern European countries. *European Economic Review, 121*, 103330.

Terzi, A., Singh, A., & Sherwood, M. (2022). *Industrial policy for the 21st century: Lessons from the past* (European Commission Discussion Paper 157). European Commission.

Tung, R. L., Zander, I., & Fang, T. (2023). The tech cold war, the multipolarization of the world economy, and IB research. *International Business Review, 32*(6), 102195.

van Dam, A., & Frenken, K. (2020). *Vertical vs. horizontal policy in a capabilities model of economic development* (Utrecht University Papers in Evolutionary Economic Geography 2037). University of Utrecht.

Wiarda, M., Janssen, M. J., Coenen, T. B. J., & Doorn, N. (2024). Responsible mission governance: An integrative framework and research agenda. *Environmental Innovation and Societal Transitions, 50*, 100820.

Chapter 8
Inclusive Innovation and a Participatory Future

The future is already here, it's just not evenly distributed.
(William Gibson)

Abstract Innovation is too often imagined as the work of elite firms, star scientists and cutting-edge labs. Yet real transformation depends on whether societies can make innovation inclusive, whether the benefits extend beyond narrow groups to reach workers, small firms and marginalised communities. This chapter explores how inclusivity shapes not only the outcomes of innovation but also its direction. It looks at experiments in participatory foresight, grassroots initiatives and citizen engagement that challenge the top-down model of technological change. At the same time, it highlights the risks of exclusionary dynamics that concentrate power, widen inequalities, and leave many on the margins of progress. By examining both pitfalls and possibilities, the chapter argues that inclusive innovation is not a luxury but a necessity if emerging economies are to build systems that are resilient, legitimate and capable of delivering futures shared by the many, not just the few.

8.1 Introduction

For years, innovation policy has been driven by the pursuit of excellence. National strategies have channelled resources into high-tech sectors, elite research institutions and globally competitive start-ups. The underlying logic was that by supporting the best, countries would increase productivity, drive growth and gain international recognition. Excellence would lead to spillover effects, and innovation would ultimately benefit the entire economy and society. In practice, however, this model has led to mixed results. Innovation flourishes in selected regions, usually in capital cities or metropolitan centres, while rural, peripheral and historically disadvantaged areas remain underserved (Ludwig & Macnaghten, 2020; Peddi et al., 2023). Certain individuals have benefited disproportionately, while others have been systematically excluded. At the same time, increasing public investment in research has not always led to greater public trust. Communities face digital divides, small firms are excluded from innovation ecosystems and social needs are often neglected. The promise of

N. Stojčić, *Elusive Innovation*, Applied Innovation and Technology Management,
https://doi.org/10.1007/978-3-032-14900-8_8

inclusive prosperity has not materialised for many (Chataway et al., 2014; Opola et al., 2021).

This chapter starts from a simple but urgent premise that innovation without inclusion is incomplete (Casadella & Tahi, 2025). It may bring efficiency or international competitiveness, but it lacks legitimacy, resilience and equity. A system that always privileges the same actors, regions and priorities risks deepening inequality and undermining public support. In today's world of polycrises, polarisation and rapidly changing technological landscapes, innovation needs to be reimagined as a participatory process (Opola et al., 2021; Planes-Satorra & Paunov, 2017). Inclusion is not only about increasing diversity at the margins, but also about changing the way innovation is defined, who is allowed to participate, whose knowledge is valued and which problems are prioritised. The challenge is not just to widen access to existing innovation systems, but to democratise them to ensure that the tools, institutions and incentives of innovation work for a wider group of people, places and purposes. This chapter explores what inclusive innovation looks like in practice and why it is essential for the future of equitable development.

When innovation is exclusive, it is not only inequitable but also inefficient. By sidelining rural entrepreneurs, frontline civil servants, informal workers and grassroots organisers, innovation systems exclude a vast reservoir of knowledge and creativity (Danse et al., 2020; Planes-Satorra & Paunov, 2017). These actors often have critical, situated knowledge that is never incorporated into research agendas, digital platforms or policy conversations. Spatial exclusion exacerbates this inefficiency (Lee, 2025). In many emerging economies, national innovation capacity is overly concentrated in capital cities with R&D funding, start-up incubators and digital infrastructure flowing disproportionately to urban centres, leaving peripheral areas underfunded despite their rich environmental and cultural capital. Such spatial centralisation narrows the geography of opportunity and misses opportunities for more decentralised and place-based innovation (Barca et al., 2012). The result is a system that not only neglects large parts of society, but also weakens its own adaptability, diversity and reach, thereby missing the chance to utilise innovation as a genuine national development force.

Social and epistemic marginalisation further distort the priorities of innovation systems (Fricker, 2007; Kidd et al., 2017; Peddi et al., 2023). When decision-makers and technologists come from similar backgrounds, certain problems dominate agendas while others are neglected. Solutions emerge in contexts with existing infrastructure, such as urban mobility apps in well-connected cities, while rural or underserved regions remain invisible to innovators. Furthermore, there is a persistent devaluation of non-formal knowledge. Indigenous practices, tacit know-how and community-led experimentation are often dismissed in favour of codified science and proprietary metrics. This leads to "innovation gaps", i.e. places or social contexts where urgent needs exist but are ignored because the people who live in these realities are excluded from the systems that are supposed to create solutions. By failing to recognise and integrate these different forms of knowledge and needs, innovation systems perpetuate inequity, hinder resilience and fall short of their transformative potential.

In many innovation strategies, inclusion is treated as a peripheral gesture, an isolated pilot project for women entrepreneurs, a one-off regional initiative or a diversity tick box on funding applications. While these efforts are valuable, they do not constitute a systemic approach. Inclusion must not be seen as an afterthought or a separate goal, but as a centrepiece of the innovation process itself (Klingler-Vidra et al., 2022). Inclusive systems are not only fairer, but also smarter. They utilise a broader range of perspectives, respond more effectively to real-world challenges and are more resilient when faced with uncertainty. They are able to recognise emerging problems early on, interpret needs more accurately and jointly develop solutions that work across social and regional boundaries. In short, inclusion increases both the relevance and performance of innovation systems, making them more responsive and legitimate, especially when it comes to managing complex societal changes such as climate change, digital transformation or healthcare emergencies.

Beyond improving performance, inclusion also strengthens the democratic legitimacy of innovation (Carayannis & Campbell, 2012; Schillo & Robinson, 2017; von Hippel, 2005). When communities are truly involved in shaping the development, use and management of technologies, outcomes are more equitable and public trust grows. People are more willing to support innovation when they see themselves reflected in the process and outcomes. Conversely, exclusion undermines this trust. The hesitant attitude towards vaccines, public resistance to AI or protests against infrastructure sites are often not an expression of ignorance, but of the feeling of being excluded from decisions that affect daily life. Major international organisations such as the OECD, UNDP and the European Commission have recognised this and made inclusive innovation a strategic priority. However, operationalising this concept remains a challenge. There is no standardised model or metric. Policymakers and institutions are often unclear about what inclusive innovation means in practice, how it can be embedded in institutional routines or how inclusion can be harmonised with other policy objectives.

This chapter explores how innovation systems can become more inclusive, not only by widening access, but also by redistributing power and reshaping the questions we ask. Who gets to be an innovator? Is innovation reserved for those with degrees, patents and venture capital, or can carers, community organisers and informal workers also be recognised for their problem-solving skills? Whose problems drive the innovation agenda? Is the focus on optimising services for those who are already connected and privileged, or on the unmet needs of marginalised communities? Who will ultimately benefit from innovation and how will the risks and rewards be distributed? These are not rhetorical questions, nor can they be answered by superficial inclusion efforts or adjustments to performance indicators. They require a fundamental rethinking of the way innovation systems are conceptualised, managed and evaluated. This chapter argues that inclusion is not just a question of access, but also a question of voice, agency and equity. It is about envisioning innovation that reflects and serves the full diversity of society.

The chapter is organised into six interconnected parts, each of which explores how innovation systems can be made more inclusive and participatory. First, it identifies the different dimensions of exclusion, geographical, social, epistemic and institutional that determine who is allowed to innovate and who benefits from innovation. These exclusions are not accidental, but are embedded in structures, policies and practices that systematically overlook certain people, places and forms of knowledge. The chapter then introduces the core concepts of inclusive innovation and clarifies how it differs from related concepts such as social innovation, grassroots innovation or impact investing. While these approaches often focus on specific projects or communities, inclusive innovation seeks systemic change in the way innovation itself is understood and managed.

The chapter then turns to practice and examines how participation can be organised in innovation processes. Through co-design, co-production and citizen participation, inclusion becomes not just a goal, but a method. Next, the chapter examines the concrete tools available to policymakers, including inclusive public procurement, regional development strategies, gender-sensitive innovation programmes and education reforms. A warning is also sounded that inclusion can be co-opted, reduced to symbolic gestures or branding exercises that do little to challenge existing power dynamics. In its final section, the chapter argues that inclusion must go beyond access to agency enabling people to shape not only innovations but the systems that produce them. Inclusive innovation is not a barrier to excellence. It is the foundation of an innovation system that is smarter, more just and ultimately more sustainable.

8.2 Dimensions of Exclusion in Innovation Systems

Innovation is often celebrated as an open, flexible and inherently inclusive field in which ideas come from everywhere and everyone can participate. However, this optimistic view masks a more complex reality. Exclusion is built into the structures, processes and norms of most innovation systems. This exclusion is rarely overt. It is hidden in everyday decisions about who receives R&D funding, which networks are tapped for expertise, what language is used in application forms and whose experience is considered "relevant". These seemingly insignificant decisions accumulate into broader patterns that consistently privilege certain actors, usually urban, well-resourced and already networked, while marginalising others. As a result, entire communities, regions and forms of knowledge are routinely excluded from innovation processes. This section examines these overlapping dimensions of exclusion and argues that they are not incidental to innovation, but constitutive of it. Without a direct engagement with these dynamics, inclusive innovation runs the risk of remaining a rhetorical endeavour rather than a systemic change that is well intentioned but limited in its impact.

Spatial exclusion is perhaps the most visible and enduring form of inequality in innovation systems (Kemeny et al., 2025; Planes-Satorra & Paunov, 2017). While national strategies often speak of innovation ecosystems in the plural, in practice funding, infrastructure and decision-making tend to be concentrated in capital cities and a handful of large urban centres (Roper & Jibril, 2024). Most incubators, accelerators, technology parks and digital platforms as well as the headquarters of national innovation agencies are located in these centres. This centralisation not only means that rural or peripheral regions are excluded from critical resources, but also that they are left out of the agenda-setting process. Innovators in secondary cities or rural areas often lack access to policy networks, visibility or legitimacy to apply for support. Regional governments are often treated as administrative implementers rather than policy co-creators. As a result, place-based potential, characterised by particular environmental, industrial and cultural assets, remains untapped, reinforcing a cycle in which only a few areas are seen as "innovative", while others are merely seen as recipients of intervention from above.

This structural imbalance exists even in contexts where place-based innovation has been officially recognised. For example, smart specialisation strategies (S3) have been introduced across the European Union to promote regional innovation through tailor-made strategies. However, in many Central and Eastern European countries, the implementation of S3 has become a bureaucratic fulfilment obligation that has nothing to do with genuine regional priorities or capabilities. Without a targeted spatial planning policy and stronger regional innovation governance, these ecosystems remain underfunded and politically marginalised. Spatial marginalisation is not just inefficient, it is also wasteful. It limits the national knowledge base and innovation capacity by ignoring areas with untapped potential. A decentralised, regionally anchored approach to innovation policy would not only promote equality of opportunity but also open up multiple pathways to change based on local strengths, needs and aspirations.

Innovation systems are not immune to the broader social inequalities that characterise opportunity and recognition (Bakker & McMullen, 2023; OECD/European Commission, 2023). Gender, ethnicity, socio-economic status, disability and migrant background all influence who is seen as a legitimate innovator. Despite decades of effort, women remain systematically underrepresented in science, technology and entrepreneurship. In 2024, only 9.37% of patent applications to the European Patent Office included a female inventor (European Commission, 2024). The barriers have nothing to do with skills, but with the structure of entrenched mentoring roles, gendered assessment criteria, limited access to mentoring and persistent cultural norms. In many emerging economies, these problems are exacerbated by weak institutional support and limited resources. Marginalised groups often face a double exclusion. They are ignored as participants in innovation systems and undervalued as holders of relevant knowledge and solutions. This invisibility reinforces a prevailing model of innovation that privileges formality, technicality and elite networks.

Young people are also rhetorically celebrated as the "future of innovation" but structurally excluded by rigid funding and regulatory systems (Bastien & Holmarsdottir, 2017; Williams, 2025). Public funding programmes often require formal incorporation, demonstrable revenue or co-funding, effectively sidelining young people with creative ideas but limited institutional backing. This contradiction, praising youth while denying them access, stifles the renewal of innovation systems and deepens the generational divide (Partanen et al., 2025). At the same time, the lack of inclusive structures means that many grassroots innovations go unrecognised. These forms of exclusion weaken the system by filtering out ideas that emerge from lived experience, cultural diversity or non-traditional knowledge. Innovation diversity is not just about fairness, but also about resilience, adaptability and relevance. If only a small part of society is allowed to innovate, the pool of ideas becomes homogeneous, blind spots increase and legitimacy diminishes. Truly inclusive innovation means dismantling the institutional philtres that determine who is seen, heard and funded.

Epistemic exclusion is another of the pervasive and less recognised barriers in innovation systems. It determines whose knowledge is seen as credible, whose expertise is honoured and which ideas are considered worthy of investment (Boogard, 2021; Ottinger, 2023). In many countries, innovation is still narrowly defined through the lens of high technology, formal research and market-driven outcomes. Community knowledge, tacit skills, traditional practices and local experimentation often do not fall within these parameters. However, these alternative forms of knowledge are often better adapted to local conditions, based on experience and better geared towards long-term sustainability. In agriculture, for example, smallholder farmers have long developed seed varieties, pest control methods and land management practices that are adapted to their environment, but this knowledge is often ignored in favour of laboratory-based, technology-heavy innovations. The same dynamic applies to healthcare, where informal providers in underserved areas develop practical coping strategies that rarely appear in policy frameworks or funding appeals.

This hierarchy of knowledge reproduces inequalities by privileging technical expertise and sidelining the contributions of those closest to the problems the innovation is intended to solve. Even promising discourses such as "frugal innovation" are often adopted without changing the underlying power dynamics. Grassroots solutions are praised rhetorically but remain structurally excluded from decision-making, funding or strategic influence. In some emerging innovation systems, there are efforts to formalise and support local innovation, but the prevailing global narratives still link innovation to patents, intellectual property and venture capital. Reversing epistemic exclusion requires more than symbolic gestures. It requires a structural change in the way knowledge is valued and who is allowed to generate, validate and implement it. This includes a rethink of selection panels, assessment criteria and standards of evidence. A more inclusive system must recognise that knowledge is not linear or singular, but plural, context-bound and co-produced. Accepting this complexity does not mean a dilution of excellence, but a redefinition of relevance.

Institutional exclusion determines who can influence the rules, priorities and incentives of innovation systems. As noted by Acemoglu and Robinson (2012), inclusive institutions drive economic and political progress. While policy purports to serve the public, the structures that design and guide it often lack meaningful input from those who are most affected. Ministries, national councils and innovation agencies tend to be dominated by representatives of established firms, elite universities and metropolitan institutions. Small and medium-sized enterprises, local governments, civil society organisations and marginalised communities, on the other hand, are excluded. Consultations, when they do take place, are often rushed, opaque or symbolic and invite feedback without having any real influence on decisions. This leads to a policy that reflects the interests and logic of insiders and reinforces an already narrow and exclusive innovation system.

This exclusion leads to inertia. Programmes are designed for actors who already have experience in dealing with bureaucracy, i.e. those who can write competitive applications, report on KPIs and speak the language of impact and scalability. In contrast, innovators from the community or grassroots groups have a hard time gaining support or influencing priorities. To change this dynamic, participation needs to be embedded in all phases of governance, from agenda setting to evaluation. Mechanisms such as participatory foresight, citizens' juries and regional innovation forums offer practical ways to bring in different perspectives. Cities such as Barcelona and Cape Town have already experimented with such approaches, while Belgian regions have piloted inclusive assemblies on digital policy. But for these efforts to last, they need to go beyond pilot status. Inclusion must become a structural principle, not an occasional project. Only then can innovation systems truly reflect and serve the society they are meant to change.

Exclusion in innovation systems is not accidental, but systemic. It reflects the way innovation has long been conceptualised, as a pursuit of excellence narrowly defined by technological progress, commercial viability and global competitiveness. This view shapes institutions, incentives and indicators in a way that systematically marginalises certain regions, groups and fields of knowledge. The result is not a few outliers who fall through the cracks, but structural patterns of exclusion that are reproduced over time. The solution to this problem cannot be achieved through isolated programmes, token consultations or rhetorical references to diversity. It requires a fundamental rethinking of what innovation is, what purposes it serves and to whom it is accountable. This does not mean sacrificing ambition, quality or competitiveness. It means broadening the definition of excellence to include inclusivity, contextual relevance and social accountability. It also means understanding that competitiveness without inclusion is ultimately fragile and that inclusion without agency is symbolic at best. Real change starts with addressing exclusion as a systemic challenge.

Exclusion in innovation systems is not a glitch, but a persistent, multidimensional reality that determines who is allowed to innovate, what knowledge counts and which future is prioritised. It limits opportunities, wastes talent and restricts the imagination of what innovation can achieve. But this exclusion is not an immutable law. It can be named, challenged and ultimately reshaped. This requires more than goodwill; it requires a rethink of innovation policy and system design. Inclusion can no longer be an afterthought or an add-on, but must become a fundamental principle. The next section presents inclusive innovation as a strategic framework, not just as a moral imperative or development policy slogan, but as a lens to make innovation systems more effective, adaptive and equitable. It explores how to innovate with and for those who have long been marginalised, and how to embed inclusion not only in the outcomes but also in the architecture of the system itself.

8.3 Concepts and Principles for Inclusive Innovation

"Innovation for whom?" This deceptively simple question is at the centre of inclusive innovation. Traditional innovation policy has long assumed that benefits trickle down, that market mechanisms reward good ideas fairly and that progress is broadly shared. However, it has been shown that exclusion is not an anomaly, but that it is built into the way innovation systems work. Various approaches have emerged in response (Mortazavi et al., 2021): grassroots innovation (Dana et al., 2021; Hossain, 2016; UNDP, 2021), social innovation (Altuna et al., 2015; Satalkina & Steiner, 2022), pro-poor innovation (Meetei et al., 2025; Stott & Tracey, 2018) or frugal innovation (Albert, 2022; De Marchi et al., 2022; Knorringa et al., 2016), all of which seek to rebalance the system. More recently, the concept of inclusive innovation has gained traction as a more holistic framework. It goes beyond specific programmes or sectors and asks deeper questions about participation, relevance and equity. In this section, the concept of inclusive innovation is not understood as a rebranding, but as a rethinking. It explores how inclusive innovation challenges prevailing norms about who is allowed to innovate, which problems are worthy of attention, and how the value created through innovation is distributed socially, spatially and institutionally.

Inclusive innovation is often seen first as a question of access, ensuring that more women pursue STEM careers, that rural or underserved regions are integrated into innovation systems or that young people have access to entrepreneurship programmes. These are important goals, especially in catch-up contexts where historical imbalances have characterised participation in innovation. However, if access efforts focus solely on integrating people into existing structures, they risk reinforcing the very systems that excluded them in the first place. Inclusion is about adapting, not changing the framework. When marginalised actors are integrated into systems that were never designed with their circumstances in mind, the result may be more visibility, but not necessarily more agency, equity or impact. True inclusive innovation shifts the focus from access to agency. It asks not just who participates, but how. Following Heeks et al. (2013), we distinguish innovation for the excluded, with the excluded and by the excluded. The first level provides solutions for marginalised groups, the second involves them in the design and implementation, and the third empowers them as primary innovators. Each level is important, but the further we move towards "by", the more likely we are to see innovations that are contextually grounded, socially embedded and systemically transformative. Agency in this context means more than participation; it means the power to define problems, design responses and shape the systems of innovation itself.

Inclusive innovation is not defined by the sector in which it takes place or the technology it utilises, but by its purpose, governance and impact. It begins by addressing problems and focusing on issues that disproportionately affect those typically excluded from mainstream innovation, such as rural health, access to clean water, inclusive mobility or financial services for the unbanked. It is also fundamentally participatory, involving communities not just as passive beneficiaries or test subjects, but as co-creators who set priorities and influence outcomes. Inclusive innovation is contextualised and draws on local culture, knowledge and lived experience rather than relying on externally imposed solutions. It is gender responsive and aims not only to improve material outcomes, but also to redistribute voice and decision-making power. Finally, it is systemic, i.e. it aims to change the structures that determine how innovation is conceived, produced and sustained. Importantly, inclusive innovation does not necessarily originate from the grassroots or take place on a small scale. Large firms, government programmes or cutting-edge technologies can all contribute, as long as they align with these core principles.

Inclusive innovation has conceptual similarities with related terms such as social innovation, frugal innovation and grassroots innovation mentioned above but differs in its systems-level focus and emphasis on structural inclusion. Social innovation focuses on new solutions to social needs such as ageing populations, homelessness or urban resilience and usually emerges from civil society or public sector experiments. While inclusive innovation overlaps with these goals, it goes further by questioning who is allowed to participate in innovation processes and how power and resources are distributed within these processes. Rather than focusing only on socially useful outcomes, inclusive innovation looks at the governance of innovation. It asks whose voices shape agendas, whose knowledge is legitimised and how systems embed or undo exclusion. In this sense, inclusive innovation is not only about developing ethical or impactful technologies, but also about embedding equity and diversity into the structure of innovation policies, processes and institutions.

Frugal and grassroots innovations are also key contributors to the inclusive innovation landscape. Frugal innovation, which often emerges in resource-constrained environments, emphasises cost-effective, efficient and accessible solutions. However, frugality does not automatically equate to inclusivity, as many frugal innovations are driven by market needs or efficiency goals rather than a commitment to equity. Grassroots innovation, on the other hand, encompasses community-driven responses to local challenges that often emerge outside of formal R&D institutions. These efforts are an example of inclusivity in action but may remain disconnected from national policy systems or lack recognition and support. Inclusive innovation embraces the values of both but goes further by calling for structural reforms in the areas of funding, evaluation, coordination and power-sharing. It is not a niche or isolated activity. Rather, it is a lens through which all innovation, whether public or private, high-tech or low-tech, can be examined, critiqued and refocused to serve broader social and territorial inclusion. Inclusive innovation is thus a strategic imperative, not a charitable add-on.

Inclusive innovation is often misinterpreted as developing separate programmes for disadvantaged groups or addressing social problems through one-off projects. This limited view reinforces the very divisions it seeks to bridge. Inclusive innovation is not a byway, but a transformative agenda to reshape the core structures of innovation systems. It requires that inclusion is anchored not just at the margins, but at the centre of the planning, funding, evaluation and governance of innovation. This means rethinking who defines national innovation priorities, what forms of knowledge are considered legitimate, who is eligible for funding and how success is measured. It means that research institutions need to open up to different epistemologies, that funding calls need to be designed to recognise community-led initiatives and that evaluation frameworks need to be introduced that consider equity and responsiveness alongside traditional metrics. Inclusive innovation is therefore not only a social commitment, but also a policy and institutional redesign challenge. It challenges outdated assumptions about merit, value and expertise and offers a more democratic and responsive vision of innovation.

Inclusive innovation is not just a question of equity or efficiency, it is also a powerful driver for better innovation. When more people, perspectives and contexts are actively involved in the innovation process, the results are more resilient, relevant and trustworthy. Inclusion allows innovation systems to draw from a broader range of experiences and knowledge, making them more responsive to real-world challenges and more adaptable to disruption. It increases legitimacy by ensuring that those who are affected by the innovation also help to shape it. Crucially, it fosters creativity by incorporating different ways of thinking, solving and imagining. This is not just theoretical. Pioneering innovations such as oral rehydration therapy, developed using local practices in rural Bangladesh, or mobile money systems such as M-Pesa in Kenya, show how inclusion can be the very source of transformative ideas. In these cases, the innovation did not trickle down to the marginalised areas. They emerged there and reshaped the systems from the ground up.

Building inclusive innovation systems requires not only good intentions, but also a principled approach to the way innovation is structured, supported and evaluated. Five key principles form the basis for this. Firstly, accessibility ensures that innovation resources such as funding, infrastructure and networks are accessible to different stakeholders, including those typically excluded. Second, recognition is about valuing informal, local and tacit forms of innovation that often do not fall under conventional criteria. Third, participation requires that communities are empowered to shape the innovation agenda and not just respond to predetermined challenges. Fourth, responsiveness requires systems that can adapt to evolving social needs rather than sticking to rigid programme templates. And finally, accountability means that success should be measured not only in terms of economic outcomes, but also in terms of equity, empowerment and social well-being. These principles are not boxes to be ticked, but provide guidance that influences funding decisions, institutional design and evaluation criteria. They mean that innovation is no longer exclusive and technocratic, but inclusive and transformative.

Inclusive innovation is not just a policy trend or a rhetorical phrase; it is a strategic and ethical imperative for building innovation systems that are robust, responsive and legitimate. It challenges us to go beyond GDP growth, the number of patents or the valuations of start-ups and instead ask: Who has been excluded and what knowledge, ideas and solutions have been lost as a result? It forces us to rethink whose voices determine progress, whose problems are prioritised and whose future we can imagine. By putting inclusion at the centre of innovation policy, countries can build systems that are not only more equitable, but also more effective in tackling complex societal challenges. The path to inclusive innovation does not end with broader access, but must continue through deeper empowerment and structural change. The next section looks at participation not just as a principle, but as a practise: How co-design, co-production and distributed governance can reshape innovation processes across communities, institutions and power structures.

8.4 Participation as a Method: Co-design, Co-production and Democratic Innovation

Participation is a word that is easily found in mission statements and strategy papers. It signals openness, responsiveness and a commitment to democratic values. In practice, however, participation is often superficial and limited to stakeholder consultation at the end of a process, community surveys to tick a box or advisory boards that have little real power. This section asks: What would it mean to treat participation not as a principle but as a method? Not something you work towards, but something that is embedded in the entire innovation process, from agenda setting and problem definition to design, testing and scaling. When participation becomes a method, it changes the way innovation is done. It questions who is in the lead, how expertise is defined, what counts as success and how risks and rewards are distributed. And it makes innovation not only more legitimate, but also more creative, relevant and resilient.

Most contemporary innovation policies refer to "stakeholder engagement", usually involving established actors such as industry representatives, academic experts and large non-governmental organisations. However, these consultations often take place late in the process and offer only limited opportunities to influence the agenda or design. The structure of participation is predetermined and power remains centralised. Participatory innovation offers a fundamentally different approach by recognising the role of stakeholders not as passive consultees but as active co-creators (Peddi et al., 2023; Planes-Satorra & Paunov, 2017). This means going beyond collecting tokenistic inputs and jointly prioritising, designing interventions and defining outcomes. It requires a shift from informing to co-deciding and from collecting feedback to co-creating. This approach is particularly important when tackling complex societal challenges such as climate adaptation, digital inclusion and health equity, where solutions must be socially legitimised, contextually relevant and democratically supported. In this sense, participation is not a box to be ticked, but a method of governance that democratises innovation and increases its transformative potential.

Co-design begins where innovation all too often misses the definition of the problem (Dubois et al., 2024; Eriksson et al., 2023). In many systems, problems are viewed through a technical, market-driven lens that focuses on efficiency, productivity or cost. This view can obscure deeper societal issues of power, equity and life experience. Co-design challenges this by engaging diverse stakeholders, community members, policymakers, service users and frontline actors in defining the real problem before arriving at solutions. It is about opening up the problem space rather than presupposing it. The UK Design Council has institutionalised this approach through its "Double Diamond" framework, which puts citizens and service users at the heart of public service innovation. Similarly, India's SELCO Foundation has used co-design with off-grid communities to co-create energy solutions that are aligned with real-life needs, solutions that would not come about through the traditional route of research and development. Beyond improving technical suitability, co-design promotes ownership, legitimacy and accountability, all of which are important qualities when innovation intersects with daily life, vulnerability and contested values.

Building on the premise of co-design, which emphasises the opening up of the problem space, co-production goes one step further by involving different actors in the development and implementation of the solutions themselves (Eriksson et al., 2023). This makes innovation a joint endeavour, not only in the prioritisation but also in the implementation of the work. In co-production, participation becomes action. It can take many forms as citizen science projects where communities help collect and analyse environmental or health data, innovation labs that bring together the insights of policymakers, researchers and residents or participatory pilot projects where users test and improve technologies in their everyday lives. Each model redistributes responsibility and integrates knowledge from different sources into the innovation process. Examples from around the world illustrate the power of co-production. In Barcelona, the Digital Commons initiative enabled residents to determine the rules for managing the city's data and who can access it and under what conditions. In Kenya, the Mathare Social Justice Centre worked with residents on informal settlements to document rights violations through participatory mapping and mobile tools, transforming both data and democratic voice. These are not token engagements but acts of co-governance. Co-production requires time, trust and repetitive facilitation, but it delivers solutions that are more legitimate, context sensitive and resilient than those developed through top-down or technocratic approaches.

Extending the logic of co-design and co-production, participatory innovation is not limited to solving current problems but also demands the right to imagine the future. Participatory futures approaches such as foresight exercises and speculative design bring a forward-looking dimension to inclusive innovation and ensure that elites, technocrats or corporate actors do not have a monopoly on long-term visions. They create spaces where communities, activists, youth and other often excluded groups can challenge assumptions, articulate hopes and highlight overlooked risks. Crucially, these are not predictions, but possibilities that allow us to navigate uncertainty together and pluralise the paths of innovation. There are numerous examples of how this has led to a reshaping of narratives and policies. In South Africa, the Human Sciences Research Council has partnered with youth to explore the future of work and education, foregrounding issues such as dignity and cultural continuity that are ignored by mainstream labour models. Meanwhile, speculative design projects, from feminist AI prototypes to Afrofuturist cityscapes, have redefined the boundaries of innovation itself. By visualising alternatives, these processes shake up standard assumptions and open up space for new coalitions and priorities. When embedded in policy-making, participatory futures do not prescribe outcomes but enable democratic negotiations about what counts as progress and for whom.

A growing number of participatory methods are enabling policymakers and innovation experts to embed inclusion not only in rhetoric but in practice. Living labs, for example, allow communities, researchers and companies to develop and test innovations together in the real world. Deliberative assemblies, such as citizens' juries, create structured spaces where diverse populations can discuss complex issues and make policy recommendations. Participatory budgeting allows residents to allocate funds based on collective priorities, including innovation or infrastructure projects. More informal formats such as innovation cafés and storytelling workshops enable the exchange of ideas across social, linguistic and disciplinary boundaries. Even open innovation challenges can become inclusive if the communities themselves define the problems to be tackled. But method alone is not enough. What really matters is intention and structure: Who gets to participate? Who formulates the questions? How are decisions made and what follow-up actions are planned? When done seriously, participatory methods foster trust, institutional learning and long-term commitment. If they are superficial, they risk reinforcing alienation, fuelling cynicism and weakening the legitimacy of innovation systems.

Participation in innovation is not just a normative commitment but offers concrete strategic benefits. When participatory methods are used wisely, they improve four core dimensions of innovation systems. Firstly, they improve relevance, as solutions are better aligned with the realities of different users and communities. Second, they increase responsiveness so that innovation systems can better adapt to changing needs, contexts and feedback. Thirdly, participation fosters resilience, as people are more likely to support and sustain innovations that they have helped to shape. And finally, participation encourages reflection by revealing assumptions, challenging blind spots and revealing new perspectives. These qualities are particularly important in times of uncertainty, such as public health emergencies, climate change or the governance of new technologies, when traditional models of top-down control often falter. In such situations, no single actor has all the answers, and participatory approaches are not only desirable but necessary. They help to build the collective intelligence and trust that innovation systems need to manage complexity and risk.

But participation is never neutral. It is a political act that reshapes the distribution of power and the question of whose votes are considered legitimate. It therefore often encounters resistance from experts who want to protect their authority, from bureaucracies that shy away from complexity or from private actors with entrenched interests. Furthermore, not all participatory processes are empowering. Poorly designed processes can become exploitative, asking communities to contribute time, ideas or legitimacy without resulting in meaningful influence, compensation or follow-up. Worse, failed participation efforts can deepen disillusionment and reinforce the very exclusions they purport to combat. Participation must therefore be institutionalised and linked to clear responsibilities. It must influence not only the outcomes of innovation systems, but also their governance and underlying assumptions. When done well, participation promotes both innovation and democracy. If it is treated as a box-ticking exercise, there is a risk that it becomes a decoration, an event rather than a method, a narrative rather than a practice.

Participation is not a panacea, but it is a powerful method for transforming innovation into a more inclusive, democratic and contextualised process. When done well, it transforms innovation from something that is imposed on communities into something that is designed with them and ultimately driven by them. This participatory turn not only increases the legitimacy of innovation, but also its quality and sustainability, as different perspectives and lived experiences feed into the entire process from problem definition to the development and implementation of solutions. However, for participation to go beyond pilot projects and isolated initiatives, it must be embedded in the structures and routines of innovation systems. This brings us to the next crucial step: public policy. What concrete measures can governments take to ensure that inclusive innovation is not just a mission statement, but a structural reality? The next section looks at the policy instruments, institutional mechanisms and programmatic designs that can turn inclusive innovation from principle into practice.

8.5 Policies for Inclusion: What Governments Can Do

If inclusive innovation is to be more than a theory or a set of aspirational values, it must be embedded in the operational core of public policy. This means going beyond temporary initiatives for marginalised groups or the occasional funding of socially beneficial projects. It requires a redesign of the architecture of innovation systems, a rethinking of who they should serve, how they allocate resources and how they adapt over time. Governments have a central role to play in this change. They are not just regulators or funders, but also shapers of markets, facilitators of different actors, standard setters and guardians of the public interest. With the right policy tools, governments can ensure that inclusion is not an afterthought, but a fundamental element of how innovation works. This section explores how public authorities can promote structural inclusion, focusing on targeted support mechanisms, regional and spatial planning policies, education and skills development, gender-sensitive approaches and the activation of local institutions and civil society actors as key partners in innovation.

One of the first steps towards inclusive innovation is to break down barriers that prevent marginalised actors from participating in the system. These can include small businesses, community-based organisations, informal innovators or people from underrepresented social groups. Funding programmes for innovation often have eligibility criteria, such as co-financing requirements, legal involvement or previous project experience, which favour established actors and systematically exclude newcomers. Application procedures are often complex, jargon-laden and inaccessible to those unfamiliar with institutional procedures. These structural philtres reinforce existing inequalities and limit the diversity of voices shaping innovation agendas. Governments can play a catalytic role by reorganising their funding structures and introducing micro-grants, simplified calls and support for first-time applicants. Giving space to newcomers is not only a matter of fairness but strengthens the resilience and creativity of the whole system by tapping into overlooked ideas and networks.

Concrete policy measures can help close these access gaps. Some governments are experimenting with inclusive tools such as innovation vouchers, challenge-based calls for proposals and support consortia involving non-traditional actors. In Slovenia, for example, regional development agencies are working with municipalities to issue vouchers to support social enterprises in rural areas and help them develop and test ideas. In Colombia, the innovation agency Ruta N has created customised funding streams for women and community-led start-ups, with special coaching and simplified processes. These programmes recognise that not all innovation follows a linear, commercial path and that value also lies in civic, social and grassroots creativity. When this targeted support through coworking spaces, incubators and peer learning platforms is embedded in the development of a broader ecosystem, it can have multiplier effects, allowing inclusive innovation to scale and sustain itself beyond isolated pilot projects.

Spatial inclusion in innovation is not just about individual participation, but also about regions beyond capital cities and dominant tech clusters being recognised as important contributors to innovation ecosystems. All too often, public investment and policy attention is focused on urban centres, while peripheral and rural areas remain underfunded and disconnected. The European Commission's Smart Specialisation (S3) strategies should address this imbalance by aligning regional strengths with innovation funding. However, as mentioned previously, in many Central and Eastern European countries, these strategies have struggled to fulfil their inclusive promise. Rather than fostering genuine regional ownership, S3 processes have often become bureaucratic fulfilment exercises that lack local ownership and capacity. Treating regional actors as implementers rather than agenda setters leads to spatial stagnation rather than spatial dynamism. Inclusion at the territorial level must go beyond rhetoric and be embedded in the way innovation systems are managed, funded and measured across diverse geographies.

Effective spatial strategies require a stronger commitment to place-based innovation (McCann & Soete, 2020; Yan et al., 2024). Governments can improve territorial inclusion by investing in regional innovation platforms that bring together universities, businesses, civil society and public organisations in collaborative arrangements. Instead of imposing project calls from above, they can fund missions that are tailored to local realities, such as sustainable agriculture in mountainous regions or circular economy initiatives in coastal areas. Regional development agencies need to be strengthened not only as intermediaries for the distribution of EU funds, but as proactive system developers. Flexible funding frameworks for locally defined priorities can also help bridge the gap between national policy and regional reality. The aim is to enable regions to innovate in an authentic way, capitalising on their unique capacities and needs.

Skills development is often seen as the gateway to inclusion in innovation systems. The predominant policy response has been to expand STEM education, promote coding bootcamps and invest in digital upskilling. While these measures are valuable, they are only part of the equation. Inclusive innovation requires more than technical expertise, it requires confidence, adaptability and the ability to creatively tackle complex problems. Without a change in institutional culture, even the best-equipped individuals can be excluded from systems that are not tailored to their circumstances. Women returning to work, youth in rural areas, older adults and ethnic minorities need more than just their skills, they need spaces where they are welcomed as equal contributors. Inclusion in this sense is not just about skills, but also about legitimacy and belonging. Removing these softer, often invisible barriers is key to making skills initiatives truly inclusive, rather than reinforcing existing hierarchies in innovation systems.

For skills policies to be truly inclusive, governments need to design interventions that reach beyond the classroom and into the community. Programmes that promote confidence in the digital world, especially among groups that have not had access to it in the past, can be transformative. Portugal's INCoDe.2030 strategy, for example, focuses on promoting digital literacy across all generations and embeds inclusion into national digital transformation goals. Kenya's Ajira Digital initiative provides digital skills training through public universities and youth centres while creating a public online work platform that connects learners in rural areas with paid opportunities. Governments can also expand STEAM approaches that integrate arts and humanities into science and technology education, promoting more diverse thinking and problem solving. Investing in community-based lifelong learning platforms such as libraries or community centres can ensure continued access to skills. Finally, recognising and certifying informal learning, including grassroots innovation, would help to add value to the different ways in which people acquire knowledge. These approaches go beyond employability and promote empowerment and sustainable engagement in innovation ecosystems.

Building inclusive innovation systems requires also the elimination of deep-rooted structural biases, particularly in relation to gender. Even though gender is often rhetorically recognised in policy as a cross-cutting issue, it is largely left out of the design and governance of innovation systems. This is a critical omission. Not only are women underrepresented in STEM subjects, start-ups and intellectual property, they are also often excluded from shaping the agendas that define what counts as innovation. A truly gender-equitable system examines how innovation priorities, funding mechanisms and success metrics are shaped by gender norms. Governments can take concrete steps by applying gender budgeting to science and innovation policy, conducting impact assessments and funding women-led research on under-researched topics such as care, reproductive health and domestic work. Ultimately, gender inclusion not only improves equity, but also the diversity, adaptability and relevance of innovation systems themselves.

Building on the need to tackle structural biases such as gender exclusion in innovation systems, another powerful lever for inclusion lies in harnessing the potential of local institutions and civil society anchors. While national governments often focus on top-down strategies and elite centres, inclusive innovation can and should often come from trusted, mission-driven institutions embedded in communities. Libraries, schools, hospitals, co-operatives and local governments already have the infrastructure, legitimacy and social capital to act as facilitators, experimenters and educators.

They can translate abstract innovation strategies into locally meaningful initiatives, trial solutions directly with users and build digital and creative confidence through accessible training. In the UK, libraries have developed into community technology centres, while in Brazil, local clinics have promoted health innovation at grass-roots level. The South Korean model of "Village Companies" enables public–social partnerships in rural areas. Although these institutions are not usually included in innovation indicators such as patents or R&D intensity, they are important actors in inclusive innovation ecosystems that embed trust, break down barriers and broaden participation from the ground up.

To truly embed inclusion in innovation systems, efforts must go beyond isolated initiatives and become institutional mandates. Relying on temporary pilot projects or the goodwill of a few progressive actors risks vulnerability and inconsistency. Instead, inclusion should be a core principle that is integrated into the structure of innovation governance and reflected in rules, processes and evaluation frameworks. This includes mandating indicators for inclusion in national innovation strategies, linking public funding not only to commercial outcomes but also to equality-oriented outcomes and giving marginalised voices an official seat at the decision-making table. It also means equipping ministries and implementing agencies with the skills and tools they need to design, measure and evaluate inclusion across the policy cycle. Such a shift means moving away from performative gestures, where inclusion is symbolic or temporary, to a structural shift, where it becomes part of the way systems work by default. Only then can inclusion become a permanent and credible part of national innovation agendas.

Governments have the tools to make inclusive innovation a systemic reality not through technological breakthroughs, but through deliberate policy choices, institutional reform and long-term commitment. This means investing in overlooked innovators, enabling regional diversity, broadening the definition of skills and values, addressing gendered power dynamic, and activating trusted local institutions as drivers of innovation. When these actions are aligned, inclusion moves from a peripheral goal to a defining feature of how innovation systems function. Nevertheless, there is a danger that inclusion will be watered down to rhetoric, stripped of its substance and reduced to checklists. Avoiding this requires vigilance by embedding accountability, maintaining commitment and resisting the pressure to go back to business as usual. As innovation systems evolve to meet global challenges, climate, inequality and digital transformation, it is not only morally necessary but also strategically prudent to ensure that they do so inclusively. The next section looks at the pitfalls of performative inclusion and explores how systems can maintain meaningful participation without falling into fatigue or co-optation.

8.6 Avoiding the Pitfalls: When Inclusion Becomes a Buzzword

The term "inclusive innovation" is now widely used in strategies, mission statements and programme brochures by governments and development agencies (Mortazavi et al., 2021; Opola et al., 2021; Planes-Satorra & Paunov, 2017). It signals good intentions, equality, diversity and participation, but all too often remains disconnected from meaningful structural change. When inclusion becomes a slogan rather than a strategy, there is a danger that inertia is masked with the language of change. This section looks at the dangers of superficiality: when inclusion is reduced to optics rather than outcomes, when communities are consulted without influence, or when programmes for "the marginalised" reinforce dependency rather than shifting power. Such practices are not harmless, they create disillusionment, weaken momentum and can deepen the very inequalities they claim to address. True inclusion requires more than representation or branding; it requires new rules, new relationships and sometimes new discomforts. If these are avoided, inclusion becomes a gesture rather than an obligation. To maintain their legitimacy, innovation systems must see inclusion not as an add-on, but as a test of whether they can truly evolve.

One of the most insidious forms of superficial inclusion is tokenism, i.e. the symbolic inclusion of marginalised groups without giving them any meaningful power (Kim & Hyun, 2025). A woman may be included on an innovation panel or a rural NGO may be listed as a "partner" in a major grant application, but these roles often have no bearing on priorities, design or resource allocation. Tokenism serves as a cloak of legitimacy and helps institutions appear progressive while decision-making remains in the hands of incumbent actors. It is particularly damaging because it leads to disappointment: Individuals and communities who are "invited" but not listened to often feel they are being exploited rather than empowered. Tokenism thus undermines both trust and effectiveness and reinforces the very marginalisation it is supposed to combat. The danger is not representation per se, but empty representation, where the existence of difference is confused with the distribution of power. Without structural changes, inclusion remains superficial and ultimately performative.

To move beyond tokenism, institutions need to understand inclusion not as participation in someone else's agenda, but as co-ownership of processes and outcomes. This requires changes in how decisions are made, who has authority and how success is defined. True inclusion means involving underrepresented stakeholders from the earliest stages of policy and programme development, not just seeking feedback after the fact. It also requires a redistribution of concrete power. Communities must be given control over budgets, programme areas or evaluation benchmarks that directly affect them. For example, youth groups could co-manage innovation grants in education; rural communities could lead the design of place-based innovation strategies. It is crucial that these forms of participation are financially secure. Participants need time, training and remuneration to be able to contribute in a meaningful way. Respect, continuity and transparency are equally important. If involvement is ad hoc or superficial, even well-intentioned efforts can backfire. Ultimately, inclusion without power is not inclusion at all. It is window dressing and innovation systems must do more than adorn the status quo.

In addition to the risk of tokenism, another serious challenge is participation fatigue (Chung et al., 2017), where people are repeatedly asked for input but this input is rarely reflected in the outcomes. This form of fatigue arises from the same basic problem: involvement without power. Communities may be invited to consultations, workshops or pilot programmes, only to find that the decisions have already been made, their ideas shelved and the benefits syphoned off elsewhere. In such cases, participation becomes an extractive method of gaining insight or legitimacy without investing in mutual benefit. Over time, this leads to disillusionment. Those who were once keen to get involved become cynical, stop coming or actively resist further participation. This is particularly common in regions where there are many short-lived donor projects or initiatives that lack consistency. To avoid this, we need to move from transactional to relational models of engagement based on transparency, continuity and mutual benefit. Participation needs to be seen as a long-term partnership rather than a ticking of boxes if innovation is to be truly inclusive and empowering.

An even more insidious challenge than tokenism or fatigue is the inclusion trap, where systems invite more diverse participants but fail to adapt their underlying structures, values or norms. Women, rural entrepreneurs or marginalised youth are granted access to innovation programmes, but success is still measured by conventional metrics such as growth rates, pitch competitions, patents or the willingness of investors. This form of inclusion is conditional; it expands the guest list without rearranging the table. The result is a system that appears to be more open but subtly reinforces the same power hierarchies and assumptions. Innovations based on care work, collective ownership, ecological responsibility or community knowledge can be dismissed as irrelevant or not scalable. To avoid this trap, policymakers need to adopt a more pluralistic definition of innovation and value. This means revising evaluation frameworks, funding models and institutional mindsets to allow for different pathways, not just those that fit the prevailing economic logic. True inclusion is not just about who participates. It's about reshaping the rules of the game to welcome different ways of thinking, creating and contributing.

While digital platforms are often hailed as tools of democratisation and inclusion, their actual impact can be much more ambivalent. Although they break down some traditional barriers to access and enable global reach, platforms often reproduce and reinforce existing inequalities. Those with higher digital literacy, better connectivity and social or financial capital tend to benefit disproportionately, while others are left behind. Dominant languages, cultural norms and algorithmic biases further marginalise underrepresented communities. Participation often ends at content creation, with users having no real say in how the platform is managed or how data is used. This creates a system in which innovation appears open, but power remains concentrated. In some contexts, platforms act as unaccountable gatekeepers that influence who receives funding, visibility or legitimacy, often in opaque and exclusionary ways. To prevent this, governments and civil society must push for transparency, ensure accessibility and promote alternative models of ownership and governance. Otherwise, platforms will not bridge the digital divide but perpetuate it.

One of the most worrying risks in the pursuit of inclusive innovation is the appropriation of its language to legitimise unjust or exploitative practises. When inclusion becomes a branding exercise, the veneer of equity can hide deeply problematic policies or technologies. For example, when a facial recognition system is labelled "inclusive" because it recognises different skin colours, the fundamental issues of surveillance, consent and civil liberties are ignored. Similarly, gig platforms can be lauded for "empowering youth" even as they perpetuate unsafe working conditions without social protections. In such cases, the language of participation, diversity or empowerment is strategically deployed to deflect criticism and preserve the status quo. This kind of performative inclusion undermines not only trust, but also the credibility of truly participatory and equity-focused approaches. To prevent this, inclusive innovations must be accompanied by a critical reflexivity that constantly scrutinises who is included, under what conditions and in the service of what goals.

If inclusion is to be more than just rhetoric, it must be treated as a structural imperative rather than a branding exercise. If the language of inclusion is used superficially, it can insulate institutions from deeper introspection and necessary reform. True inclusion means confronting uncomfortable questions about who has the power, whose knowledge counts and what values shape innovation systems. It requires more than symbolic gestures or short-lived initiatives. Instead, inclusion must be substantive, linked to real changes in the distribution of resources and decision-makers. It must be sustainable, embedded in long-term planning rather than dependent on project cycles. It must be accountable, with clear mechanisms for measuring outcomes, and contextualised to reflect the lived realities, histories and priorities of different communities. As this chapter concludes, the ultimate goal is to move from mere access to agency, inviting people into existing systems and reconceptualising innovation itself as a democratic, equitable and pluralistic process.

8.7 Conclusion

For far too long, innovation policy has treated inclusion primarily as a question of access, ensuring that more people can be connected to existing systems. Programmes are expanding connectivity, promoting STEM careers for women, offering workshops for rural entrepreneurship and opening up funding competitions to underrepresented groups. These measures are important, but they often miss the deeper question: Who is in charge in these systems? Inclusion is not just about being there, it's about shaping what happens. It's about influencing priorities, deciding how problems are defined, and determining what success looks like. In this chapter, we have argued for a fundamental shift from access to agency. Agency means the power to shape outcomes, challenge prevailing norms and create space for other values such as justice, sustainability and dignity. True agency also requires rethinking the way innovation is funded, regulated, designed, practised and measured to ensure that inclusion is not an afterthought but embedded in the DNA of innovation systems.

This reorientation is particularly important for catching-up and emerging economies where innovation systems are still being built. These countries have a unique opportunity to avoid simply copying exclusionary models from other countries. Instead, they can build systems that are inclusive by default, rooted in local realities and globally networked. Such systems can recognise and support diverse innovation practices, from grassroots problem solving to community-based entrepreneurship. In more advanced economies, where innovation is often more institutionalised, inclusion takes on a different urgency. Here, it is about growing public scepticism, democratic deficits and the alienation caused by top-down technological change. Inclusion in these contexts is not only important for equity, but also for resilience, helping societies to adapt to change, rebuild trust and ensure that innovation serves collective rather than narrow interests.

Of course, moving from rhetoric to real reform is far from easy. Institutional inertia, entrenched power dynamics and performative gestures often stand in the way. Building inclusive innovation systems requires more than just new policies, but also political will, new alliances and persistent effort. It also requires a willingness to face discomfort, challenge dominant narratives and be mindful of the risks of co-optation. But the rewards are profound: a more legitimate, responsive and ultimately more creative innovation ecosystem. Inclusion is not a barrier to performance, but a driver of relevance and adaptability. In the final chapter of this book, we broaden the perspective even further and ask: How can innovation be managed in a time characterised by uncertainty, crisis and complexity? Ultimately, inclusion is more than a moral claim; it is a survival strategy for thriving in a turbulent world.

References

Acemoglu, D., & Robinson, J. A. (2012). *Why nations fail: The origins of power, prosperity and poverty*. Crown Business.

Albert, M. (2022). Assessing the sustainability impacts of frugal innovation — A literature review. *Journal of Cleaner Production, 365*, 132754.

Altuna, N., Contri, A. M., Dell'Era, C., Frattini, F., & Maccarrone, P. (2015). Managing social innovation in for-profit organizations: the case of Intesa Sanpaolo. *European Journal of Innovation Management, 18*(2), 258–280.

Bakker, R. M., & McMullen, J. S. (2023). Inclusive entrepreneurship: A call for a shared theoretical conversation about unconventional entrepreneurs. *Journal of Business Venturing, 38*(1), 106268.

Barca, F., McCann, P., & Rodriguez-Pose, A. (2012). The case for regional development intervention: Place-based versus place-neutral approaches. *Journal of Regional Science, 52*(1), 134–152.

Bastien, S., & Holmarsdottir, H. B. (2017). *Youth as architects of social change: Global efforts to advance youth-driven innovation*. Springer.

Boogard, B. K. (2021). Epistemic injustice in agricultural development: Critical reflections on a livestock development project in rural Mozambique. *Knowledge Management for Development Journal, 16*(1), 28–54.

Carayannis, E. G., & Campbell, D. F. J. (2012). *Mode 3 knowledge production in quadruple helix innovation systems*. Springer.

Casadella, V., & Tahi, S. (2025). Inclusive national innovation systems: Rethinking institutions in the light of inclusion imperatives. Journal of Institutional. *Economics, 21.*

Chataway, J., Hanlin, R., & Kaplinsky, R. (2014). Inclusive innovation: An architecture for policy development. *Innovation and Development, 4*(1), 33–54.

Chung, G. H., Choi, J. N., & Du, J. (2017). Tired of innovations? Learned helplessness and fatigue in the context of continuous streams of innovation implementation. *Journal of Organizational Behavior, 38*, 1130–1148.

Dana, L.-P., Gurau, C., Hoy, F., Ramadani, V., & Todd, A. (2021). Success factors and challenges of grassroots innovations: Learning from failure. *Technological Forecasting & Social Change, 164.*

Danse, M., Klerkx, L., Reintjes, J., Rabbinge, R., & Leeuwis, C. (2020). Unravelling inclusive business models for achieving food and nutrition security in BOP markets. *Global Food Security, 24.*

De Marchi, V., Pineda-Escobar, M. A., Howell, R., Verheij, M., & Knorringa, P. (2022). Frugal innovation and sustainability outcomes: Findings from a systematic literature review. *European Journal of Innovation Management, 25*(6), 984–1007.

Dubois, L.-E., Le Masson, P., & Weil, B. (2024). That was fun, now what?: Modelizing knowledge dynamics to explain co-design's shortcomings. *Design Studies, 95.*

Eriksson, E., Williams, S., & Hellstrom, A. (2023). Dis/value in co-production, co-design and co-innovation for individuals, groups and society. *Public Money & Management, 43*(1), 17–25.

European Commission. (2024). *She Figures 24*. European Commission.

Fricker, M. (2007). *Epistemic injustice: Power and the ethics of knowing*. Oxford University Press.

Heeks, R., Amalia, M., Kintu, R. & Shah, N. (2013). *Inclusive innovation: Definition, conceptualization and future research priorities* (Development Informatics Working Paper no. 53). SSRN.

Hossain, M. (2016). Grassroots innovations: A systematic review of two decades of research. *Journal of Cleaner Production, 137*, 973–981.

Kemeny, T., Petralia, S., & Storper, M. (2025). Disruptive innovation and spatial inequality. *Regional Studies, 59*(1).

Kidd, I., Medina, J., & Pohlhaus, G. (2017). *The Routledge handbook of epistemic injustice*. Routledge.

Kim, T.-S. B., & Hyun, E. (2025). Beyond tokenism: A contingency model of board gender diversity and environmental innovation in Korean and Japanese firms. *Asia Pacific Business Review*, 1–23. Online first.

Klingler-Vidra, R., Glennie, A., & Lawrence, C. S. (2022). *Inclusive innovation*. Routledge.

Knorringa, P., Peša, I., Leliveld, A., & van Beers, C. (2016). Frugal innovation and development: Aides or adversaries? *The European Journal of Development Research, 28*, 143–153.

Lee, N. (2025). Inclusive innovation in cities: From buzzword to policy. *Regional Studies, 59*(1), 1–12.

Ludwig, D., & Macnaghten, P. (2020). Traditional ecological knowledge in innovation governance: A framework for responsible and just innovation. *Journal of Responsible Innovation, 7*(1), 26–44.

McCann, P., & Soete, L. (2020). *Place-based innovation for sustainability*. Publications Office of the European Union.

Meetei, L. A., Bhowmick, B., & Barai, P. (2025). Bottom of the pyramid education: Innovation by intermediary organisations and their stakeholders. *Management Decision*. Online First.

Mortazavi, S., Eslami, M. H., Hajikhani, A., & Vaatanen, J. (2021). Mapping inclusive innovation: A bibliometric study and literature review. *Journal of Business Research, 122*, 736–750.

OECD/European Commission. (2023). *The missing entrepreneurs 2023: Policies for inclusive entrepreneurship and self-employment*. OECD Publishing.

Opola, F. O., Klerkx, L., Leeuwis, C., & Kilelu, C. W. (2021). The hybridity of inclusive innovation narratives between theory and practice: A framing analysis. *The European Journal of Development Research, 33*, 626–648.

Ottinger, G. (2023). Responsible epistemic innovation: How combatting epistemic injustice advances responsible innovation (and vice versa). *Journal of Responsible Innovation., 10*(1), 2054306.

Partanen, M., Kettunen, M., & Saarinen, J. (2025). Community inclusion in tourism development: Young people's social innovation propositions for advancing sustainable tourism. *Tourism Recreation Research, 50*(1), 58–73.

Peddi, B., Ludwig, D., & Dessein, J. (2023). Relating inclusive innovations to indigenous and local knowledge: A conceptual framework. *Agriculture and human values., 40*, 395–408.

Planes-Satorra, S. & Paunov, C. (2017). *Inclusive innovation policies: Lessons from international case studies* (OECD Science, Technology and Industry Working Papers, No. 2017/02). OECD Publishing.

Roper, S., & Jibril, H. (2024). Understanding the geographical distribution of innovation in England: density, accessibility and spillover effects. *Regional Studies, 58*(6), 1320–1338.

Satalkina, L., & Steiner, G. (2022). Social innovation: A retrospective perspective. *Minerva, 60*, 567–591.

Schillo, R. S., & Robinson, R. M. (2017). Inclusive innovation in developed countries: The who, what, why and how. *Technology Innovation Management Review, 7*(7), 34–46.

Stott, N., & Tracey, P. (2018). Organizing and innovating in poor places. *Innovation: Management Policy and Practice, 20*(1), 1–17.

UNDP. (2021). *Grassroots innovation: An inclusive path to development*. LSE Capstone report for UNDP Accelerator Labs.

von Hippel, E. (2005). Democratizing innovation: The evolving phenomenon of user innovation. *Journal fur Betriebswirtschaft, 55*(1), 63–78.

Williams, K. S. (2025). Youth-driven innovation, engagement and empowerment. In P. Eriksson, T. Montonen, P.-M. Laine, & A. Hannula (Eds.), *Elgar Encyclopedia of Innovation Management*. Edvard Elgar.

Yan, S., You, L., Growe, A., & Wang, Q. (2024). Propositions for place-based policies in making regional innovation systems. Evidence from six high-tech industrial development zones in China. *Cities, 154*, 105322.

Chapter 9
Governing Innovation in the Age of Uncertainty

The present is theirs; the future, for which I really worked, is mine. (Nikola Tesla)

Abstract The world of innovation is no longer shaped by steady progress but by turbulence. Financial, environmental, geopolitical and technological crises have made uncertainty the defining condition of our age. This chapter explores what it means to govern innovation when predictability is scarce and shocks are frequent. It examines how traditional governance models, built on stability and linear planning, struggle to adapt to volatility and complexity. In their place, more experimental and adaptive approaches are emerging, policies designed to learn from failure, institutions that prioritise resilience and governance frameworks that seek to balance agility with accountability. Yet these shifts are fraught with tension. Too little structure breeds chaos and too much rigidity stifles creativity. The chapter argues that in times of uncertainty, governing innovation requires not mastery over change but the capacity to navigate it while embracing risk, encouraging experimentation and building systems that can bend without breaking.

9.1 Introduction

Innovation, once hailed as the engine of boundless progress, is now at a crossroads. Despite an unprecedented abundance of technology, talent and investment, societies feel more fragmented than ever. Institutions that once provided stability are now struggling to respond to fast-moving crises. We live in a world characterised by transitions: ecological, digital, geopolitical and the one of inequality. The COVID-19 pandemic has shattered illusions of preparedness, the energy crisis has exposed fragile global interdependencies and recent rivalries of global powers have shed light on strategic vulnerabilities of countries integrated in global value chains. Meanwhile, artificial intelligence continues to challenge the ethical and legal framework that is supposed to govern it. In this climate of turbulence, a deeper reckoning is taking place. Both citizens and policymakers are beginning to ask themselves: Who really benefits from innovation? Who gets to decide which problems deserve attention? And

N. Stojčić, *Elusive Innovation*, Applied Innovation and Technology Management,
https://doi.org/10.1007/978-3-032-14900-8_9

what kind of future are we building? These questions go to the heart of innovation governance and concern not only how we innovate, but also why, for whom and with what consequences.

In this new era, innovation systems can no longer be judged solely on their contribution to GDP or global competitiveness. They are called upon to tackle major societal challenges, from climate protection and health security to democratic renewal and social cohesion. To do so, they must evolve beyond linear, market-driven models and become more resilient, inclusive and reflective. This is not just a technical adaptation, but a fundamental change in governance. Innovation systems need to become faster without becoming ruthless, strategic without becoming rigid and adaptable without losing direction. They need to strike a balance between ambition and diligence, disruption and equity, and experimentation and trust. In short, they need to be governed differently. This final chapter begins with this premise. It summarises the core arguments of this book and explores the question of what it means to govern innovation in an age characterised not by stability but by volatility. What ethos, institutions and strategies are needed when uncertainty is the only certainty?

For much of the twentieth century, innovation policy was primarily about accelerating technological progress, driving industrial modernisation and improving national competitiveness. This involved instruments such as research and development tax credits, venture capital and science parks, which were often modelled on high-income countries. Success was portrayed as a race to the frontier, where it was assumed that knowledge would spread naturally and capacity would emerge through imitation and integration. But as this book shows, this model no longer reflects the complexities of today's world. Innovation does not simply spread. It is shaped by power relations, institutional readiness and persistent asymmetries between multinational companies and local actors. The catch-up process is fraught with systemic weaknesses, especially in developing countries that lack the institutional and financial buffers of advanced systems. It is not enough to simply adopt existing models. Structural gaps, policy incoherence and market failures make the failure of innovation a systemic risk rather than a temporary setback.

Furthermore, the role of innovation itself is changing. It is no longer about producing more efficient gadgets or slightly improving productivity. Today, innovation must tackle major societal challenges: the climate crisis, the ageing population, the digital transformation and threats to democratic governance. These are not just technical puzzles; they require political negotiations, inclusive processes and new institutional capabilities. Innovation systems that exclude certain communities, regions or forms of knowledge reduce their resilience and legitimacy. Narrow definitions of innovation that focus only on patents, scalability or high-tech R&D overlook alternative models such as grassroots innovation, care-based economies and place-based experimentation. The assumption of linear progress has been replaced by the reality of a polycrisis: multiple, overlapping crises with no single solution. In this environment, innovation must be managed differently. It must become more strategic, more inclusive and more reflexive. The challenge is not only to create innovation, but also to redesign the purpose, structure and governance of innovation systems for an age of uncertainty.

Governing innovation in today's volatile world requires more than a well-stocked policy toolbox; it requires a rethinking of the policy ethos. Traditional tools such as grants, incubators and university–industry partnerships are still valuable, but they are no longer enough to steer innovation through complexity and crisis. What matters now is not only what is funded, but the underlying logic: why we innovate, how we involve different actors, and for what purpose. This chapter argues that innovation governance must go beyond technocratic management and adopt a value-driven, reflexive approach. This means that we need to move from linear planning to anticipatory governance, from narrow efficiency to systemic resilience, from pure expertise to participatory and inclusive models. This requires embracing mission-oriented and place-sensitive strategies and the acceptance that uncertainty cannot always be controlled, only managed. In essence, innovation systems must learn to learn. They must be able to adapt, challenge their assumptions and evolve their direction to respond to the changing needs of society and the shocks of a turbulent century.

The crossroads at which today's innovation systems find themselves is not just a question of technical capability or economic optimisation, it is profoundly existential. We must ask ourselves whether innovation will continue to function according to the logic of extraction, acceleration and exclusion, or whether it can be redirected towards values of solidarity, sustainability and collective action. This book argues that such a reorientation is not only desirable, but essential. Yet it is anything but guaranteed. What the innovation of the future will look like depends on decisions made now by governments setting priorities, by funders incentivising, by researchers setting frameworks, by firms determining strategies and by communities demanding a say. Whether innovation becomes an instrument of collective well-being or reinforces the inequalities of the status quo depends on whether governance is seen as a mechanical optimisation task or as a generative, inclusive and political process of collective design.

In the previous chapters, we have outlined both a diagnosis and a vision for action. The failure of innovation must be understood as systemic, not just technological. Knowledge transfer is not a passive process, but a contested terrain characterised by power asymmetries. Multinational companies need to be managed, not just welcomed. Inclusion is not charity, but a source of resilience and legitimacy. Learning systems, not just delivery mechanisms, are essential for change. Funding must be redirected to public purpose missions, ecosystems must be designed for adaptability, and governance must evolve to become more participatory and trustworthy. This chapter brings these insights together and applies them to the question of governance in uncertain times. It begins with an examination of the nature of contemporary uncertainty, why today's polycrisis renders traditional policy models inadequate, and what kind of new institutional ethos is needed to meet this challenge.

9.2 The Nature of Contemporary Uncertainty

Every innovation is associated with uncertainty. No one can predict which technologies will prevail, how markets will react or what unintended consequences might arise. This has always been the case. But the uncertainty facing innovation systems today is deeper, broader and more entangled than ever before. We are no longer dealing with isolated risks that are neatly modelled and managed through contingency plans. We are in a situation that complexity theorists refer to as a polycrisis, i.e. a state in which multiple systemic risks interact in unpredictable ways, reinforcing each other and cascading on top of each other. Climate breakdown, geopolitical instability, pandemics, technological disruption, the erosion of democracy, each of these factors on its own would pose a major challenge for policymakers. Together, they create an environment of radical uncertainty made of not only unknown outcomes, but also unknown futures. In such a world, innovation systems cannot simply optimise, predict and scale. They must adapt, learn and navigate under conditions of surprise and stress. To do this, we must first understand the nature of contemporary uncertainty and why it challenges the core assumptions of how innovation policy has traditionally been designed.

In policy discourse, the terms "risk" and "uncertainty" are often used interchangeably. But they refer to very different phenomena. Risk means that a number of possible outcomes are known, the probabilities of which can be calculated. Think of a loan default, a product recall or a weather forecast. Risks can be priced, insured and managed. Uncertainty, on the other hand, refers to the space beyond probability calculation, where outcomes are unknown, probabilities are undetermined and surprises are not only possible but likely. It is the difference between a game of roulette and exploring a jungle that no one has mapped. For decades, innovation systems were designed to manage risk. Funding agencies evaluated proposals based on technical maturity and expected return on investment. Venture capitalists hedged their bets across multiple portfolios. Governments used forecasts to evaluate and prioritise sectors. But in a world of rapid feedback loops, technological convergence, environmental fragility and geopolitical volatility, these tools are often inadequate. We no longer navigate risk. We live in uncertainty.

So what makes the present moment different? Several overlapping forces are shaping the terrain on which innovation is taking place. The contemporary landscape is defined by the instability of the planet, putting environmental volatility at the centre of innovation governance. Climate change is no longer an abstract future threat, but a current disruptor that is reshaping economic and social systems alike. Heatwaves damage infrastructure, floods displace communities and changing weather patterns threaten food and energy security. For innovation systems, this means navigating a constantly shifting terrain where assumptions of stability no longer apply. The transition to clean energy is an example of this challenge. It requires not only new technologies, but a comprehensive rethinking of geopolitics, behaviour, infrastructure and equity. Technologies such as solar or hydrogen are embedded in a complex web of dependencies on rare earths, cross-border policy trade-offs and local adaptation requirements. The uncertainty here is multidimensional, environmental, economic and political, and innovation systems must be able to adapt in real time. Static roadmaps and isolated programmes are no longer enough. Governance must evolve to deal with unpredictability and not just optimise efficiency.

This environmental volatility is overlaid by a rapidly changing geopolitical order. The era of relatively open global integration has turned into an era of strategic competition, selective decoupling and techno-nationalism. Innovation, once imagined as a borderless flow of knowledge, is now embroiled in power struggles over chips, data and digital infrastructures. The rivalry between the United States and China, the debates over the regulation of artificial intelligence in the EU and national subsidies for the semiconductor industry reflect a deeper change where science and technology have become instruments of sovereignty and security. For emerging innovation systems, this means both danger and room for manoeuvre. They run the risk of being squeezed between the strategic interests of the major powers or being excluded from global supply chains. However, the realignment also creates space to assert regional autonomy, join forces with alternative blocs or develop niches in areas that are neglected by the dominant players. Innovation policy must therefore recognise these disruptions not only as risks, but also as spaces for strategic positioning, while keeping an eye on their normative implications.

At the same time, the technological frontier itself is converging in a way that increases uncertainty. Artificial intelligence, biotechnology, quantum computing and synthetic biology are not only advancing rapidly, but also colliding with each other, leading to unpredictable interactions and exponential effects. This convergence raises not only technical challenges, but also profound ethical, legal and social dilemmas. In particular, AI is redrawing the boundaries between human and machine intelligence, disrupting labour markets and raising questions about surveillance, bias and governance. Policymakers face a delicate balancing act; they must promote innovation while protecting public values. Institutions of many emerging innovation systems are unprepared for this and are constrained by outdated mandates, fragmented powers or a lack of capacity. Societal fragmentation and the stress of democracy create additional uncertainty. Polarisation, mistrust in science and backlash against perceived elitist goals threaten the legitimacy of innovation initiatives. In many contexts, communities no longer trust that innovation will serve them. This creates a legitimacy gap that traditional top-down approaches cannot close. Governance must therefore address uncertainty not as a technical obstacle, but as a political and cultural condition that requires reflexivity, participation and institutional renewal.

In this new era of deep uncertainty, innovation policy must move beyond linear models of planning and control. Traditional approaches, such as setting targets, building pipelines, allocating funds by sector and monitoring results, are no longer sufficient in a context characterised by volatility and rapid change. What we need are governance systems that are able to anticipate change without assuming predictability, that continuously adapt to changing circumstances and that incorporate different forms of knowledge. It is crucial that we learn not only from successes, but also from failures, friction and feedback. Governance must become reflexive and iterative, based on the realisation that ambiguity is not a temporary obstacle to be removed, but a permanent condition to be navigated. The goal is not to enforce certainty, but to create resilience and responsiveness in all institutions. Innovation systems must be able to think ahead together, engage fully and change course when necessary. The next section looks at anticipatory governance and foresight, tools that are essential for managing innovation in a turbulent world.

9.3 Anticipatory Governance and Strategic Foresight

In a world increasingly characterised by rapid change and overlapping crises, innovation policy can no longer be based on assumptions of linear progress or stable baselines. Extrapolating from the past is often misleading, and waiting until a crisis occurs is economically, socially and politically costly. Governing innovation in the twenty-first century requires a forward-looking orientation that accepts complexity and uncertainty. This is the core premise of anticipatory governance, developing the ability to not only react to disruption, but to imagine and shape a potential future before it fully materialises. It is a shift from reactive to proactive policymaking, from firefighting to shaping the future. Anticipatory governance does not promise security, it rejects it. Instead, it cultivates institutional imagination, strategic flexibility and systemic awareness. It calls on politicians, researchers and citizens alike to think in terms of the possible rather than the inevitable and to view the future as something they can help shape rather than just endure.

Anticipatory governance goes beyond isolated exercises in foresight or scenario planning. It aims to embed future thinking into the very architecture of innovation systems: How policy is made, how investments are prioritised, how regulations evolve and how the public is involved. Strategic foresight is a pillar of this system and provides tools such as horizon scanning, scenario building and trend mapping. However, the real change happens when these tools are institutionalised and linked to budget cycles, embedded in government mandates and used to inform long-term missions or adaptive regulations. Importantly, anticipatory governance is not confined to technical analyses. It is also a normative and participatory practice that answers who envisions the future, whose voices count and whose interests shape the options considered? For anticipatory governance to be meaningful, silos must be broken down, time horizons equalised and a culture of reflexivity promoted. This section examines why this shift is so important for innovation policy and what is needed to move from rhetoric to institutional reality.

Anticipation is a central element of innovation. Yet innovation policy often relies on lagging indicators, such as the number of patents, R&D intensity or the survival rate of start-ups. While these indicators are useful, they reflect what has already happened. They offer only limited guidance for navigating uncertain, rapidly changing futures. In today's world, where climate breakdown, digital disruption, demographic change and political instability are reshaping the innovation landscape, such backward-looking frameworks are increasingly inadequate. Policymakers run the risk of managing innovation systems with the equivalent of a rear-view mirror, which is useful for reflection but dangerous for orientation. Governing innovation in this environment requires a conscious shift from performance monitoring to forward-looking capacity. This means not only measuring what has worked but asking what should work and for whom in possible future contexts. Forward thinking is no longer a luxury. It is a necessity for responsible innovation, especially in catch-up economies where the margin for error is smaller and the cost of late adaptation is higher.

The need for anticipatory governance becomes clear when we examine the recent blind spots that have caught many governments and institutions unprepared. The rapid spread of generative AI, for example, has blown up the regulatory and ethical framework, creating both opportunities and disorientation. Global vaccine supply chains, long taken for granted, buckled under the pressure of a pandemic, despite warnings of the scenario. Heatwaves now regularly disrupt energy infrastructure and reduce labour productivity, yet few innovation systems prioritise climate adaptation technologies. Platforms like TikTok have reshaped education and labour dynamics, while remote working has upended urban planning assumptions without coordinated policy foresight. In each of these cases, foresight tools existed but were marginalised or disconnected from policy levers. The result is reactive governance that attempts to contain risks that could have been anticipated and better managed strategically. Anticipatory governance closes this gap. It integrates foresight into institutional routines, links futures thinking to public priorities and builds the adaptive capacity to respond not only to what is probable, but also to what is plausible, disruptive and not yet imaginable.

Strategic foresight is a powerful set of practices designed to help policymakers, institutions and societies deal with uncertainty. In contrast to traditional forecasting, which is often based on the present, foresight deals with multiple, divergent futures. Techniques such as scenario planning allow stakeholders to imagine radically different worlds, such as those characterised by climate crises, AI revolutions or demographic changes, and consider the impact on today's decisions. Horizon scanning uncovers weak signals and emerging trends that might otherwise be overlooked. Delphi surveys capture the collective intelligence of different expert communities, while backcasting helps to chart a path from a favoured future to the present. Future literacy initiatives, increasingly promoted by UNESCO and other organisations, aim to develop the everyday ability to question assumptions and explore alternatives. These tools not only enrich strategic thinking but also democratise it by inviting more voices into conversations about where we are heading and how we can prepare. Used correctly, they make innovation policy more forward-looking, inclusive and responsive.

Examples from around the world show how foresight can be institutionalised to shape national strategies. Finland's Parliamentary Committee for the Future is a pioneering example that has recently been also embraced by countries such as Lithuania, Philippines, Paraguay or Chile. These bodies regularly conduct foresight exercises and ensure that these are integrated into legislative debates and policy planning. In Singapore, the Centre for Strategic Futures acts as a foresight centre within the government, directly tied to the Prime Minister's office and tasked with identifying long-term challenges and incorporating these into cross-ministerial decision-making. South Africa's Vision 2030, led by the National Planning Commission, utilised participatory foresight methods to engage youth, academics, business and civil society in shaping the country's long-term development agenda. These cases show that foresight is not just about producing reports or trend maps. When embedded as a governance function, it helps to build resilience, align policies across sectors and time horizons, and recognise deep societal values that should guide innovation. The challenge is not only one of technical capacity, but also of political commitment to see the future not as something given to be extrapolated, but as a space of choice, reflection and co-creation.

While strategic foresight provides the tools to explore possible futures, anticipatory governance ensures that these insights are translated into institutional action. This requires embedding foresight at the core of policymaking and linking it to budgetary decisions, regulatory priorities and programme design. Genuine anticipatory governance goes beyond isolated foresight units by promoting coordination across government ministries and integrating long-term thinking into all policy areas. Feedback loops are established to monitor how the future evolves and to adapt policies accordingly, turning innovation systems into learning systems. Regulatory sandboxes and test environments allow experimentation with emerging technologies such as AI, financial technology or mobility before they are fully rolled out. Public involvement becomes key as it ensures that citizens participate and prioritise the development of the future. The European Commission's Joint Research Centre advocates "mainstreaming the future" by including foresight at every stage of the policy cycle, from impact assessment to participatory dialogues. Some governments are now piloting future councils and ethics commissions that work alongside innovation agencies to ensure that long-term societal values are aligned with economic goals.

Despite its growing importance, anticipatory governance faces some persistent challenges that hinder its widespread adoption. A key obstacle is the short-term focus of political cycles, where elected officials favour immediate outcomes over long-term foresight and often view the latter as speculative or politically risky. In addition, institutional silos are a structural barrier. Foresight activities are often confined to planning units and disconnected from core policy functions, resulting in lessons learnt but rarely acted upon. A technocratic bias also undermines inclusivity, as foresight exercises tend to rely heavily on expert input, while community perspectives and non-dominant knowledge systems are sidelined, leading to elite visions of the future. Furthermore, many scenario-building efforts fall into the trap of "scenario paralysis" and produce elaborate reports without actionable results. Finally, in many emerging economies, a lack of institutional capacity and financial resources limits sustained engagement in futures research. Donor-led projects may offer temporary support but often lack continuity and local ownership.

To address persistent barriers, anticipatory governance must become a systemic practice, not an occasional add-on. This requires the integration of foresight into core budgetary and planning cycles to ensure that it informs real decisions and does not remain a peripheral issue. Public officials need to be trained in futures literacy to apply foresight in a meaningful way, while institutions should establish formal functions such as futures units, innovation observatories or resilience commissions to embed anticipatory endeavours. Cross-sector platforms are essential to link foresight with regulation, strategy and investment, enabling learning across silos. Crucially, broader participation of citizens, artists, social scientists and young people will help foster pluralistic and inclusive visions of the future. Real-world examples show that this is possible: Rwanda embeds futures research into district-level planning; Canada's Policy Horizons challenges prevailing policy assumptions through futures research; Tunisia cultivates a grassroots democratic futures community through participatory workshops. These cases show that anticipation is not about prediction, but about preparation, and preparation must be treated as a strategic imperative.

Anticipatory governance is not about accurately predicting the future but about enabling wiser decision-making in the present amidst uncertainty, complexity and constant change. It encourages a shift in the way innovation systems operate away from pure acceleration towards spaces for exploration, learning and adaptation. Instead of reacting passively to disruptions, anticipatory systems actively prepare for them, making management more flexible and responsive. This approach redefines the role of foresight by embedding it as a core capability for navigating volatile environments. As we move forward, attention must shift from the cognitive tools of anticipation to the institutional foundations of resilience. The key question is: What structures, networks and guiding principles enable innovation systems to not only survive shocks, but to adapt and evolve? In a world where disruption is inevitable, resilience must be more than survival. It must be about learning to change and maintaining the ability to shape an uncertain future.

9.4 From Agility to Institutional Resilience

In response to a wave of global disruptions ranging from pandemics to energy crises and geopolitical tensions, governments have increasingly turned to agility as a guiding principle for innovation governance. The term epitomises speed, responsiveness and a willingness to experiment. Public organisations are being encouraged to shed their bureaucratic inertia, create flexible frameworks and embrace the ethos of "failing forward". In the field of innovation, agility is seen as essential to keep pace with new technologies, support fast-moving start-ups and seize fleeting opportunities. It reflects the transition from rigid, top-down planning to dynamic, adaptive policy-making. However, while agility can accelerate processes and enable rapid changes of direction, it remains an incomplete response to systemic uncertainty. Agile systems may be successful in the short term but can prove fragile when confronted with persistent or layered crises. As complexity and the frequency of shocks increase, agility alone is no longer enough and calls for elevation of resilience to a core institutional imperative.

Resilience provides a deeper, more enduring foundation for managing innovation than agility alone. While agility enables movement, resilience ensures continuity, coherence and adaptability under pressure. A resilient innovation system responds quickly, absorbs shocks, learns from disruption and reconfigures itself without losing its purpose or integrity. This is particularly important for emerging economies and fragile institutional frameworks, where vulnerabilities are amplified and the cost of failure is higher. Resilience requires a different orientation from quick fixes to system-wide learning and from ad hoc responses to embedded capabilities. It depends on trust, coordination, institutional memory and the ability to compromise over time. In this context, resilience is not a rhetorical phrase, but a practical design principle. This section explores how innovation systems can cultivate this resilience through robust structures, adaptive norms and targeted capacity building. The aim is not to replace agility, but to anchor it in a more stable and sustainable framework that endures, evolves and supports change through turbulence.

Resilience in the ecological sense refers to the ability of a system to absorb shocks and reorganise itself during change while retaining its core functions, structure and identity. In innovation policy, this concept is equally important. Resilience is the ability of an innovation system to adapt to disruption and continue to create public value despite uncertainty. This is becoming increasingly important as innovation systems are exposed to unpredictable, compounding shocks. A pandemic can paralyse laboratories and change research plans overnight. A war can disrupt supply chains, restrict the exchange of knowledge and drain capital. Extreme climate events can paralyse production, strain digital infrastructure and change demand patterns. Even political upheaval can abruptly dissolve agencies and undo years of strategic planning. In such contexts, survival and continuity do not depend solely on agility or speed. Instead, resilience stems from deep systemic properties such as institutional memory, functional redundancy, diversity of actors and approaches, and strong feedback mechanisms that enable systems to intelligently reorganise and evolve in the face of disruption. Resilience is not a single attribute. It is an emergent property that arises from how institutions, actors and infrastructures are organised.

Resilient innovation systems are not characterised by uniform excellence, but by heterogeneity. When systems rely heavily on a small group of actors, sectors or technologies, they become vulnerable to shocks that disrupt these specific areas. In contrast, resilience grows from a rich diversity of actors, knowledge sources and innovation models. This includes a balance between large firms and SMEs, support for both formal scientific institutions and grassroots experimentation, and the promotion of both technology- and demand-led innovation. In addition, innovation activities need to be spread from a few elite institutions to a broader range of actors in all regions and sectors. Such pluralism can be more complex to coordinate and less comprehensible to funders, but it offers adaptability when established pathways are blocked. A resilient system therefore does not focus all resources on flagship universities or single industry clusters but distributes support across a diverse innovation landscape that enables multiple pathways to problem solving and reduces systemic dependence on a single node.

In an era of efficiency-driven governance, redundancy is often misunderstood as waste. But in resilient innovation systems, redundancy plays an important role as a kind of insurance against failure. It creates buffer zones and fallback options that cushion shocks and enable iterative learning. This can take the form of overlapping mandates between different authorities so that responsibilities do not collapse if one actor fails, or in the form of different funding streams so that a failed funding programme does not derail an entire sector, or in the form of a backup infrastructure for research labs and digital systems. Redundancy is particularly important in emerging economies where reliance on centralised institutions makes systems fragile. A strategic buffer can be achieved by investing in decentralised capacities such as regional hubs, community innovation programmes or grassroots labs that reduce dependence on capital cities or flagship institutions. Such investments make innovation ecosystems less vulnerable and more able to maintain coherence under pressure, even if certain programmes or infrastructures are disrupted or delayed.

Resilient innovation systems are both responsive and self-aware. They have feedback mechanisms that enable learning, correction and further development. Rather than relying solely on retrospective assessments, these systems utilise real-time monitoring, embedded learning teams and iterative assessment tools to detect early signs of stress or underperformance. Reflexivity goes beyond collecting data and fosters a culture that sees learning as an end in itself. For example, innovation agencies can deploy embedded evaluators who work directly with programme teams to support continuous learning, rather than simply reviewing outcomes after the fact. Such practices help systems to change course before failures become systemic. An institutional memory that documents what was tried and why is also critical and allows stakeholders to build on past experiences rather than repeating mistakes. Ultimately, systems with lots of feedback are not only efficient but also adaptable. They are able to recalibrate in response to internal and external signals without losing momentum or direction.

A final set of building blocks focuses on the balance between autonomy and coordination and the role of trusted intermediaries. Institutions in resilient systems need enough autonomy to experiment and adapt, but also enough coordination to contribute to common national or regional missions. This requires clear mandates, legal flexibility and budget systems that allow for iteration. Finland offers a model where agencies such as Business Finland focus on national missions such as the green transition but remain flexible in partnership models and programme instruments. However, resilience is not only found in institutions, but also in networks. Intermediaries such as development agencies, local universities and innovation centres are important links between the public, private and civil sectors. They support vulnerable actors in times of crisis, mediate between national policies and local realities and help maintain continuity in times of disruption. During the COVID-19 crisis, such intermediaries often outperformed the response capacity of central authorities. Healthy, trust-based networks are therefore critical to system-wide resilience.

Building resilience in emerging innovation systems poses particular challenges. Fragile institutions, limited financial resources and unpredictable policy changes make resilience seem like an unaffordable luxury. Many innovation systems in these contexts are already overstretched and struggle to fulfil basic requirements. However, resilience does not require massive new expenditure, but a rethink in administration. It is about developing funding mechanisms that tolerate risk and experimentation and allow failure as part of the learning process. It is about maintaining organisational flexibility to enable adjustments rather than enforcing rigid efficiency. Resilience also means fostering collaboration between public actors and supporting digital and social innovation infrastructures that are rooted in communities. Crucially, it reduces structural dependence on foreign donors or multinational firms for key innovation capacities. In this sense, resilience is not an additional burden, but a smarter way of dealing with uncertainty, a governance approach that favours long-term adaptability over short-term optimisation.

Furthermore, building resilience in this environment depends on cultivating governance capabilities rather than acquiring expensive technologies. This includes investing in foresight, facilitation, systems thinking and adaptive leadership, skills that strengthen the ability of institutions to learn, respond and evolve. These skills are often underestimated but can be developed through targeted training, peer exchange and practical experimentation. Encouragingly, some catching-up countries are already making progress. Rwanda has built flexible digital infrastructures that enabled rapid, decentralised responses during the COVID-19 crisis. Estonia's modular e-governance systems were designed with resilience in mind and allow for iterative upgrades without a complete overhaul. In the Western Balkans, innovation funds in Serbia and North Macedonia are beginning to adopt sandbox approaches and test new policy instruments. These examples show that resilience cannot be imported across the board. Instead, it must be anchored locally and built on an understanding of specific institutional strengths, vulnerabilities and societal needs. The aim is to develop resilience strategies that fit the context and not to imitate models that have been developed elsewhere.

One of the main pitfalls of crisis-driven innovation policy is the tendency to treat resilience as a purely reactive trait, focusing on getting back on its feet quickly rather than questioning whether a return to the previous state is even desirable. True resilience must go beyond first-order adaptation to include second-order learning, i.e. the ability to reflect on and revise the assumptions that shape policy. This requires innovation systems to critically evaluate the indicators they use to measure success, reassess narrow definitions of what counts as "good" innovation and create institutional space for dissenting voices, alternative visions and marginalised perspectives. Without this deep reflexivity, systems can become agile but stagnate and remain trapped in a pattern of short-term fixes that fail to deliver real development. A resilient innovation policy must therefore enable learning not only from failures, but also from the framework conditions that guide decision-making. This ensures that crises become catalysts for change rather than mere disruptions to the status quo.

Agility enables systems to move quickly, but resilience enables them to persist and evolve. Resilience is not limited to institutional design, but is embedded in the relationships between actors, in the narratives that shape policy goals, in the infrastructures that support experimentation and in the everyday routines that enable adaptation. In an era characterised by disruption, the most durable innovation systems will not be those that are merely efficient or technologically advanced. Rather, they will be those that cultivate diversity, foster strong and distributed networks, support reflexive learning and remain anchored in a clear sense of public purpose. These systems are not only better equipped to absorb shocks, but also to use disruption as an opportunity for change. Crucially, resilience is not just a technical capability, but also a social and political one. For this reason, the next section turns to the topic of trust and legitimacy, as no innovation system can thrive without public trust and meaningful civic engagement.

9.5 Trust, Legitimacy and Public Engagement

Even the most technologically advanced innovation system cannot thrive without public trust. Satellites can orbit the earth, quantum computers can perform mind-boggling calculations and vaccines can be developed at unprecedented speeds, but if the institutions behind these breakthroughs are not trusted, if citizens feel unheard or unprotected, the system loses its foundation. Trust is the invisible infrastructure that enables innovation to function and thrive. It weaves together the relationships between scientists and citizens, businesses and regulators, politicians and the public. When this fabric is strong, societies can be resilient in the face of uncertainty, have open debates about risks, make informed compromises and work towards common goals. But when trust wanes, even the most carefully crafted policies are met with resistance, mistrust or rejection. In recent years, these cracks in the trust infrastructure have become more apparent, revealing the vulnerability of innovation systems that fail to invest in legitimacy, inclusiveness and genuine public engagement.

Across the world, trust in public institutions, scientific expertise and innovation systems has steadily eroded, sometimes gradually, sometimes in dramatic collapses. While the causes vary from region to region and culture to culture, the consequences are strikingly similar: vaccine hesitancy even during health crises, public resistance to climate policies, fears of artificial intelligence, rejection of digital ID systems and criticism of innovation funding that benefits elites rather than society. This erosion of trust is not necessarily a rejection of the technology itself, but often a reaction to the opaque processes and unequal power relations that surround its development and deployment. People are increasingly asking: Who decides what gets funded? Whose interests are prioritised? Who bears the risks? When innovation is perceived as an imposition rather than a collective endeavour, or worse, as a mechanism for private gain at the expense of the public, it loses legitimacy. Innovation systems cannot afford to ignore these perceptions without risking public disengagement and resistance.

For many communities, especially those who have faced exclusion or exploitation in the past, the problem is not a rejection of science or progress, but a deep scepticism of the institutions behind it. The erosion of trust stems from the repeated experience of being overlooked, misled or harmed. This makes innovation appear to be a continuation of systemic injustice rather than a solution to common challenges. In this context, trust cannot be reduced to a mere attitude or PR objective. It must be understood as a relationship based on consistent accountability, transparency and mutual respect. Nevertheless, for too long innovation policy has assumed that public support would automatically follow from technological success or economic gain. Public involvement was seen as an afterthought or a communication task, not a fundamental component of innovation policy. This assumption no longer holds. As public scepticism grows, innovation systems must face the reality that legitimacy is not granted, but must be earned through inclusive, participatory and trustworthy processes that reflect the needs and values of diverse publics.

Innovation systems that operate without legitimacy face three interrelated and escalating risks. First, there is policy resistance where even the best-intentioned initiatives such as green transitions, digital platforms or innovation zones can lead to backlash when communities feel excluded or threatened. The Gilets Jaunes protests in France, originally sparked by a fuel tax, show how perceived exclusion from policymaking can trigger widespread unrest. The second point is the loss of social acceptance. When technologies such as AI, biotechnology or new energy systems are introduced without genuine consultation, they are often met with public resistance, delays, reputational damage or even legal and political obstacles. The third point is the erosion of systemic credibility. When innovation is repeatedly associated with increasing inequality, intrusive surveillance or the privatisation of public goods, trust in the system collapses. Citizens begin to see "innovation" as a means of exploitation rather than progress. The ultimate threat is not just resistance, but disengagement, a state where people no longer see innovation as something done by them or for them, and both democratic participation and inclusive progress are at risk.

It is possible to restore trust in innovation systems, but it will take more than clever messaging or institutional rebranding. It requires a fundamental shift in governance away from closed, technocratic models towards open, participatory and accountable approaches. This does not mean that every citizen must be involved in every technical decision. Rather, it means ensuring that those who are affected by innovation have real opportunities to prioritise, understand trade-offs, challenge assumptions, propose alternatives and hold institutions accountable. Participation must be structured, meaningful and sustainable, not symbolic or performative. To build such trust, multiple layers of participation must be created, from citizens' assemblies and community consultations to transparent decision-making processes and open data platforms. Together, these efforts form a broader architecture of legitimacy that strengthens the social contract around innovation. When people feel that they are seen, heard and respected, trust can grow and innovation can move from something that is done for them to something that is done with and for them. Only then can innovation systems claim lasting public legitimacy.

Trust cannot be delegated or outsourced but must be intentionally integrated into the core of institutional practice. This starts with transparency. Institutions must disclose how decisions are made, how funding is allocated and what criteria are used to evaluate success. It also means disclosing who is consulted, what perspectives are gathered, and how these inputs influence outcomes. Responsiveness is equally important. Feedback loops should not only collect concerns, but actively address them. Representation ensures that governance structures such as advisory boards or regulatory councils include voices beyond technocrats and industry elites, especially from the communities most affected by the innovation. Procedural justice strengthens legitimacy by ensuring fair, consistent and inclusive processes. Studies show that even controversial decisions are more likely to be accepted if the processes are perceived as fair. Finally, innovation must align with shared values and demonstrate a commitment to goals such as environmental justice, digital dignity and labour rights. These are not peripheral ideals, they are central to gaining and maintaining public trust.

These principles are already being tested and implemented in various contexts. In Canada, the Public Policy Forum has promoted deliberative processes that bring citizens and experts together to address the ethics of artificial intelligence and data governance, creating space for informed public input. In Spain, regional innovation agencies have used participatory foresight methods to ensure that innovation priorities reflect local values, needs and visions for the future. These and similar examples show that building trust is not a vague ideal, but a concrete practice that can be embedded in the architecture of innovation systems. By creating inclusive spaces, embedding accountability and aligning innovation with the public good, institutions can begin to repair broken relationships and lay the foundation for long-term legitimacy. In doing so, they transform innovation from a source of division into a collective tool for shaping a just and resilient future.

Many public engagement initiatives aim to raise awareness through science communication, exhibitions or education campaigns. While these are important, they are essentially one-sided. They treat citizens as passive recipients of information rather than active co-creators of knowledge. A more transformative approach recognises the public as a source of collective intelligence. People bring lived experiences, contextual insights and ethical perspectives that no expert model or algorithm can fully replicate. Farmers can sense climatic changes before they are captured by data; patients can recognise side effects of drugs that were overlooked in clinical trials just as teachers know which technologies actually work in the classroom. Harnessing this intelligence requires structured spaces for dialogue, co-creation and deliberation, places where different forms of knowledge are respected and integrated. This includes lived experience, tacit understanding and cultural knowledge as well as technical expertise. Instruments such as consultative assemblies, living labs, citizens' forums and participatory budgeting are not simply democratic innovations, but essential instruments for restoring trust and legitimacy in innovation policy and improving policy quality.

Trust in innovation is not only characterised by institutional design or procedural fairness, but also by narratives. The stories we tell about innovation in political discourse, media coverage, education and funding rhetoric shape public understanding and legitimacy. When innovation is portrayed as an elitist competition for patents, a race for dominance or a disruptive force that creates clear winners and losers, it often alienates the very public it is meant to serve. In contrast, narratives that portray innovation as a collective effort to overcome real-world challenges, based on fairness, inclusion and imagination, can foster connectedness and inspire engagement. Governments and innovation agencies must therefore learn to develop and disseminate better stories. These should bridge the gap between science and society, link technology to justice and present experimentation as an act of care, not just calculation. In a time of increasing scepticism, narrative becomes an important tool to restore legitimacy and make innovation feel human, relevant and shared.

In an era characterised by great uncertainty and accelerated change, trust is no longer a soft or secondary issue, but a strategic asset that is as important to innovation systems as infrastructure, funding or skilled talent. Without trust, innovation becomes fragmented, controversial or easily captured by narrow interests. With trust, systems gain the legitimacy, resilience and inclusivity needed to manage complexity and achieve long-term progress. However, trust cannot be imposed from above. It must be earned and cultivated through consistent transparency, meaningful engagement, fair processes and alignment around shared values. It is built slowly, through reciprocity and sustained attention to how innovation impacts people's lives. The conclusion of this chapter is that the way forward is to weave trust into the fabric of innovation policy. The next section summarises the key findings from this book and calls for a new policy ethos that is purpose-driven, reflexive, pluralistic, resilient and accountable. In today's world, shaping the future means earning the public's trust.

9.6 Governing Transformative Innovation: Towards a New Policy Ethos

Throughout this book, we have observed a growing tension within innovation systems. They are tasked with tackling increasingly complex and urgent societal challenges such as decarbonising the economy, overcoming social inequalities, responding to global shocks and maintaining technological sovereignty in an increasingly fragmented world. Yet they continue to operate within a policy framework that stems from a bygone era characterised by assumptions of linear growth, institutional stability and relatively predictable trajectories. This misalignment has led to a growing gap between the transformative outcomes we demand from innovation systems today and their actual design and ability to deliver them. Bridging this gap will not be achieved through improved instruments or incremental reforms alone. It will require a fundamental shift in the way we think about innovation governance, a new policy ethos that is explicitly purpose-led, adaptive to uncertainty, committed to continuous learning and anchored in democratic legitimacy. The following section outlines this ethos, not as a rigid blueprint, but as a set of guiding principles for forward-looking innovation policy.

At the centre of every innovation system is a series of fundamental questions: What are we innovating for? And for whom? These questions are not abstract or rhetorical, because they define the priorities we set, the outcomes we value and the voices we amplify. Are we pursuing innovation to drive growth, improve competitiveness, promote inclusion, create sustainability or strengthen resilience? Are we designing it for global markets, national elite champions or for marginalised communities and future generations? All too often, innovation is treated as an inherently good and self-correcting force, its direction assumed to be progressive and its benefits naturally widespread. But as this book has shown, innovation is not neutral. It reflects institutional choices, political dynamics and social structures. It can reinforce inequalities or challenge them, degrade the environment or contribute to its restoration, strengthen communities or leave them behind. To steer transformative innovation, we need to face these choices openly, rather than leaving them to markets or entrenched interests. Based on the arguments set out in this book, we propose five interlocking pillars that form an ethos for innovation policy in the twenty-first century:

The first pillar of a new policy ethos is directionality. Innovation must be guided by clear, collective goals and not driven solely by the logic of the market or abstract notions of progress. This means reorienting innovation systems towards tackling urgent societal challenges such as climate change, digital inequality, circular production or equitable access to health and care. Competitiveness is still important, but it should serve public missions and not override them. A mission-oriented policy is one way to structure this orientation, but the most important prerequisite is clarity of purpose. Innovation must be at the service of objectives that have been defined together with society and are open to democratic deliberation. This also requires selective governance based on understanding that not every innovation is useful. Some technologies or business models may contradict sustainability goals, deepen inequalities or undermine public trust. Effective governance must be able to reject not only ineffective ideas, but also those that steer innovation systems in a direction that is not compatible with the long-term well-being of society.

The second pillar is reflexivity, i.e. the ability of innovation governance to be self-aware, adaptive, and capable of learning. In a complex, uncertain environment, failures, surprises and challenges are not exceptions, but part of the landscape. Reflexive governance builds this understanding into its design by embedding feedback loops, encouraging iterative learning and supporting policy experimentation. Pilot programmes, regulatory sandboxes and real-time evaluation mechanisms are all tools that allow systems to adjust course when necessary. Reflexivity also means revisiting assumptions and being open to change, even if it disrupts existing plans or metrics. Crucially, it requires abandoning the illusion of top-down control. Complex systems are about directing, not commanding, cultivating adaptability and not just operational agility. Reflexive systems are not fragile. They are resilient in the face of uncertainty because they can absorb new insights, respond to disruptions and evolve their own frameworks as challenges change. This makes reflexivity an essential prerequisite for managing transformative innovation.

The third pillar is plurality. Innovation systems must recognise that no single model is suitable for all places or purposes. What works in a technology centre like Berlin may not work in a post-industrial city in Croatia, and solutions that work in urban Nairobi may not work in rural Poland. Innovation governance must therefore be contextualised and pluralistic, supporting different actors, approaches and knowledge systems. This includes valuing social and cultural innovation alongside technological and commercial innovation and recognising that meaningful solutions often emerge not only in laboratories or boardrooms, but also in communities, on farms and in everyday life. Policy must take a portfolio approach that supports high-tech and low-tech, formal and informal, radical and incremental innovation. Prioritising relevance, resilience and inclusivity over speed and hype ensures broader societal benefits. Plurality must also extend to governance structures, acknowledging that some systems can benefit from centralised coordination, others from decentralised experimentation. The key is to maintain flexibility while ensuring coherence and equity.

The fourth pillar is resilience. Innovation systems must not only be designed for peak performance under stable conditions, but also for continuity and coherence under stress. This includes building institutional buffer capacities, supporting redundancies in critical infrastructures, diversifying funding sources and investing in regional capabilities and social networks. Resilience also means ensuring that communities can adapt with innovations rather than being harmed or displaced by them. An innovation system that deepens precarity or undermines public trust may appear successful in the short term but remains structurally fragile. The fifth pillar, accountability, strengthens all others by basing innovation governance on democratic legitimacy. This includes inclusive governance structures, participatory agenda-setting, monitoring of public investment and ethical scrutiny of new technologies. Accountability ensures that those who bear the risks of innovation also have a say in shaping innovation and that the benefits are shared fairly. Public engagement is not a PR strategy, but a governance imperative that ensures innovation is aligned with public values and societal needs.

Introducing a new policy ethos for innovation has concrete implications for the way governments and institutions operate. It means that funding frameworks need to be reorganised to align with public missions and inclusive objectives and ensure that innovation serves societal needs and not just economic indicators. Evaluation systems need to be redesigned to reward learning, adaptability and contextual relevance, not just efficiency or output. Governments should also strengthen the intermediaries that bridge the gap between national policy and local experimentation so that innovation can emerge from diverse settings. Foresight and anticipatory governance must become core functions rather than peripheral tasks, while policy teams must be equipped with new skills: systems thinking, participatory facilitation and long-term accountability. These changes require not only technical adaptations but also a cultural shift in the way innovation is imagined and governed. Transformative innovation cannot be achieved within the confines of an outdated institutional logic. It requires new mandates, new benchmarks and, in many cases, completely new organisational forms that do justice to the complexity of today's challenges.

Examples of this change can be found in various regions. In Europe, initiatives such as the European Innovation Council and the Horizon Europe missions demonstrate a move towards mission-oriented and purpose-driven approaches. In Africa, the African Union's Science, Technology and Innovation Strategy for Africa 2024 (STISA) explicitly links innovation to inclusive development and human well-being. In Latin America, countries such as Uruguay and Chile are experimenting with participatory technology assessments, civic engagement in policymaking and open science frameworks. These efforts reflect the growing recognition that innovation needs to be managed in a way that is inclusive, reflexive and accountable. However, in many emerging economies, innovation policy remains anchored in older paradigms that are narrowly focused on technology transfer, start-up support or digital infrastructure. The real opportunity lies not only in technological leapfrogging, but also in governance leapfrogging, i.e. adopting models that are more adaptable, democratic and mission-aligned from the outset. In this way, these countries can build innovation systems that are not only competitive, but also socially anchored, resilient and trustworthy.

A twenty-first-century policy ethos does not diminish the role of the state but redefines and enhances it. Rather than simply acting as a funder or regulator, the state must lead the way, bring together different actors and become a long-term steward of inclusive innovation ecosystems. This means setting strategic priorities without micromanaging, enabling bottom-up experimentation while maintaining coherence, and managing digital and social platforms not just individual firms. Crucially, it must actively create the conditions for innovation to take root in communities and regions that have long been excluded from its benefits. The role of the state is expanding from overseeing transactions to shaping change. This is a challenging role that requires institutional creativity and the political will to align innovation policy with broader goals of equity, sustainability and social solidarity. Only by embracing this broader mandate can the state ensure that innovation serves as a tool for collective progress rather than selective advantage.

Innovation is not a force of nature, but a creative space characterised by choices, values and governance. It can be steered towards inclusive, sustainable outcomes or drift towards inequality and exploitation. The policy ethos described in this chapter provides a compass for navigating this space, not a rigid map, but a set of guiding principles for managing innovation with clarity of purpose, democratic legitimacy and adaptability. In a world characterised by complexity, volatility and accelerated change, innovation governance needs to be refocused to serve long-term societal goals. The final section of this book takes a step back to consider what it means to govern innovation in the contemporary moment in history when short-termism has become dangerous, uncertainty is a constant and the future we face must be approached not with control but with humility, imagination and care. In this context, governing innovation is not about prediction, but about purposeful, responsible and collective design.

9.7 Conclusion

This book began with a simple but far-reaching question: Why do innovation systems fail, and what can be done about it? In the course of the book, we have argued that failure is rarely just technical, but often systemic. Emerging innovation systems face profound structural obstacles of weak knowledge flows, weak institutions and limited autonomy in navigating the global technological landscape. While multinationals are central to capability building, they can also perpetuate dependencies and extractive dynamics. We have seen that inclusive innovation is not an optional add-on, but a fundamental element of resilience and legitimacy. And we have argued that innovation policy must evolve from a narrow focus on R&D and competitiveness to a broader commitment to social change, equity and sustainability. These findings point not to fixes at the margins, but to the need for a new policy ethos, one that embraces complexity, rethinks directions and puts governance at the centre of innovation.

Perhaps the most important conclusion is that governance of innovation is not about controlling the future, but about making conscious, value-led choices in the present that determine what future remains possible. We live in a time in which short-term urgencies and long-term consequences coexist and collide. Climate crises, changes in artificial intelligence, demographic upheavals and growing inequality all require immediate attention, but their impact will determine the decades to come. In this context, innovation must be understood not only as a tool for economic upgrading, but as a collective societal capability. An ability to imagine, to adapt and to deal with uncertainty with courage and prudence. Managing innovation today means embracing complexity rather than reducing it, reconciling ambition with humility and building systems that learn, integrate and endure.

Managing innovation today means recognising complexity, uncertainty and responsibility. It requires recognising that not all innovation is inherently beneficial, that some risks are incalculable, that value cannot always be reduced to GDP or intellectual property and that legitimate knowledge comes from many sources, not just labs or companies, but also communities, ecosystems and lived experience. This requires humility in the face of uncertainty and a commitment to stewardship. This means investing not only in physical infrastructure, but also in institutions that are able to learn and adapt. It is about fostering diverse knowledge systems, building trust across social boundaries and establishing feedback loops that connect current decisions with future needs. Above all, it requires an ethic of care for people, places and the planet. Innovation policy must move beyond the blind pursuit of acceleration and instead focus on inclusive, regenerative and democratically grounded pathways to transformation. It is not about a quick fix, but a deeper, ongoing commitment.

Yet this is not a gloomy message, but a hopeful one. An ethos of innovation governance broadens the horizons of what innovation can be and for whom it is intended. It empowers countries, especially those in transition, to determine their own development path based on their context, values and vision, rather than adopting outdated or misaligned models. It invites communities, not just experts, to participate in the governance of technologies that shape their lives, opening up space for deliberation, co-creation and collective responsibility. And it offers the opportunity for innovation policy to serve solidarity, dignity and a shared future, rather than as an instrument of exploitation or marginalisation. At a time when ecological, technological and political crises are escalating, such an approach is not a luxury, but a necessity. We cannot predict the disruptions ahead, but we can prepare for them by building systems that are inclusive, reflexive and resilient. These systems will not only survive turbulence but will also be able to shape it towards more equitable and sustainable outcomes.

MIX
Papier aus verantwortungsvollen Quellen
Paper from responsible sources
FSC® C105338

If you have any concerns about our products,
you can contact us on
ProductSafety@springernature.com

In case Publisher is established outside the EU,
the EU authorized representative is:
Springer Nature Customer Service Center GmbH
Europaplatz 3, 69115 Heidelberg, Germany

Printed by Libri Plureos GmbH
in Hamburg, Germany